C.E.A.S.E. for Equity isn't about red or blue, left or right, or where you live – whether in the heart of a bustling city or the quiet of a rural town. It's not about political affiliation, geographic location, or drawing lines between who is right and who is wrong. It's not asking you to ignore the past but to confront it with courage and compassion. At its core, this book is about cultivating empathy and sustaining ecosystems for equity – elements, habitats, interactions that support all people, not just a privileged few. It requires you to see the humanity in every person you encounter. It encourages you to break free from narratives that divide. It challenges you to begin the long-overdue process of collective healing and liberation.

C.E.A.S.E. for Equity invites every reader to take personal responsibility – for your choices, your language, and your actions. This book encourages you to contribute with the intent of reforming the social and economic structures that allow prejudice, oppression, exclusion, and erasure to persist. It's a vision rooted not in blame but in accountability, transformation, and love. Above all, *C.E.A.S.E. for Equity* is about peace, justice, and a sincere concern for the human soul. It's a call to walk and work together – not simply as acquaintances or allies, but as accomplices seeking a more just and compassionate world for all humanity.

C.E.A.S.E. for Equity

C.E.A.S.E. for Equity

Cultivating
Empathy
And
Sustaining
Ecosystems for Equity

Michael S. Gordon

2025 by Michael S. Gordon
All rights reserved. Published 2025
Printed in the United States of America

No part of this book may be used or reproduced in any manner whatsoever without the written permission of the author or publisher.

Published in the United States of America by
Team US Empowerment Solutions, LLC Westport

Library of Congress Cataloging-in-Publication Data

Names: Gordon, Michael S., 1971-author.
Title: C.E.A.S.E. for Equity: Cultivating Ecosystems And Sustaining Ecosystems for Equity / Michael S. Gordon.
Description: Westport : Team US Empowerment Solutions, LLC, 2025 304 pages, 23.4 cm
Includes bibliographical references.
Identifiers: LCCN 2025915889 | ISBN 979-8-9996367-0-6 (hardcover) | ISBN 979-8-9996367-2-0 (paperback) |
ISBN 979-8-9996367-1-3 (ebook)
Subjects: LCSH: Empathy-Psychological aspects. | Social Justice. | Empathy-Social aspects. | Economic justice. | Environmental justice. | Social Marginality. | Ethics-Social aspects. | Equity (Social sciences). | Love-Social aspects. | Self-actualization (Psychology). | Compassion. | Oppression (Psychology). | Sustainable development-Moral and ethical aspects. | Identity (Psychology)-Social aspects. | Education-Personal growth through education.
Classification: LCC BF575.E55 .G67 2025 | HM821 .G67 2025 | LC149 .G67 2025 | DDC 152.41-dc23

Text design and composition by Michael S. Gordon

*Thanks be to God for creating me,
my Lord and Savior Jesus Christ for sustaining me,
and the Holy Spirit for guiding me.*

For my wife, my children, and all of my family members.

I dedicate this book to all who have the mind and the will to behave and speak with more patience, kindness, compassion, grace, consideration, and forgiveness; to see the humanity in everyone – moment by moment, blink by blink

Be quick to listen, slow to speak, and slow to anger.
– James 1:19

CONTENTS

Foreword by Dr. Scott J. Silver-Bonito	ix
Preface	xii
Introduction	1
I. Empathy	7
Getting to Know Me	9
Understanding Empathy	19
II. Ecosystems	31
Natural Ecosystems	33
The Primary Man-Made Ecosystems	38
The Human Condition	46
Nature and Nurture	50
Human Behavior Mirrors Natural Ecosystems	54
C.E.L.L. Development	57
III. Sammā-sati (aka The Active, Watchful Mind)	71
Belief	73
Emotions	78
Let's Play a Game (A Reflexive Exercise)	83
The Criticality of Language	86
SO! What Should We Do About the n-word?	90
Your T.E.A.M.	96
IV. Consider the "Facts"	107
V. Actionable Steps	123
Improve Your C.O.R.E.	125
Eradicate H.A.T.E. with L.O.V.E.	128
Be Intentional	136
It's Really About R.A.C.E.	137
Desist…	145
…and C.E.A.S.E. for Equity	256
References	277

Foreword

We are all unified by a universal thread, and empathy is what weaves us together. Michael's message in this book rings loudly and resonates deeply. Having known Michael for nearly 12 years, reading this book felt like a warm, engaging conversation with him. Some books tackling the profound topics of equity and liberation can lean too heavily on statistics, losing the essential human narrative. Michael, however, strikes a perfect balance between lived experience, community stories, and universal data, creating a grounded and achievable framework for moving toward a community of liberation.

One of the first things that struck me was how familial this book felt as I read it. His observations, stories, and jokes make for an enjoyable reading experience, despite the challenging nature of the work and topics discussed. When working with Michael in our district, I was always impressed by how he never dismissed anyone's thinking, lived experiences, or theories. Together, we worked to uncover, identify, and shift our patterns of thought to better serve all our students. Michael's generosity with his time, experience, and guidance was always evident in our collaborations, and it shines through in his writing. He was always so welcoming when discussing difficult topics. These memories of Michael and our work together permeate the narrative he creates, making me feel welcomed and valued as a reader. Michael's masterful prose doesn't deliver a didactic text, but rather presents a community of listening and learning.

Having extensively studied empathy as a foundation for sustainable and equitable problem-solving, I believe Michael masterfully provides a roadmap for moving beyond identity politics, partitioned communities, and aggressive finger-pointing. His approach fosters a community of astute listeners and problem-solvers, ready to tackle the pervasive issues facing the United States. Michael's emphasis on centering problem-solving around listening, empathy, and empowerment is pervasive throughout his text and aligns deeply with my own research and experience. What Michael does beautifully is bring empathy back to the forefront: we are unified in our humanity, our stories are all valid and powerful, and we are all worthy of liberation and equity.

By sharing his own journey, Michael highlights his experiences and builds an incredible foundation for why he is an amazing champion for transformative change. His many roles—as a church leader, martial artist, teacher, husband, and musician, among others—illuminate how we all come to the table with diverse and interconnected roles, talents, and responsibilities. Through each of these lenses, we can build a more just society. As I wrote my doctoral dissertation, one piece of research I encountered highlighted that problem-solving should be a culturally sensitive, reciprocal, and empowering process between those experiencing the problem and those helping to solve it. When solutions are imposed rather than co-created, their sustainability is transient. However, when the problem-solving process is truly collaborative, empathetic, and elevates local culture and expertise, the solution will be evergreen.

Michael's profound life experiences traveling the world, his interactions in his work, and his keen eye for a panoramic investigation of issues from different angles guide the reader toward a path of liberation for all humans. He skillfully elevates the cultures, experiences, and beliefs of others—both local and global—to make the case for how we can shift the patterns of thinking and policy that have trapped our society in a system of unbalanced, incremental change that has served few and harmed many. Michael tackles issues such as policy creation, financial education and sustainability, educational opportunities, and the importance of receptive and reciprocal empathy throughout his presentation of how we move toward a liberated society. He uses anchored language, acronyms, and his own experience to guide the reader on how they can, in large and small ways, enact change within themselves and their communities to bring about true equity. In fact, Michael's written guidance feels more like a companionship stroll and a commitment to being with the reader as they embark on their own journey of transformative learning and work toward a liberated society in the United States.

Michael's story is compelling, his pathway forward engaging and relatable, and his heart's intention is clear in his championing of empathy, understanding, and connection. This

Foreword

book is a must-read for all communities. His warm and inviting nature shines through clearly as you read *CEASE for Equity*. By the time you finish this book, you'll feel an attainable and sustainable call to action, realizing this is merely the start of a conversation, a journey. Michael's words are clear: we are all tied by our humanness in this journey, and when we are a liberated society, our horizon is endless and our collective soul will be boundless.

Dr. Scott J. Silver-Bonito

C.E.A.S.E. for Equity

<u>Preface</u>

Full disclosure, I had many, many critical points while writing this book – literal occurrences and times of deep self-criticism. Many moments in which I critically reflected on what I believe, what I know, how I feel, and what I understand about the concepts we call:

Diversity	Inclusion	Equity	Power
Liberation	Race	Identity	Discrimination
Belonging	Agency	Supremacy	Bias
Marginalized	At-Risk	Freedom	Privilege

I questioned and re-examined my perspectives about these terms, as well as my C.O.R.E., while seeking connections (i.e. strategies to guide the citizens of these United States of America toward truly becoming a peaceful, welcoming, successful, healthy, educated, prosperous, unified civil society). I did my best to consider multiple perspectives about each of the concepts listed above, exploring how each affects, influences, and motivates the language and behavior choices for the vast majority of people in these United States of America.

The terminology, phrases, and imagery I use might resonate with you in ways that are familiar, comforting, and/or affirming. Or they might be challenging, disruptive, and/or triggering. I ask that you keep an open mind and do your best to explore your own knowledge, understanding, beliefs, and feelings about them.

I find the following process of self-inquiry helpful, and you might too:
1) **What** are my current feelings/beliefs about [insert culture or concept here]?
    a. Are they positive or negative?
    b. Are they based on facts or my imagination?
2) **Why** do I feel/think this way about [insert culture or concept here]?
    a. Family conversations/expectations?

Preface

        b. Family values?
        c. Opinions of family members?
        d. Opinions of peers, friends, acquaintances, opps?
3) **Where** did/does my knowledge about [insert culture or concept here] come from?
        a. Peer-reviewed research in professional publications?
        b. Social media influencers?
        c. Casual conversations?
        d. News media?
        e. Conferences/seminars?
        f. Books (such as this one)?
        g. Podcasts?
        h. How do I know if my sources are reliable?
            ➤ Do I *believe* they are **OR** am I trusting each source based on facts?
4) What do I know to be factual about [insert culture or concept here]? In other words, what have I confirmed or debunked about the information presented by the sources identified in #3?
5) How do I authentically and truthfully improve my understanding about [insert culture or concept here]?
        a. Through experience/experimentation?
        b. Through reading?
        c. Through formal interviews?
        d. Through observations?
        e. Through studying theoretical ideas?

    Like a cut gemstone, I firmly believe the multiple facets of offensive, stigmatizing, harmful, traumatizing, destructive, and hateful language and behaviors have been purposefully crafted - carefully planned to create multiple distorted and polarizing perspectives. Likewise, the habitats that contribute to offensive, harmful, and destructive words and actions within the man-made ecosystems of these United States of America were purposefully formed to influence 1) what we observe, 2) what we experience, and ultimately 3) how we speak and act toward each other.

It's important to acknowledge and emphasize that the social and economic ecosystems were intentionally designed to maintain dominance, power and control over descendants of enslaved Africans, people of the Indigenous tribes, and non-European migrants (particularly Asian and South American) living in these United States of America.

Cultivating empathy is the impetus for this book because it's the foundation of meaningful human connection. Empathy motivates individuals and encourages communities to truly understand, and support, one another without seeking financial, political, or personal gain. As a musician, educator, gardener, martial artist, and elder in the church, I've developed skills and language to guide others toward greater empathy. Each role contributes toward the skills that help me successfully navigate challenging situations, take full advantage of unique opportunities, and gain valuable insights for understanding human emotion, discipline, and the importance of community – shaping my approaches to fostering compassion in others.

As a musician, I've experienced firsthand how music transcends barriers and fosters emotional connections. Music speaks where words fail, conveying joy, sorrow, and hope in ways that resonate deeply with listeners. Teaching and performing music have provided me with opportunities to help others experience the emotions behind phrases, melodies, harmonies, rhythms, articulations, dynamics, and lyrics, subsequently fostering a deeper understanding of the human experience. Whether guiding students in expressing emotions through their instruments or collaborating with fellow musicians as part of an ensemble, I've used music as an approach to encourage sensitivity, emotional awareness, self-management, relationship building, and responsible decision making in others.

Almost three decades as an educator have reinforced my faith in the transformative power of empathy. Teaching and

Preface

learning require patience, understanding, and the ability to consider circumstances from a student's perspective. By adapting lessons to meet diverse learning styles, and addressing students' unique struggles, I strive to cultivate an environment in which individuals feel heard and valued. Education extends beyond academics – it's about shaping character, fostering self-awareness, and nurturing a sense of responsibility toward others. Through my teaching, I emphasize active listening and open dialogue, both essential to developing empathy.

Over 30 years as a martial arts practitioner has taught me that true strength lies not in physical prowess alone but in self-awareness, respect, and emotional control. My martial arts training has always emphasized humility, discipline, and the understanding of others' struggles – traits which are fundamental to empathy. In this environment, I have the honor of mentoring students in managing their emotions, resolving conflicts peacefully, and respecting diverse perspectives. Through sparring and cooperative training, practitioners learn to anticipate and respond to others' movements and emotions, reinforcing the importance of awareness and connection.

My service as an elder in the church deepens my commitment to guiding others toward empathy through faith and service. Spiritual leadership requires compassion, patience, and the ability to counsel others through personal hardships. By offering guidance, support, and a listening ear, I've helped individuals navigate challenges and strengthen their relationships. The teachings of faith emphasize love, kindness, patience, and understanding - values that I consistently seek to increase in my life while amplifying them in those I counsel. Through sermons, community outreach, and ecclesiastical care, I encourage individuals to practice empathy in their daily lives.

Life choices shape your ability to effectively guide others toward becoming more empathetic. Each experience reinforces the importance of active listening, emotional intelligence, and compassionate leadership. By fostering connections through music, encouraging understanding in education, promoting discipline in martial arts, and nurturing faith-based empathy, I strive to inspire others to approach the world with greater sensitivity, patience, awareness, kindness, compassion, and understanding. In a society that often prioritizes individual success over communal well-being, cultivating empathy remains a vital and transformative mission of mine.

Let's turn our attention to how human systems and Earth's ecosystems are deeply interwoven, reflecting principles of balance, adaptation, and interdependence. Ecosystems reflect and influence human life, with our individual and collective thoughts, emotions, and actions shaping the landscapes of each environment. Many traditional philosophies, including those of Indigenous, African, Asian, Puerto Rican (Taíno), and Indian (Hindu/Buddhist) cultures, recognize that humans are not separate from nature but part of it. When we live in harmony with nature, we thrive; when we disrupt ecosystems, we face dire consequences.

The interconnectedness of political, social, economic, and academic systems closely mirrors the dynamics of Earth's ecosystems. Each system functions best when it maintains equilibrium, adapts to challenges, and ensures the sustainability of resources. Understanding the parallels between the man-made and natural ecosystems will guide us toward more sustainable decision-making in governance, resource management, healthcare, criminal justice, and education; ensuring that human society thrives just as resilient ecosystems do. Studying and respecting the principles of nature is vital to the manifestation of what we call equity; building a more balanced and enduring future for humanity.

It's ***impossible*** for us to thrive and coexist peacefully in unhealthy environments – #FACTS! Just as natural ecosystems thrive through biodiversity and equilibrium, human societies must embrace interconnectedness and ecological stewardship to ensure a sustainable future for all life to thrive. With that in mind, understanding Earth's ecosystems will help us better understand the considerations, the approaches, the actionable steps, and the behaviors we must demonstrate toward each other on a daily basis, in our desire and quest to be truly inclusive and achieve what we are championing as equity.

Equity is more than just a concept to me – it's a lived experience, a lifelong pursuit, and a principle that has guided my personal and professional endeavors. With almost 30 years of experience as an educator, over 30 years as a martial arts practitioner, and an intimate understanding of the institutional challenges faced by marginalized communities, I bring scholarly insight and real-world experience to the conversation on equity. My journey, shaped by the realities of growing up in the inner city – in a single-mother household without the presence of my father – has given me a firsthand understanding of barriers that many individuals face in accessing opportunities, as well as the resilience needed to overcome them.

As a first-generation college student, I encountered a multitude of obstacles while navigating the complexities of higher education, without the guidance of family members who had "been there and done that." The lack of familiarity with academic expectations, financial aid, and career pathways created additional hurdles that many of my peers and I had to face. My perseverance in overcoming these barriers deepens my understanding of the structural inequities that often hinder the success of students from underrepresented backgrounds. These experiences fuel my commitment to ensuring that others facing similar struggles receive the support and resources they need to thrive.

As an educator, I've dedicated over three decades to creating inclusive learning environments that empower students from diverse backgrounds. My work has centered on dismantling institutional inequities within educational organizations and advocating for policies that ensure all students (regardless of "race," socioeconomic status, or personal circumstances) have access to quality education and the resources necessary for successful outcomes. I've mentored numerous students, many of whom came from communities afflicted by resource deficiency and limited exemplars; helping them navigate obstacles very similar to the types I once faced. These experiences provide me with deep insights regarding how biases, institutional structures, and socio-economic disparities impact learning and success.

My experiences in the martial arts have further enhanced my understanding about equity. In martial arts, discipline, respect, and perseverance are fundamental, but so is the acknowledgement that every individual begins their journey from a unique starting point. I've trained and taught in spaces where people from vastly different backgrounds come together, and I've witnessed firsthand how access to mentorship, training, and encouragement can transform lives. The martial arts aren't just about physical skill. They're about cultivating a mindset of resilience, fairness, and balance – qualities that are essential to the pursuit of equity in every habitat.

Beyond professional and athletic endeavors, my personal story is deeply intertwined with the realities of inequity. Growing up in a landscape where resources were scarce and opportunities often felt out of reach, I learned early on that hard work alone isn't always enough. The absence of my father meant that my mother bore the full weight of raising and supporting our family. Her perseverance and sacrifices instilled in me a profound appreciation for the struggles that many families endure. These early experiences shaped my belief that equity is not about giving everyone the same resources, but about 1) ensuring that each person has what they need to succeed, 2) acknowledging the unique challenges they face, and 3) empowering them to determine their path to manifest a healthy, prosperous, and peaceful way of living.

An amalgamation of choices and experiences informs my perspective on equity. This book goes beyond an academic discussion; it's a compilation of the lessons I've learned through years of teaching, mentoring, training, and living in constructed ecosystems that often fail those who need them the most. Equity is not just a policy or a routine; it's a commitment to identifying, understanding, and removing disparities; it's about transforming landscapes and habitats so that individuals and communities are able to reach their full potential.

Introduction

Let me be clear about something up front – The work of making real changes to cultivate empathy and sustain ecosystems for equity is **self-work** (read that again)! Things will not change for the better on their own; governments are not going to suddenly enact legislation to liberate and empower marginalized communities; there's no magic potion that will help us see the humanity in each other. You, the reader, along with me, the author, have to make daily personal decisions that will ensure people in our sphere of influence are liberated, empowered, and free to pursue peaceful, healthy, prosperous, joyful lives.

Some have said I should be afraid – that I'm creating unsafe situations for myself and my loved ones. How dare I, a "black" man, openly state that the concept of equity has become another institutionalized tool used to divide humanity, perpetuate suffering, and concentrate wealth, resources, and power in the hands of a few.

Speaking out against the prevailing narratives of equity and inclusion is not just controversial – it's dangerous. You might believe you are standing for truth, logic, and unity, but opposing the dominant ideology today can cost you socially, professionally, and personally. In the current climate throughout these United States of America, publicly rejecting the ideas of "white privilege," "black" victimization, and "systemic" oppression can make you a target for criticism, alienation, and even career ruin.

The ideology of equity, often paired with inclusion, is deeply entrenched across the institutions of academia, corporations, media, and politics in these United States of America. Aligned with social justice movements, it has redefined how we discuss "race," privilege, oppression, and erasure. Equity has shifted from an academic or philosophical concept to a moral litmus test for personal and professional credibility.

To question the narrative of "diversity, equity, inclusion, welcome, and belonging" is to brand yourself as an outsider, even a threat. The ideology is fiercely defended by those who see it as a path to justice, and opposition is swiftly condemned. Speaking against this narrative means accepting the risk of being labeled a traitor, a sympathizer with oppression, or someone ignorant of racialized realities.

In this day and age, one of the most significant risks is being "canceled." Cancel culture has damaged careers and ruined reputations of those who challenge dominant social justice narratives. Academics, professionals, and private citizens have lost jobs, had wealth stripped away, and faced public shaming simply for deviating from the accepted discourse.

As an educator and instructional leader for equity and inclusion, I recognize my position of influence. Yet, the moment I challenge the mainstream narrative, my credibility comes under attack. Students, colleagues, and administrators loyal to the dominant ideology may view my stance as dangerous and call for action against me. I could face investigations for creating a "hostile environment" and immense pressure to either resign or conform.

Beyond professional risks, there are personal costs. Speaking out against these ideologies often leads to social isolation. Friends and family who support the prevailing equity framework distance themselves. I'm seen as out of touch or unwilling to acknowledge the struggles of marginalized communities. I'm judged as being a traitor "to the cause," as "forgetting where I came from," and as "part of the problem."

Throughout your reading, let the following statement saturate your soul – *cease* means "to immediately stop; immediately put an end to" something that's already occurring or was previously ongoing:

> 1st **Cease making excuses** for your own behaviors and language that cause fear, anxiety, damage, trauma, destruction, and death. You must stop overlooking the impact of your actions for the sake of comfort and/or convenience. For example, descendants of enslaved

Introduction

Africans in these United States of America often complain by saying, "I don't have the same opportunities as 'white' people," instead of admitting, "My thinking, my choices, my language, and my behavior determine my level of success – not the melanin level in my skin." Another example involves electric vehicles – they seem great, but how are lives and ecosystems being impacted where the raw materials are being mined? How is the production of electricity for charging stations – the burning of fossil fuels, nuclear power, or renewable sources – impacting communities and environments here in these United States of America?

2ⁿᵈ Cease making exceptions for (aka justifying) the triggering, terrorizing, traumatizing, and -cidal (suicidal, homicidal, genocidal etc.) language and behaviors of influencers in your life (e.g. family members, friends, loved ones, tech execs, politicians etc.).

3ʳᵈ Cease accusing others of ill intent. You and I must strive to become more considerate, trusting, and forgiving. Speak to edify, not instigate…Listen to understand, not respond.

4ᵗʰ Cease blaming others for your situation. YOUR choices make the conditions that determine your success, prosperity, and health.

5ᵗʰ Cease being detached from the circumstances of others, particularly those who look, sound, think, and behave differently. You and I must make time to initiate, develop, and sustain authentic and genuine relationships with people of diverse languages, experiences, perspectives, and customs; this requires consistent and honest interactions.

C.E.A.S.E. for Equity

My experiences have taught me that achieving equity requires awareness and advocacy, coupled with introspection and action. I firmly believe the protests of late 2019 and throughout 2020 were a turning point in these United States of America. Said protests put the "racist," offensive, destructive, and traumatizing practices, legislation, institutions, policies, language, and behaviors under the proverbial microscopic lens. Citizens in every section of these United States of America are now keenly aware that inequities persist. Despite the advances and victories that resulted from the Civil Rights movement of the 1960s, disparities still exist, and people are still being terrorized based on the amount of melanin in their skin (aka skin tone), perceived accent, physical/mental abilities, ways of speaking, gender, and beliefs (cultural, religious, etc.).

C.E.A.S.E. for Equity is about 1) identifying, disrupting, and destroying the manufactured ecosystems that foster negative outcomes (e.g. oppression, dependence, inequity, disparity, trauma, erasure, genocide, homicide, suicide, terrorism etc.), in addition to 2) transforming those ecosystems to liberate and free people, empowering them to positively collaborate and improve the conditions of their community.

Throughout *C.E.A.S.E. for Equity*, I'll use comparisons, analogies, references, and stories gleaned throughout my decades in the roles I listed previously. I'll utilize the terms "man-made," "fabricated," "manufactured," and "synthetic" ecosystems interchangeably. I'll share practical approaches for examining your beliefs. I'll challenge you to inspect your language and behaviors, for the purpose of becoming a more empathetic, more inclusive, and more cohesive society. I aim to highlight reflexive practices, offering perspectives that are both deeply personal and professionally informed. My sincere hope is to move you from the meaningful dialogue you're having to actually manifesting systems that improve grace, compassion, community development, and personal growth – real change toward cultivating empathy and sustaining ecosystems for equity. Perhaps you will be able to 1) admit that

Introduction

lasting equity requires a holistic, ecosystemic approach and 2) work toward liberating individuals and communities – particularly the disenfranchised and the marginalized – removing dependency on government programs and subsidies. Let's get into it…

I. EMPATHY

1. Getting to know me…
2. Understanding Empathy

I. Empathy

1. <u>Getting to know me…</u>

On this journey to cultivate empathy and sustain ecosystems for equity, it's important that I start by sharing my story with you. It's important that you know about some of the critical periods that have impacted my life thus far…Instances I recall some of the elements and habitats in the manufactured ecosystems altering my circumstances, situations, and life choices…Occasions when my desire to feel included, seen, heard, valued, and free challenged my beliefs, influenced the language I chose to use, and the behaviors I chose to exhibit…Times of questioning, and trying to establish, my identity while seeking acceptance…Moments during which my longing for a place to feel welcome, where I truly belonged, was amplified by the language and behaviors of peers, friends, family members, and strangers. As you read the following portions of my story, it's important that you focus on my identity, culture, and vision more than my hardships.

I need you to realize something. Sharing our stories isn't merely an act of self-expression – it's a vital means of cultivating empathy and sustaining ecosystems for equity. For communities shaped by historical inequalities, storytelling is a transformative act; it allows people to reclaim their narratives, assert their humanity, and envision futures that center on justice and joy. Sharing stories helps us connect across differences, better understand lived experiences that diverge from our own, and reimagine structures that have too often ignored or silenced marginalized voices.

Storytelling plays a crucial role in building empathy, which I believe is the cornerstone for equity. When people hear firsthand accounts of exclusion, struggle, or perseverance, they're more likely to move beyond apathy or defensiveness. This shift in perspective leads to deeper solidarity, more authentic collaboration, and collective advocacy for structural changes. Empathy, cultivated through storytelling, encourages listeners to care and act; changing language and behaviors through voting, donating, organizing, and challenging prejudice, discrimination, exclusion, and inequities within their own spheres of influence.

The social ecosystem includes elements such as educational institutions, justice systems, and public policy frameworks. The narratives we tell and the voices we amplify profoundly influence this ecosystem. When individuals from marginalized communities share their stories, they shed light on injustices that data and theory often overlook. Stories of racialized profiling, housing insecurity, and lack of access to quality education reveal the human cost of inequity as well as the resilience and resistance within these communities. Listening to these stories should prompt more responsive and humane decisions from people in positions of influence, as they better understand how policies and institutions impact real lives.

Economic ecosystems also benefit from inclusive storytelling. In these United States of America, the traditional economy often prioritizes efficiency and profit over people, ignoring the experiences of workers, consumers, and communities. Yet, when people share their economic struggles, they highlight the need for more equitable economic models; struggles related to insufficient wages, navigating unemployment, or lacking access to capital. These stories have fueled movements for fair labor practices, ethical investing, and community-based entrepreneurship. They've helped shift business practices, from shareholder-centered models to stakeholder-driven ones that value social and environmental outcomes alongside financial success.

Ultimately, the stories we tell, listen to, and amplify shape our society. In order to develop and nurture ecosystems that affirm dignity, opportunity, and justice, we must make opportunities for diverse voices and experiences to be shared authentically. Sharing your stories isn't a luxury; it's a necessity for empathy, equity, and enduring change. Through storytelling, we make the invisible visible, challenge the status quo, and co-create more just and inclusive communities; we

I. Empathy

nurture hope and strengthen the elements needed to sustain ecosystems for equity.

<u>...Pequannock</u>

As I reflect on my life, I think of the fabricated ecosystems; particularly how they impact disparities in healthcare, opportunities for academic success, housing, and economic freedom in my community. Based on conversations with my mother, I get the sense that I shouldn't be alive. You see, the man who impregnated her – the man who I would eventually come to call "Dad" – had sex with her under questionable circumstances. From the tone of my mother's voice, and the carefully crafted words she used when telling me about my conception, I understood my mother questioned whether I should enter this world or not.

Although I don't recall the moment of my actual birth (duh…who would, lol), I imagine it wasn't the welcoming experience portrayed in films and on television – a time filled with extreme joy, optimism, and positive hope. Physically, I was born with an issue that affected one leg, so I had to wear a corrective brace as a toddler for a time. To this day I still experience issues on that side of my body and question the quality of health care my mother had received throughout her pregnancy with me – Were there any indicators in the ultrasound that I would be born with a leg issue? I wonder about the attitudes of the medical professionals who had delivered me – Did they pay less attention, or deliver me with less care, because of prejudices regarding my mother's perceived culture, "race", or economic status? Only God knows at this point.

My early childhood was spent in the projects known as Pequannock Apartments, located in the south end of Bridgeport, CT. During this time, I was the youngest of three children, being raised by my hard-working single mother. Despite the love and attention she showered on me, I struggled with feeling accepted in my community. I was always trying to show the other kids I was capable – to prove that I belonged.

This usually resulted in my humiliation and self-isolation. I didn't have fighting skills, like my older sister and brother – so it seemed like I was always getting picked on. I didn't have speed, dexterity, agility, or stamina like most of the other boys and girls, who played sports – so I spent most of my time playing alone in the dirt. "What's wrong with me?" and "Why can't I ever say or do the 'right' things?" were constant questions.

It's important for you to know that a tragic event happened to me when I was two years old. You see…I bit an electrical cord while it was still plugged into the wall. The electrocution burned a hole in the corner of my mouth, which resulted in a noticeable scar. Don't judge me, lol – I was TWO! As a toddler, I remembered seeing my mother do something behind the T.V. sometimes, before she turned it on. I got angry at the T.V. because it wouldn't turn on for me (I really wanted to watch Sesame Street). Needless to say, I'm alive today by the mercy and grace of God. I tell you this because "I should have died when I was two…life would be better for everyone if I didn't exist," was the chorus to the theme song of my life while growing up in the projects.

One of my grade school teachers, 3rd grade I recall, was an organism in the ecosystem for equity that impacted the trajectory of my life. In every ecosystem, there are predators and prey. This particular teacher was the predator, and I was the prey. For reasons unknown, she lowered a grade on my report card after it had already been written. This prevented my acceptance into a program known as Project Concern. This program was instituted in the 1960s, whereby children from impoverished/marginalized communities were bused to more affluent school districts – districts where access to high-quality resources and academic opportunities were abundant, in addition to other socioeconomic advantages. My older brother and sister, along with friends from the projects, were already beneficiaries of this program. I was next in line to continue the legacy of my family. However, the lowered grade resulted in

I. Empathy

my continued status as a ward of the Bridgeport Public School system.

Although I didn't directly experience racialized discrimination in my community, the limited amount of melanin in my skin and thick curly hair caused some to question whether I was "a little Puerto Rican," a "black" kid, or some other ethnicity. I walked to and from Roosevelt Elementary School, along with other kids who shared experiences and struggles that were similar to mine – single-mother household, not having the latest "gear" (aka styles of outfits), and meals that were acceptable nutritionally but not always balanced nor plentiful. Yet I always felt separated from everyone – I always felt different - and desired inclusion. So much so, that I would steal money from my own mother to buy friendship - so I would feel like I was "part of," so I would feel like I belonged.

At the start of the summer in 1979, I was eight years old. My pregnant mother, two siblings, and I made a cross-country move from Bridgeport, CT, to Anaheim, CA. In addition to my thoughts of, "I get to be around my aunts, uncles, and cousins," during the chartered bus ride, I was filled with the hope of finding my fit. "Maybe there will be more kids like me." I was looking forward to finally feeling like I belonged somewhere.

One day, my siblings and some of my cousins were going to a community swimming pool. I was much younger than everyone else and, from what I remember, the adults forced them to let me tag along. Needless to say, I didn't feel like I was welcome on this excursion. This was when I had my second near-death experience. An older kid pushed me into the deep end of the swimming pool, and I nearly drowned. Thankfully, a teenager/young adult rescued me. Instead of experiencing joy at being alive, I felt like more of a misfit and a burden as I cried during the walk home. Cue the music and scroll the lyrics playing in my mind, "I should have died when I was two…life would be better for everyone if I didn't exist…"

C.E.A.S.E. for Equity

...The East End

My remaining elementary through high school years were spent growing up on the East End of Bridgeport, still struggling with my identity. The influence of the social and economic ecosystems on the human condition were palpable to me. Was I supposed to be a tough guy? (I don't like hurting people.) Was I supposed to be a player? (I don't have the looks nor the words to get the ladies.) Was I supposed to be a baller? (I didn't have the money.) Was it ok that I preferred comic books over pornographic magazines? (I still don't understand the attraction nor the excitement). Those were just some of the questions I had, as a boy who was developing into a manling.

I no longer walked to school but caught the school bus on the corner of Central Avenue and Williston Street, outside of Tony's store. I went to High Horizons Magnet School with children of diverse melanin levels, economic backgrounds, social standings, cultural traditions, religious beliefs, and familial connections. My classmates and friends included children of two-parent and single-parent homes; free spirits and rigid rule followers; church goers and agnostics; smokers, drinkers, and drug dealers; hard rockers, B-boys and gang members; dancers, rappers, band kids, and singers; taggers and other visual artists. Although my fighting skills were still questionable, I was becoming more comfortable with my sense of style and felt less alone.

I was book smart but didn't possess the street smarts exhibited by some of my peers and siblings. My mother did her best to make sure I didn't get "caught up in the streets." However, I would sneak down to the corner store on Deacon Street to play video games, despite her warnings that drugs were being sold there and her threats of punishment if she caught me in there.

In the 5th grade, I joined the school band. Since my mom couldn't afford to rent an instrument, my friend Gina agreed to share her clarinet with me. On days when she wasn't going to band, I would use her instrument. In our young minds, this was a brilliant plan, but it was neither practical nor

I. Empathy

sustainable, especially when we were in band class at the same time, smh. Skin color didn't matter…ethnicity didn't matter…gender didn't matter…socio-economic status didn't matter…cultural and religious beliefs didn't matter. Gina was doing her best to help a friend feel welcome and find a place where I felt like I belonged. Needless to say, I had to choose a school instrument – the French horn.

I remember coming home one day to discover someone had violated our private space. They had broken into our second-floor apartment and robbed us. The police went through the motions of taking our statements and writing the report, but it did little to make my family feel safer in the community – to help us feel empowered and free.

Fast forward to my years at Central Magnet High School. I was still among many of the same peers and friends as in elementary school, but there was a noticeable segregation within the student body at large. Kids were visibly shunned and excluded, verbally demeaned and intimidated, and physically assaulted because of prejudices and perceived differences. There were clear "groups" that you were either part of or you weren't. This was the first time I felt targeted or pressured because of my "race."

In high school, I had my first genuine encounter with the threat of gang violence. Viral organisms of the social and economic ecosystems affected my sense of safety, challenging me to change my belief about guns and my desire to obtain one. Despite this challenge, high school was where I felt closer to a sense of being "welcome" – the primary community being the band. I was among people who understood my ways of thinking, accepted my perspectives about society, related to many of my experiences, and shared my joy for learning and performing music. Questions about my identity began shifting more toward my enslaved African and (according to family elders and historians) Indigenous ancestors. I tried spending more time with great-uncles and great-aunts, to hear their stories and learn from their wisdom.

Throughout my grade school years, I liked, "dated," and "went out with" girls who were:
- Americans descended from enslaved Africans,
- Hispanic (specifically Puerto Rican),
- "White" (specifically Italian and Greek),
- Asian (specifically Vietnamese),
- Caribbean (specifically Jamaican, Haitian, and Cape Verdean),
- Hearing impaired and non-English speaking,
- Catholic, Protestant, Pentecostal, and non-Denominational.

Neither melanin level (aka skin complexion), accent, speech pattern, nor body type mattered to me. I was drawn to the kindness in a girl's eyes, the joy in her smile, the confidence in her words, and the grace in her actions.

...Hilltop and Main

Exiting high school and entering college expanded my awareness about the fabricated ecosystems affecting my life, my family, and my community. Being away from home for the first time, living at the hilltop on a college campus, caused my struggles with welcoming and belonging to resurface. My attention was fragmented into a desire for academic success, a self-imposed expectation of being the first member from our family to obtain a college degree, a longing for a romantic relationship, and a deep concern for family situations and circumstances back home.

I was secure in my faith as a Christian, which boosted my confidence as a manling. Yet, I continually sought validation about my cultural ancestry and heritage. The passing of many family elders fueled my desire to search for documentation, specifically about my Indigenous lineage. I sought proof and guidance as to where I could experience and learn more about the culture and traditions of my ancestors.

Fast-forward to my adult life throughout the past few decades, to my journey from being a passionate educator in my

I. Empathy

hometown of Bridgeport, CT, despite limitations imposed by administration, to my inclusion as part of a supportive learning community in Wilton, CT. When the thought of "I abandoned my students, my own people," pops into my head, I recall how my then-assistant principal asked me during a meeting, "Can't you just play 'them' (aka the students) CDs to listen to?" – instead of teaching them how to create, perform, respond to, and make connections through music. I recall how my then-principal allowed a parent to literally cuss me out and call me out of my name for 45 minutes straight – with the principal saying nothing to stop it!

With disappointment, I remember the comment made to me by a colleague soon after my arrival in Wilton – "These kids are so lucky that *you're* here." (I was one of two "black" teachers at the school and one of a handful of "black" teachers working in the district). I shake my head as I think about a colleague who recently singled me out of the group with, "You *have* to see this," in her excitement to show me pictures of her daughter dating a "black" guy.

On the flip-side of that coin, I'm filled with joy as I recall how the superintendent and principal, during my welcome interview in Wilton, assured me that family always comes first. In refreshing opposition to the negative memories, I think about how I can have open, honest, and confidential racialized conversations with my current principal and friend.

I often wonder:
- Where would I be in my life today if I had been accepted into Project Concern?
- How might life have been different for my friends and me if our parents had been able to afford the costs associated with extracurricular activities? (e.g. participation fees, equipment, transportation, etc.)
- Would my experiences growing up have been different if my mother had been able to send me to a sleepaway camp? Would I have been more confident and resilient

growing up? Would I be less reflective about how ecosystems for equity impact my life?
- Why was it difficult for my family to "get off" Section 8 housing assistance?
- Why were we unable to escape the threat of criminal activity?
- Why did it seem like families in my community were plagued by health conditions such as diabetes, heart disease, high cholesterol, alcoholism, and drug addiction?
- Why is it so difficult for me, and other descendants of Indigenous tribes and enslaved Africans, to find concrete evidence of our ancestry, heritage, and lineage?
- What would it feel like to connect with unknown family members? What traditions, ceremonies, and celebrations might they know? How would my children and future heirs benefit?
- Why do we accept the classification of which subjects are "academic" and which subjects are "special?" Shouldn't all subjects be valued equally for the development of the "whole child?"
- How long would I have stayed employed in Wilton if I had made a complaint to HR or responded directly with "Is it because I'm 'black'?" or "Do you say that to every new teacher?"
- How would my colleagues label me and treat me if I had responded with, "Why am I the only one who 'has to see this?' or "Your 'white' daughter with a 'black' boy doesn't impress me."

To answer these questions and more, reflecting on ways to cultivate empathy and sustain ecosystems for equity is critical. To state the obvious, it begins with cultivating empathy. So, let's get 'er done!

I. Empathy

2. <u>Understanding Empathy</u>

Make time to understand that empathy is a complex human experience, involving physiological responses and cognitive processes. When you experience empathy, your body and brain undergo changes that affect your perception, decision-making, and interactions with others. Needless to say, empathy is a crucial component of human connection, influencing relationships, education, leadership, and cultural exchange. It manifests in various ways across cultures and disciplines, thus shaping the way individuals interact with the world. To put it simply, empathy is the ability to understand and share the feelings of another.

In many Indigenous traditions, empathy is deeply tied to the relationship between humans, nature, and the spirit world. An example is that of the Lakota Sioux concept of "Mitákuye Oyás'iŋ" (mee-tah-koo-yay oh-yah-seen), which means "we're all related." This philosophy teaches that all living beings are interconnected, and to harm another is to harm oneself. One story is that of a Lakota medicine man called Black Elk, who had visions of unity and healing. He believed that true wisdom and compassion came from seeing oneself in others, including animals, plants, and even the land itself. In practicing empathy, Indigenous communities have traditionally emphasized listening, patience, and understanding before taking action.

Asian cultures, particularly those influenced by Confucianism, Buddhism, and Taoism, emphasize empathy as a guiding principle for social harmony. In Chinese philosophy, the concept of "ren" (仁) is central to Confucian teachings, representing human-heartedness and benevolence. An enlightening story from Japan is that of a wandering monk, Ryōkan, who lived a humble life of kindness and compassion. One night, a thief broke into his hut, only to find nothing worth stealing. Instead of reacting with anger, Ryōkan offered the thief his robe, saying, "I wish I could give you the moon." This act of deep empathy turned the thief's heart. This story highlights the power of understanding and non-judgment. In

Buddhist traditions, the practice of "metta" or loving-kindness meditation encourages individuals to cultivate empathy, not just for loved ones but also for strangers and even enemies.

The African philosophy of Ubuntu, meaning "I am because we are," reflects the deep sense of empathy and interconnectedness present in many African cultures. I recall a story of Nelson Mandela's empathizing with his jailers during his imprisonment. Rather than harboring hatred, he sought to understand their fears and humanity, ultimately leading to reconciliation and the end of apartheid in South Africa. Another example from Africa involves a tribe where, when someone commits a wrongdoing, the entire village gathers around them. Instead of punishment, each villager takes turns reminding the person of their good deeds and innate goodness. This act of communal empathy reinforces the belief that people can learn and grow through understanding rather than condemnation.

"La Bendición" (The Blessing), where children are taught from a young age to bless their elders, is one way respect and empathy are demonstrated in Hispanic and Latino cultures. This simple yet powerful tradition reinforces a lifelong practice of recognizing the emotional and spiritual needs of others. "Familismo," a strong value of family and communal support, is also emphasized; amplified in times of crisis as families and neighbors come together to provide comfort and assistance. During Hurricane Maria in 2017, countless Puerto Ricans demonstrated empathy by opening their homes, sharing food, and helping rebuild their communities despite their own struggles. These demonstrations of resilience and collective support embody the spirit of empathy in action.

In addition to the cultural value, you must also consider and explore empathy as a skill that is demonstrated in a variety of professions and activities. In the field of education, highly effective teachers understand that students come from different backgrounds with unique challenges. Just as teaching styles must be adjusted to meet the unique learning needs of each

I. Empathy

student, empathy requires adapting one's approach to connecting with others. Struggling students need encouragement and honest feedback, not sarcasm and ridicule; students who shout out must not be viewed as impulsive but require a more "conversational" structure; an overly talkative child may simply be seeking attention due to boredom or loneliness. By being considerate of the students' unique perspectives (influenced by their experiences and background), an educator cultivates empathy by preparing the learning environment to encourage trust and growth.

In martial arts, empathy is often seen in the relationship between sparring partners. While the goal is to challenge one another, true martial artists understand that their training partner is not an enemy but a mirror for self-improvement. The best fighters are those who understand not just their own techniques but also their opponent's movements, mental state, and limitations. A story of Bruce Lee emphasizes this idea – he believed martial arts were not just about fighting but about understanding others. He taught that a true warrior must feel their opponent's energy and respond with both strength and compassion.

As a gardener, I can't force a plant to grow. Instead, I must provide the right conditions (sunlight, water, removal of weeds, and nutrients) for it to thrive. Similarly, empathy requires attention, patience, and care. An empathetic person recognizes different individuals need different forms of support, just as a gardener understands different plants require different conditions and nutrients for healthy development. For example, a young sapling might need protection from the wind, just as a grieving friend might need quiet comfort rather than words of advice. The gardener's role is not to control but to nurture, mirroring the essence of empathetic relationships.

In my experience, the performance of music is one of the most profound expressions of empathy. In addition to listening to his/her own instrument (including the human voice), a musician must also focus on demonstrating the following 5 social emotional competencies, adapted from those outlined by the Collaborative for Academic, Social, and Emotional Learning (CASEL)[1]:

1. Understanding how thoughts, prior experiences, emotions, and values influence technique, language, and behaviors (Self-awareness)
2. Managing emotions, thoughts, language, and behaviors to achieve the goal of reading and translating the written music composition, as well as accurately interpreting and conveying the composer's intent. (Self-management)
3. Having a keen and intimate understanding of what the other musicians are playing/singing (Social awareness)
4. Building and maintaining healthy relationships by reflecting on how his/her personal performance impacts others (including the audience), focused on balancing and blending his/her sound with other members of the ensemble. (Relationship skills)
5. Playing/Singing to enhance and support the composition for the greater good of the ensemble (Responsible decision-making)

In an ensemble, every musician must be attuned to the entire group, adjusting the tempo, pitches, dynamics, articulations, phrases, and rhythms based on the collective sound. Jazz musicians, for example, engage in call-and-response improvisation, where they must deeply listen and react to their fellow musicians in real time. This ability to anticipate, adjust, and connect mirrors the way empathy functions in daily life.

As a church leader, I serve as a consultant, advocate, confidante, and guide, providing spiritual and emotional support. It's imperative that I patiently and actively listen to

---

[1] Collaborative for Academic, Social, and Emotional Learning (CASEL). *Core SEL Competencies.* CASEL, https://casel.org/fundamentals-of-sel/what-is-the-casel-framework/

I. Empathy

the thoughts, complaints, struggles, concerns, and perspectives being shared. I do my best to understand, sympathize with, and relate to the experiences and emotions being shared; offering words of comfort and wisdom with kindness, compassion, and careful consideration for the impact I might have.

True empathy in religious leadership means not just preaching doctrine but being able to relate to the real-life hardships of individuals. For example, the Biblical story of the Good Samaritan teaches the essence of empathy – not just feeling pity for the injured man but taking action to help him. This story transcends religious boundaries, illustrating that empathy requires not just thought but meaningful action.

Empathy is a universal human experience that transcends culture, profession, and personal background. Whether through the wisdom of Indigenous interconnectedness, the mindfulness of Asian traditions, the communal values of African and Puerto Rican societies, or the practical applications in education, martial arts, gardening, music, and faith, empathy remains a guiding force in fostering understanding and unity.

Now, I must highlight that empathy is not just an abstract concept – it has tangible physical manifestations. When you feel empathetic toward another, your body responds in ways that reflect the emotions they are experiencing. These responses include changes in brain activity, hormonal fluctuations, muscle contractions, and autonomic nervous system reactions.

The mirror neuron system (MNS) plays a crucial role in the experience of empathy. These specialized neurons fire both when an individual performs an action and when they observe someone else performing the same action.[2]

The MNS is thought to be crucial for understanding the emotional and physical experiences of others by simulating those experiences internally. This causes you to internally simulate another's experience, which fosters an intuitive under-

---

2 Rizzolatti, G., & Craighero, L. (2004). The mirror-neuron system. *Annual Review of Neuroscience, 27*, 169-192.

standing of their emotional state. When you witness someone in distress, your brain may activate in a way that mimics the emotions of the distressed person, leading to shared physical sensations such as tension or discomfort. This neural mirroring allows you to feel as if you're experiencing another person's emotions firsthand.

Functional MRI (fMRI) studies have shown that when people observe someone in pain, the same regions of the brain responsible for processing their own pain – such as the anterior cingulate cortex and the anterior insula – become active[3]. This suggests that empathy has a strong somatosensory component, whereby you vicariously experience the emotions of others at a neurological level.

Empathetic engagement can lead to physiological changes in heart rate and blood pressure. Research has shown that witnessing someone in emotional pain can trigger increased heart rate variability (HRV), which reflects an individual's ability to regulate emotional responses; providing insight into how effectively the human body can adapt to stress and recover from it. When you observe someone else in distress, your own heart rate may increase or decrease, depending on the type of empathetic response[4]. For example, compassionate empathy, which involves a desire to help, is often associated with parasympathetic activation, leading to a calming effect. Conversely, prolonged exposure to distressing situations can result in increased heart rate, blood pressure, stress-related responses, and emotional exhaustion. This personal distress empathy, where you feel overwhelmed by another's suffering, is sometimes referred to as compassion fatigue.

Empathy-related interactions also influence hormonal responses. Oxytocin, often called the "love hormone" or

---

[3] Singer, T., Seymour, B., O'Doherty, J., Kaube, H., Dolan, R. J., & Frith, C. D. (2004). Empathy for pain involves the affective but not sensory components of pain. *Science*, *303*(5661), 1157-1162.

[4] Decety, J., & Meyer, M. (2008). From emotion resonance to empathic understanding: A social developmental neuroscience account. *Development and Psychopathology*, *20*(4), 1053-1080.

I. Empathy

"bonding hormone," plays a crucial role in promoting social bonding and empathetic behavior[5]. When you engage in empathetic interactions, your oxytocin levels rise, reinforcing feelings of connection and trust. Studies have shown that higher levels of oxytocin are associated with greater empathetic accuracy and pro-social behavior[6], leading to greater emotional attunement with others.

On the flipside of this coin, cortisol, a stress hormone, may also be released when witnessing another's suffering, leading to heightened emotional responsiveness or distress. When you witness intense suffering, your body may enter a stress response, making it more difficult to engage in compassionate action. Chronic exposure to distressing empathetic situations can lead to burnout, partially due to prolonged elevation of cortisol levels[7].

Facial mimicry is another physical response associated with empathy. Facial electromyography (EMG) studies have shown that individuals automatically mimic the facial expressions of those they observe[8]. You unconsciously imitate the facial expressions of those you're are interacting with, a behavior facilitated by mirror neurons. This mirroring effect helps you recognize and internalize the emotions of others. When someone smiles, as an empathetic observer you may unconsciously smile back; if someone is crying, your face may show sadness; observing someone in pain might lead to furrowed brows. Similarly, muscle tension in your body can increase when witnessing another person's pain, reinforcing the shared emotional experience.

In addition to the physical experiences, empathy is also

---

[5] Hurlemann, R., Patin, A., Onur, O. A., Cohen, M. X., Baumgartner, T., Metzler, S., ... & Kendrick, K. M. (2010). Oxytocin enhances amygdala-dependent, socially reinforced learning and emotional empathy in humans. *The Journal of Neuroscience, 30*(14), 4999-5007.

[6] Barraza, J. A., & Zak, P. J. (2009). Empathy toward strangers triggers oxytocin release and subsequent generosity. *Annals of the New York Academy of Sciences, 1167*(1), 182-189.

[7] Figley, C. R. (2002). Compassion fatigue: Psychotherapists' chronic lack of self-care. *Journal of Clinical Psychology, 58*(11), 1433-1441.

[8] Dimberg, U., Thunberg, M., & Elmehed, K. (2000). Unconscious facial reactions to emotional facial expressions. *Psychological Science, 11*(1), 86-89.

a cerebral process that involves perception, reasoning, and decision-making. Your brain must analyze the emotions of others, evaluate the context, and determine an appropriate response. This complex process often involves several cognitive steps, including perspective-taking, emotional regulation, moral reasoning, and decision-making.

The first step in empathetic thought processing: recognizing and identifying the emotions of others. This requires interpreting facial expressions, body language, and verbal cues. Dr.'s Uta Frith and Christopher D. Frith identified the temporoparietal junction (TPJ) and medial prefrontal cortex (mPFC) as key brain regions involved in this cognitive empathy process[9]. In social settings, you rely on context to make sense of emotional expressions. For example, seeing a friend with tears in his/her eyes could indicate sadness, relief, or joy, depending on the situation. Your brain rapidly analyzes contextual clues to attribute the correct emotion to the observed individual.

Another fundamental cognitive aspect of empathy is perspective-taking, which allows you to mentally place yourself in another person's situation. This ability is closely linked to the concept of the Theory of Mind (ToM), introduced in the 1978 article *Does the chimpanzee have a theory of mind?* by Dr. David Premack and Guy Woodruff[10]. ToM refers to imagining yourself in another person's situation and predicting their thoughts and feelings. When engaging in empathetic reasoning, you reflect on:
- How would I feel in this situation?
- What might the other person be thinking or experiencing?
- What external factors might be influencing their emotions?

Considering these questions will lead you to 1) a more accurate

---

[9] Frith, C. D., & Frith, U. (2003). Development and neurophysiology of mentalizing. *Philosophical Transactions of the Royal Society of London. Series B: Biological Sciences, 358*(1431), 459-473.

[10] Premack, D., & Woodruff, G. (1978). Does the chimpanzee have a theory of mind? *Behavioral and Brain Sciences, 1*(4), 515-526.

I. Empathy

understanding of another's emotional state and 2) responses that are more compassionate.

Research has shown that different brain networks are activated during emotional empathy (feeling others' emotions) versus cognitive empathy (understanding others' emotions) [11]. Shamay-Tsoory and others identified the anterior insula and limbic system as significant for emotional empathy, while the prefrontal cortex is crucial for cognitive empathy.

Empathy requires a balance between emotional engagement and cognitive control. Without emotional regulation, you might become overwhelmed by another's suffering, leading to personal distress rather than constructive support. Failing to maintain this self-other distinction can result in empathetic distress rather than compassionate empathy [12]. Effective empathetic individuals regulate their emotional responses to avoid becoming overwhelmed by another person's suffering. The prefrontal cortex, responsible for higher-order thinking, helps regulate emotional responses, allowing you to maintain a level of detachment that prevents emotional burnout while still providing meaningful support. For example, an educator working with a distressed student must regulate his/her own emotions to remain calm to provide effective guidance and care, rather than becoming emotionally paralyzed.

Empathetic thinking often involves moral reasoning, particularly when deciding how to respond to another's pain or struggles. You weigh ethical considerations, asking questions such as:
- Is it my responsibility to help?
- What is the most ethical course of action?
- Will my intervention improve or worsen the situation?

These considerations engage multiple brain regions, including

---

[11] Shamay-Tsoory, S. G., Aharon-Peretz, J., & Perry, D. (2009). Two systems for empathy: A double dissociation between emotional and cognitive empathy in inferior frontal gyrus versus ventromedial prefrontal lesions. *Brain, 132*(3), 617-627.

[12] Decety, J., & Lamm, C. (2006). Human empathy through the lens of social neuroscience. *The Scientific World Journal, 6,* 1146-1163.

the prefrontal cortex and anterior cingulate cortex, which are responsible for ethical decision-making and social behavior.

After analyzing an empathetic situation, you must then decide how to act. The logical process behind this decision-making involves weighing potential actions (your intent) and the consequences (the impact). Some possible responses include:
- Offering verbal or physical support,
- Taking direct action to alleviate another's distress,
- Expressing understanding and solidarity,
- Choosing to disengage in order to protect your own emotional well-being

Your chosen course of action depends on various factors, such as personal values, past experiences, and situational constraints. It's believed that people who score high in cognitive empathy can analyze situations logically and detach themselves from emotional distress, allowing them to offer more constructive support. Likewise, individuals who experience high empathy may also be more inclined to engage in altruistic acts, even at a personal cost. Studies on charitable giving have shown that people with higher activation in brain regions associated with empathy and reward processing are more likely to donate time and money to those in need[13].

Empathy is most effective when the physical and cognitive responses are aligned (working in harmony). When you experience strong physical sensations without logical regulation, you'll eventually become overwhelmed. This results in distress, inaction, and apathy. Conversely, if empathy is purely cognitive, it may lack the emotional depth necessary for meaningful connections. Striving to balance the physical and cognitive aspects increases your capacity for compassionate and effective responses in social interactions.

As an educator, martial artist, musician and church leader, it's important that I improve on my approaches for

---

[13] Harbaugh, W. T., Mayr, U., & Burghart, D. R. (2007). Neural responses to taxation and voluntary giving reveal motives for charitable donations. *Science, 316*(5831), 1622-1625.

I. Empathy

managing my empathetic responses. I must consciously maintain emotional engagement to provide support, while using cognitive control to prevent burnout. This balance ensures that empathy remains a source of connection rather than emotional depletion.

At this point, you should have a clearer understanding of the multifaceted process of empathy, involving both physical sensations and logical thought processes. Your body reacts to empathy through changes in brain activity, hormonal fluctuations, heart rate variations, and muscle mimicry. Simultaneously, your brain engages in logical analysis, employing perspective-taking, emotional regulation, moral reasoning, and decision-making. Examining the dual nature of empathy provides insight into how you connect with others and how you can cultivate compassionate interactions while maintaining emotional well-being. Scrutinizing the physiological and cognitive dimensions of empathy helps you increase your capacity, and improve your ability, to cultivate empathy with others, while safeguarding your physical, mental, and emotional health.

II. ECOSYSTEMS

1. Natural Ecosystems
2. The Primary Man-made Ecosystems
3. The Human Condition
4. Nature and Nurture
5. Human Behavior Mirrors Natural Ecosystems
6. C.E.L.L. Development

II. Ecosystems

From what I remember being taught in science classes, an ecosystem is a complex and dynamic community of living and non-living things interacting with one another in specific environmental conditions. Understanding Earth's natural ecosystems requires an examination of how different living things (humans, animals, plants, and microorganisms) interact with their environment (air, water, soil, and climate). Likewise, understanding man-made ecosystems requires an honest evaluation of how beliefs, traditions, practices, policies, institutions, and legislation influence the ways we communicate and interact. Ecosystems for equity regulate the success of individuals, impact the health of families, shape the trajectories of communities, and alter the human condition. Let's start with a refresher about natural ecosystems.

1. Natural Ecosystems

Living organisms (e.g., plants, animals, fungi, bacteria, and other microorganisms) are one of the most fundamental elements of any ecosystem. Each of these organisms plays a specific role within the ecosystem, operating through an intricate balance of biological and chemical interactions to ensure 1) the flow of energy and 2) the cycling of nutrients. These processes are made possible by three primary groups of organisms: producers, consumers, and decomposers.

Producers form the foundation of all ecosystems. These are primarily plants and algae that harness energy from the sun through the process of photosynthesis. By converting sunlight into chemical energy, producers generate the biomass that fuels the rest of the food web. In terrestrial ecosystems, grasses, trees, and shrubs serve as producers, while in aquatic environments, algae and phytoplankton play a similar role.

Consumers are organisms that rely on producers or other consumers for energy. Each level of consumers plays a vital role in maintaining ecological balance by regulating population sizes and transferring energy from one group of living things to another in the food chain. They're divided into three primary categories:

- Herbivores, which feed exclusively on plants (e.g., deer, rabbits, and cows).
- Carnivores, which prey on other animals (e.g., hawks, snakes, and wolves).
- Omnivores, such as bears and humans, consume both plant and animal matter (e.g., humans, chickens, and racoons).

Decomposers are critical for recycling nutrients back into the ecosystem. Worms, bacteria, and fungi break down the bodies of dead plants and animals, returning vital nutrients to the soil and water. Without decomposers, ecosystems would become overwhelmed with organic waste, and essential nutrients would remain locked in unusable forms.

Together, producers, consumers, and decomposers form a self-sustaining cycle that allows ecosystems to function effectively. This natural cycle supports biodiversity and keeps ecosystems resilient in the face of environmental changes.

Equally important are the non-living components of an ecosystem. These include sunlight, water, air, minerals, and climate. The non-living components provide the necessary conditions for life and significantly influence the types of organisms that can survive in a particular ecosystem. For instance, climate determines temperature and rainfall patterns, which in turn affect plant growth and animal behavior.

A critical process that sustains ecosystems is the flow of energy. You might recall that this energy primarily comes from the sun. Plants, algae and phytoplankton (producers) capture solar energy through photosynthesis, converting it into chemical energy. Herbivores then consume these producers, gaining energy, and are themselves consumed by carnivores and omnivores. Decomposers complete the cycle by breaking down dead organisms and returning nutrients to the soil, which plants can then use again.

Another vital process in ecosystems, closely linked to energy flow, is nutrient cycling. Key elements like carbon, nitrogen, and water continuously move through living

II. Ecosystems

organisms and the physical environment in complex cycles. These cycles ensure essential nutrients are reused and remain available within the ecosystem, supporting ongoing life and growth.

Natural ecosystems are broadly categorized into two main types: terrestrial and aquatic. Terrestrial ecosystems are land-based and include forests, deserts, and grasslands. They play a significant role in sustaining biodiversity, regulating climate, and providing critical resources for life on Earth. On the other hand, aquatic ecosystems (indispensable to the health of the planet) exist in water environments. Freshwater ecosystems provide drinking water, irrigation, and habitat for a multitude of species. Marine ecosystems, meanwhile, are fundamental in global climate regulation and marine biodiversity.

Understanding the unique functions of natural ecosystems provides us with insight into the resilience of life and the adaptability of organisms to Earth's diverse landscapes. Each habitat plays a crucial role in supporting life, regulating the environment, and sustaining human societies. Based on this understanding, you must choose to be better about appreciating, not appropriating, the complexity of life and act in ways that pre-serve (carefully and critically consider your intentions, and the potential impact you will have on) and con-serve (collaborating with, not controlling) these natural environments for future generations.

Recognizing the interconnectedness within ecosystems and preserving them is essential for ecological balance and future generations. It goes without saying that human well-being is intimately connected to the health and stability of the ecosystems mentioned above. Earth's natural ecosystems provide resources and services that are essential to human survival and prosperity. However, dismissive attitudes and negative activities, elements of the manufactured ecosystems, are depleting natural resources and damaging the aforementioned natural services.

C.E.A.S.E. for Equity

As stewards of this planet, it's our responsibility to care for the intricate web of life that sustains us all. We must commit to protecting the ecosystems. Conservation, sustainable practices, and environmental awareness are essential to repairing the damage and ensuring that natural ecosystems continue to thrive. Each small change will have a big impact, so protecting and understanding ecosystems is crucial for the wellbeing of Earth's future!

I must take a moment to review the concept of ecosystem services, mentioned previously. They can be grouped into four broad categories: provisioning, regulating, supporting, and cultural services.

1. Provisioning services are the products we get directly from ecosystems (aka the things provided by nature), the most obvious being food and materials for housing.
2. Regulating services are the natural processes that help keep the environment stable and livable, by regulating the environment. They include climate regulation, oxygen production, and water purification.
3. Supporting services form the foundation upon which all other ecosystem services depend. These essential functions are not always immediately visible or directly beneficial to humans in tangible ways, but they're critical for sustaining life on Earth and ensuring that ecosystems remain healthy and productive. They include nutrient cycling, soil formation, photosynthesis, and habitats for species – sustaining the basic ecological processes that make life possible. Without them, provisioning, regulating, and cultural services would simply not exist. For example, the natural pollination of crops by pollinators (e.g., bees, birds, and other insects) is vital to global food security.
4. Cultural services represent the non-material benefits that people derive from ecosystems. Unlike

II. Ecosystems

provisioning or regulating services, which offer tangible goods or environmental regulation, cultural services enrich human life through psychological, spiritual, and intellectual experiences. These services highlight the deep and often personal connections between humans and the natural world, underscoring the intrinsic value of nature beyond physical needs. They deepen our connection to the Earth, enrich our lives, and remind us of the importance of conserving and preserving the natural world for both present and future generations. Recreation, tourism, aesthetic appreciation, and educational inspiration are some examples, in addition to the spiritual and religious value mentioned previously.

Each of the aforementioned services contributes to human health, economic stability, and cultural practices. Without functioning ecosystems, humanity would struggle to survive, let alone thrive. Ecosystems provide numerous benefits, yet they're increasingly under threat due to debilitating human attitudes and behaviors. The growing pressures of human development, motivated by selfish ambitions, have threatened these systems on a global scale; unsustainable practices have pushed many ecosystems toward collapse.

Deforestation destroys habitats, impacts climate change, and degrades the stability of land masses. Pollution corrupts air, water, and soil quality across the globe. Runoff containing fertilizers and pesticides contributes to algal blooms in aquatic systems, depleting oxygen levels and killing marine life. Plastic pollution and heavy metal contamination have long-lasting effects on both biodiversity and human health. Sustained fluctuations in climate (e.g., shifting weather patterns, increasing and decreasing temperatures around the globe, and greater frequency of extreme weather events) exacerbate problems. For example, coral reefs are highly sensitive to rises in sea temperature, which consequently threatens the diverse marine life that depends on them.

Humanity is the only threat to, and the only hope for, the health and longevity of ecosystems. Hold yourself accountable for what you consume and discard – Yeah, I said it! Discover what it takes to produce those items. What's the production process? How is the waste discarded? What's the impact on the environment and/or local community where the resources originated? Active preservation and conservation efforts are critical.

Reforestation projects help restore ecosystems, sequester carbon, and improve biodiversity. Marine protection zones safeguard parts of the ocean from human interference, allowing fish populations and coral reefs to recover. Sustainable practices in agriculture, fishing, and industry must concentrate on reducing environmental harm while maintaining productivity. Some include regenerative agriculture (practiced by Indigenous tribes for generations), crop rotation, organic farming, water conservation, and responsible consumption.

Educating communities, helping people experience the importance of conservation, and involving them in ecological stewardship are crucial aspects of protecting ecosystems. When people intimately understand the value of ecosystems and feel empowered to take action, positive change becomes more achievable.

2. The Primary Man-Made Ecosystems

Human beings don't exist in a vacuum; we thrive – or falter – within environments designed and maintained by our collective choices. Human societies are not merely organic outgrowths of history and nature; they're complex, intentionally designed constructs to govern our interactions, distribute resources, and impact our collective well-being. Central among these constructs are the two primary man-made ecosystems – economic and social. They determine the organization of resources, relationships, and opportunities.

II. Ecosystems

The economic and social ecosystems function similarly to biological ecosystems, where various elements interact dynamically to sustain or destabilize the whole. Just as natural ecosystems rely on balance and interconnectivity to thrive, these manufactured systems require a harmonious integration of various components to sustain equity, amplify justice, and promote societal health. By viewing these two aspects of the human condition through an ecosystemic lens, we will better understand the interconnected roles of psychology, cultural norms, infrastructure, politics, legislation, education, healthcare, and housing in shaping societal outcomes.

This might not surprise you, but equity isn't a natural outcome of these manufactured ecosystems. Instead, it must be cultivated and sustained through intentional, coordinated efforts across all the domains listed above. Equity isn't a destination but a process, continuously shaped by the choices you make. It demands policies that are inclusive, culturally competent, and rooted in justice. Most importantly, it requires elements that prioritize human dignity and shared prosperity. It calls for a collective commitment to reimagining the world not as it is, but as it should be, trusting in the creativity and resilience of people themselves – a world where every individual has the opportunity to thrive within healthy and equitable environments.

Let's start with a brief explanation of these two man-made ecosystems, followed by examining how elements function within the broader contexts of them, and conclude with considering how the elements of psychology, cultural norms, infrastructure, politics, legislation, education, healthcare, and housing are interconnected with sustaining equity.

The economic ecosystem consists of the structures and institutions that dictate the production, distribution, and consumption of resources. It includes employment, labor markets, wealth distribution, access to capital, industry trends, and entrepreneurship. Equity in this ecosystem means equality of opportunity and fairness in outcomes, ensuring all individuals have access to the resources and the support necessary for full participation and meaningful benefit (this speaks to affordability).

The social ecosystem encompasses the norms, relationships, networks, and institutions that bind communities together. This includes families, shared values, academia, cultural expectations, and social services. Equity in this area means fostering inclusive environments where all identities, voices, and experiences are acknowledged, respected, and valued.

As noted, the economic ecosystem influences all things pertaining to income and entrepreneurship. Within these lie mechanisms that can either foster opportunity or perpetuate inequality. Wealth and income inequality is a defining challenge of modern economies. Capital tends to accumulate among those who already possess the finances to access resources without hardship, leading to a widening gap between the wealthy and the impoverished. Without corrective mechanisms—such as impartial taxation, inclusive financial systems, and fair labor practices—economic ecosystems can exaggerate institutionalized disparities.

Labor markets are pivotal in determining access to economic mobility. However, when these markets are saturated with discrimination, wage stagnation, and inadequate labor protections, they limit upward mobility and marginalize groups even more. Access to decent work, affordable job training, and worker protections are crucial to creating and sustaining inclusive economic opportunities. Worker cooperatives and solidarity networks prioritize shared prosperity over profit. These models ensure workers benefit directly from the value they create, fostering dignity and community resilience.

Entrepreneurship is a powerful tool for wealth creation, especially in underserved communities. However, access to capital, mentorship, and markets is a daunting barrier. Supporting small business development and reducing bureaucratic obstacles to business formation will unlock latent economic potential in marginalized communities.

II. Ecosystems

Social ecosystems encompass collective behaviors that define how you interact and find meaning within society. They shape your sense of belonging, identity, and mutual responsibility. Strong families and community networks offer emotional support, social capital, and informal safety nets. However, social fragmentation, intergenerational trauma, and exclusion erode these foundations. Revitalizing community life through local initiatives, shared spaces, and intergenerational dialogue is essential for fostering social equity.

Cultural narratives inform your understanding of success, failure, and fairness. In societies where individualism is prized over collectivism, it's easy to ignore institutional inequalities since the focus is based on ability and talent, rather than social status or wealth. This is often vocalized as the meritocratic myth that "hard work equals success," which often simplifies reality and creates false expectations by ignoring how unequal access to education, healthcare, and job opportunities affect outcomes (especially for marginalized groups). Promoting inclusive cultural narratives that recognize structural barriers and value cooperation can shift mindsets toward collective responsibility.

It's important that we acknowledge the role the media plays in reinforcing societal perceptions. Each form of media (social, print and digital, news and entertainment) has a responsibility in the way people are portrayed. Marginalized groups are often stereotyped or rendered invisible. This significantly influences public sentiment and policy decisions. Ensuring diverse and authentic representation in all forms of media is a powerful equalizer for cultural equity.

Technology is another element of the social ecosystem that can increase access to education, healthcare, and entrepreneurship. Initiatives that provide internet access, digital skills training, and tech incubators in underserved communities can close opportunity gaps.

Achieving equity requires a multi-dimensional approach that integrates diverse aspects of human life. We must stop hiding behind "the government," relying on government programs and subsidies, when it comes to empowering communities (specifically those that have been historically and institutionally targeted). Sustaining equity means extending empowerment beyond government dependency. Community grassroots and private sector initiatives, promoting self-sufficiency and resilience, must be at the forefront of our work. Government assistance should be a complement, not a prerequisite, to said initiatives.

Psychological well-being (stigmatized by the term "mental health") is foundational to individual agency. The trauma of poverty, discrimination, racialized dynamics, and exclusion inhibits a person's, and by extension a community's, belief in their own potential. Empowerment must begin at the psychological level. According to Proverbs 23 verse 7, in the Christian Bible, *"As a man thinks in his heart, so is he."* Programs that incorporate coaching, therapy, trauma-informed care, resilience training, and access to psychological health resources are vital for personal empowerment and social cohesion. They can help individuals overcome personal barriers that institutional reforms alone can't address.

Cultural norms influence everything from work ethics to family structure to the way success is defined. They influence how you perceive your own worth and that of others. In some communities, deeply ingrained narratives discourage risk-taking, education, or intergenerational planning, while in others, they reinforce exclusion and bias. For sustainable equity, we must investigate and amplify cultural narratives, challenge stereotypes, celebrate diverse forms of expression and success, adopt inclusive perspectives of value and contribution, nurture joy in heritage, and combat internalized oppression. Cultural festivals, inclusive curricula, and public art are some suggestions for serving the purpose of transforming social dynamics.

The constructed environment (aka infrastructure) significantly affects quality of life. Where you live determines your access to clean air and drinking water, safe neighborhoods, quality schools, and stable jobs. Environmental

II. Ecosystems

discrimination, racialized inequality, redlining, and urban neglect have created physical landscapes of inequity. Poor urban planning leads to food deserts, transportation disparities, and environmental hazards that disproportionately affect low-income communities. Compassionate urban design (green spaces, walkable neighborhoods, and clean infrastructure) promotes community health, personal mobility, and economic activity, while also supporting well-being and inclusion.

Governments can't create equity on their own, but they play a vital role in shaping the playing field. Public policies codify societal values and priorities. Legislation about housing, taxation, healthcare, education, nutrition, and labor establishes the mindset and commitment to sustain equity by transforming these social landscapes. The commitment to equity must include advocacy for laws that ensure affordability and expand access to resources. Equity-conscious policymaking includes dismantling barriers to participation in elections (e.g., voter suppression laws), undoing harm (e.g., ending mass incarceration), and funding support systems that balance the scales. However, it's crucial these efforts foster self-reliance while eradicating dependency on government assistance.

I firmly believe education remains one of the most powerful tools for equity. However, disparities in funding, quality supports for educators, and curriculum persist, perpetuating social stratification. In low-income communities, schools are often under-resourced, overcrowded, and less safe. Universal access to high-quality education, inclusive pedagogy, and lifelong learning opportunities are essential.

Schools must be places of safety and empowerment, especially for marginalized students. Reimagining private and public education means prioritizing equity in school funding, integrating culturally affirming teaching practices, and incorporating life skills to prepare students not just for tests, but for life. Students must be empowered through representation, history, and relevance – it will increase engagement and achievement.

C.E.A.S.E. for Equity

Charter schools, homeschooling co-ops, and vocational training programs can fill gaps left by public schools. With that said, learners who are failed by conventional approaches might be better served by pathways outside traditional academia; ways that provide relevant, empowering education outside traditional institutions – community schools, trade apprenticeships, experiential learning, and skill-based certification programs that fast-track employable skills (e.g., coding bootcamps). Exposure to mentors and role models who reflect the identities and experiences of marginalized individuals is vital for boosting self-efficacy and aspiration. Programs connecting youth with professionals, entrepreneurs, and community leaders will break cycles of poverty and disenfranchisement.

Likewise, teaching financial literacy from an early age will help individuals make informed decisions about budgeting, saving, investing, credit management, and entrepreneurship. Initiatives like matched savings accounts, microloans, and cooperative banking will sustain long-term wealth creation.

Physical health and psychological wellness (aka mental health) are prerequisites for success in any ecosystem. Equitable access to healthcare is critical for sustaining a productive and just society. Disparities in care, exacerbated by social determinants of health, must be addressed through community-based initiatives, mobile clinics, and universal coverage. Psychological wellness deserves equal attention, with services that are culturally competent and destigmatized. Poor health limits work capacity, learning, and social engagement. Yet healthcare remains deeply unequal in these United States of America.

Sustaining equity in this environment requires universal access to affordable high-quality care, trauma-informed services, and preventive programs. Clinics embedded in communities, mobile health units, and partnerships with trusted institutions (e.g., churches, barbershops, etc.) will bridge gaps and remove stigma in underserved areas, without the need for

II. Ecosystems

inserting government systems. Community members should be trained to help others navigate complexities inherent in health and preventive care systems. In addition to the infrastructure elements stated previously, holistic efforts to improve health – fitness and nutrition programs such as walking trails, community gardens, food processing and preparation classes (e.g. farm to table), and bike lanes – must be supported, implemented, and fully funded.

It's important to note that change is sustained when people feel they have a stake in their society. Empowering local communities to identify and address their particular needs fosters ownership and effectiveness. Grassroots organizing, through civic engagement, goes a long way toward accomplishing this by building power from the ground up. Training citizens in advocacy, leadership, and policy engagement enhances democratic participation (equating to control over resources and decision making) and empowers each person to manifest success, prosperity, and safety in ways that align with their cultural beliefs, customs, and traditions.

Housing is both a basic need and a determinant of opportunity – it's the foundation for employment, education, and health. Without stable housing, individuals face constant insecurity, which makes growth nearly impossible. Unaffordable housing, evictions, and homelessness erode social stability.

Solutions include a) mixed-income housing developments, b) rent control and tenant protections, c) housing-first policies, and d) pathways to home ownership that prioritize dignity and autonomy to build intergenerational wealth. Likewise, community land trusts will prevent displacement by keeping land under community ownership, and sweat equity programs will ensure individual residents obtain ownership stakes in housing developments, in exchange for their labor. Zoning reform advocacy must leverage local organizing to legalize duplexes. Accessory Development Units (ADUs), and mixed-use development to increase affordable options.

Churches, mosques, temples, libraries, recreation facilities, and cultural centers play a vital role in offering support, moral guidance, and a sense of belonging. These institutions often provide food, shelter, and education, while also serving as spaces for collaboration and support. Faith-based and cultural organizations are tactically situated to provide services that can minimize, or even eradicate, the need for government aid.

Sustainable equity can't depend solely on government programs and subsidies. We must stop hiding behind "the government" when it comes to empowering communities, specifically those that have been historically and strategically marginalized. Community grassroots and private sector initiatives are essential to rehabilitating, manifesting, transforming, and sustaining ecosystems for equity.

3. The Human Condition

Before we explore some ways that human behaviors mirror natural ecosystems, let's take the next four-ish pages to gain a better understanding of the human condition. It's what every human being experiences – encompassing your thoughts, emotions, struggles, and triumphs as you navigate life. It's shaped by universal themes such as love, suffering, purpose, mortality, freedom, and connection. The human condition is the through line, connecting all of humanity regardless of culture, geographic location, beliefs, traditions, affiliation, status, or position of influence.

Across cultures, philosophies, and spiritual traditions, the human experience is understood not as a simple narrative but as a profound and often paradoxical journey. At the heart of what it means to be human is the constant tension between opposites: joy and suffering, hope and despair, freedom and responsibility, life and death. These dualities shape your life, your identity, and your quest for meaning. From the wisdom of ancient traditions, to the insights of modern thought, humanity continues to wrestle with these contradictions. It's in the very act of grappling with them that you uncover the essence of being human.

Human beings are unique in their capacity for self-awareness. Unlike other animals, you possess the ability to think about your thoughts, to reflect on your actions, and to question your very existence. This remarkable trait is both a gift and a burden. On one hand, self-awareness fuels your creativity, your dreams, and your capacity to imagine futures not yet realized. It enables you to create art, pursue knowledge, and shape societies. On the other hand, it also brings with it anxiety, fear, and the existential weight of knowing that your life is finite.

Many spiritual and philosophical traditions have a profound perspective on this duality. For instance, Buddhism teaches that self-awareness is the root of suffering; that your ability to understand, to crave, and to fear stems from a reflective mindset. Yet, it's this same awareness that offers the path to enlightenment. By recognizing the impermanence of all things, you learn to let go, to live more fully, and to awaken to a deeper truth. One of the most persistent questions in the human psyche is: *What is the purpose of my life?* From the earliest myths to contemporary philosophies, this question echoes through every culture and every age.

Some find answers in religion, drawing meaning from divine purpose and spiritual duty. Others look to relationships, nature, or personal passions for a sense of fulfillment. Still others, particularly within existentialist traditions like those of Jean-Paul Sartre or Friedrich Nietzsche, argue that life has no inherent meaning, that you must create it yourself through your actions and choices. These views can be liberating and daunting, two sides of the same coin. They demand that you take responsibility for your life, that you become the author of your own story.

Humans are deeply emotional beings, with these emotions coloring every aspect of our existence. Yet, they often stand in tension with your rational mind. Love, for example, gives life richness and depth, but it also exposes you to the pain of loss and rejection. Fear can protect you from danger, but it can also paralyze you or prevent you from pursuing your dreams. Suffering is undeniably painful, yet it also increases your resilience, compassion, and wisdom.

Philosophers of ancient Greece and Rome taught that much of human suffering comes not from external events, but from our attachment to them. By learning to accept what you can't control, and to master your inner responses, you cultivate your emotional maturity. Learning to balance emotion and reason isn't about suppressing feeling; it's about navigating both with patience and wisdom.

From birth to death, human beings are inherently social creatures, shaped by our relationships – family, friends, communities, and even adversaries. You seek connection, belonging, and love. Yet, these desires can make you vulnerable, afraid of rejection, loss, and dependency. The African philosophy of *Ubuntu*, which means "I am because we are," captures this beautifully. It's a reminder that your humanity isn't found in isolation, but in connection. You're made whole through your interdependence with others, not through self-sufficiency. However, in the modern world, with its emphasis on individualism and competition, many feel isolated and disconnected. The challenge, then, is to reclaim the communal spirit, to build bridges, to cultivate empathy, and to recognize that your well-being is tied to the well-being of others.

Perhaps the greatest contradiction of all is this – you live knowing you will one day die. This awareness casts a shadow over all human endeavors, while also giving life its urgency and beauty. Death instills fear in some, but in others it brings a sense of clarity and purpose. The Hindu philosophy of *Samsara* (the cycle of life, death, and rebirth) teaches that death is not an end, but a transition. In this view, life is part of a larger, sacred continuum, and death serves as both teacher and guide. By accepting mortality, you learn to appreciate and embrace life more fully. You begin to value your time, to

II. Ecosystems

cherish your relationships, and to seek a legacy that extends beyond your physical existence.

Every human has the potential for both compassion and cruelty, generosity and selfishness. The struggle between good and evil is not abstract and external – it resides closer than you think, in your heart. Some traditions see evil as a product of social conditions or ignorance, while others see it as an inherent aspect of human nature. The Cherokee story of the Two Wolves illustrates this internal battle: *Within each person, there are two wolves – one good, one evil. The one that prevails is the one we choose to feed.* This story speaks to the moral responsibility of each individual. While you might not control your circumstances, you can always choose your response. You can strive to foster kindness, courage, and integrity, even in a world full of injustice.

Humans long for freedom – to choose, to learn, to create, to travel, to express ourselves. Yet we also crave structure, order, and predictability. Too much freedom can lead to chaos; too much control can become oppression. The wisdom of Taoism, an ancient Chinese philosophy, offers a path through this conflict. It teaches that the best way to live is in harmony with the natural flow of life, to avoid forcing or resisting what is. I often use the expression that life is a river and sometimes it's best to go with the current instead of working against it, learning to be content in every situation and circumstance. By learning to "go with the flow," you discover a kind of freedom that is not about domination, but about alignment. True wisdom lies in balancing autonomy with responsibility, spontaneity with discipline, and freedom with the needs of the greater good.

Needless to say, the human condition is full of contradictions. You seek happiness, yet it's pain that often teaches you the most. You crave connection, but fear the vulnerability that comes with opening yourself up to others. You long for truth, yet sometimes deceive yourself with comforting illusions. Still, it's precisely within this struggle that the beauty of humanity is revealed. Your capacity to dream, to create, to love, and to learn from suffering speaks to an incredible resilience. Across cultures and eras, the search for balance between opposites has given rise to profound wisdom, art, and meaning.

Contrary to the language and behavior of some people, being human is not about perfection. It's about doing your best to be in the present moment. It's about embracing the messiness of life with courage and compassion. It's about seeing yourself in others, finding meaning in the mundane, and turning your wounds into wisdom. At the end of the day, the human condition is not a problem to be solved, but a mystery to be lived – one breath, one choice, one relationship at a time.

Our collective efforts to enact structural changes that 1) eradicate unjust institutional practices, 2) eliminate discriminatory legislation and policies, and 3) fight corrupt methods, will manifest a society where opportunity isn't limited by wealth, birth, or background. In doing so, we not only improve individual lives but also strengthen the social fabric and future potential of our global society. The human condition improves when resources are affordable, opportunities are accessible, and rights are ethically applied for the well-being of every person, family, and community (not just the privileged few).

4. <u>Nature and Nurture</u>

The human condition is a rich and complex tapestry of experiences, shaped by countless internal and external factors that influence how you think, feel, speak, and behave. Understanding these elements will help you make sense of yourself and navigate life with more awareness, compassion, and purpose. From your biology to your beliefs, from the society you live in to the time periods you live through, every aspect contributes to who you are and how you experience the world. Let's uncover some of the diverse forces that shape human life, and examine their impact on your development, challenges you might face, and your pursuit of meaning.

II. Ecosystems

Your journey as a human being begins with the body, the brain, and the soul. Biology lays the foundation for how you interact with the world, from your genetic makeup to the chemical workings of your nervous system. Genetics play a powerful role in determining your inherited characteristics, influencing everything from your health conditions to your temperament, intelligence, and talents. Aging also reminds you of your mortality and biological limitations. As your body changes over time, you're continually confronted with the impermanence of life. This biological awareness of death shapes your priorities, and this inspires you to seek purpose, connection, and legacy.

And of course, there's also your brain chemistry, which significantly impacts your perception, your perspective, your choice of language, and ultimately your actions. Neurotransmitters such as dopamine and serotonin regulate your psychological traits (mood, motivation, and emotional well-being). For example, someone with high dopamine levels may exhibit natural optimism and drive, while someone with low serotonin might struggle with depression or anxiety.

Beyond biological elements, the mind plays a pivotal role in shaping the human condition. Your thoughts, beliefs, and sense of identity deeply affect how you experience and respond to the world. Cognitive patterns, of optimism or pessimism, influence your resilience and problem-solving skills. For instance, when you see failure as a learning opportunity, you're more likely to grow from setbacks, while someone who perceives failure as a personal shortcoming may be more prone to discouragement.

Beliefs and experiences pertaining to emotions such as love, anger, fear, and joy are powerful motivators in human behavior. They influence your relationships, decisions, and even your health. Likewise, your identity (the way you see yourself) is formed through your experiences, beliefs, and social roles. Self-awareness is a hallmark of human consciousness – it allows you to reflect on your past, imagine your future, and make choices that align with your values.

C.E.A.S.E. for Equity

     Humans are inherently social beings, with family life providing the earliest framework for understanding the world. Your upbringing, the societal norms, and your cultural values all have a profound influence on your beliefs, language, behavior, and ultimately your opportunities. Whether you were raised in environments of love and stability or chaos and neglect, the early experiences forge your emotional foundations and shape your coping mechanisms. Cultural values and societal norms further guide your understanding of right and wrong, shaping everything from your clothing preferences, to your language and dialect, to your career choices and gender roles.

     Refer to what I shared about the primary man-made ecosystems. Social class and economic background affect access to education, healthcare, housing, and employment, which influence your aspirations and psychological health. In this digital age, media and technology also play major roles in shaping your perspectives. Social media, for instance, not only connects you but also manipulates your expectations, comparisons, and sense of self-worth. A child raised in a collectivist society that emphasizes family and discipline may grow up with a different worldview than one raised in a culture that prizes individualism and self-expression. These social and cultural contexts are inescapable and deeply formative.

     The physical environment in which you live also shapes the choices you make, the emotions you display, your physical and psychological well-being, and the survival strategies you employ. The infrastructure we fabricate, climate, topography, geography, and natural events all contribute to how you navigate the daily realities of life and plan for the long-term. People living in areas prone to natural disasters or affected by climate change face unique psychological health and survival challenges, often shaped by trauma, uncertainty, and resilience.

     Living in a warm, coastal village, for example, might foster a laid-back lifestyle and close community bonds, while life in a cold, urban metropolis might cultivate a sense of hyper awareness, efficiency, and independence, along with increased

II. Ecosystems

stress. I have a theory – the need to be hyper-aware is the primary reason many inner-city children are mis-diagnosed with conditions such as attention-deficit disorder (ADD) and attention-deficit/hyperactivity disorder (ADHD). Perhaps that will be another book...I'm just saying ;-)

Urban versus rural life is another key distinction. Cities may offer access to education, healthcare, and entertainment but often come with higher stress levels and a fast-paced lifestyle. Rural areas may provide peace and connection to nature, but also isolation and limited resources. The physical environment affects your physical survival (by way of your emotional health), your relationship to nature, and your access to opportunities.

Perhaps the most distinctively human trait is the soul, which drives your need to find meaning in life. Spiritual and philosophical beliefs shape your values, ethics, and sense of purpose. Religions around the world offer frameworks for understanding existence, suffering, morality, and what happens after we pass from this life. Faith can bring comfort, community, and a moral compass. A devout Muslim, Christian, Buddhist, or practitioner of any similar tradition often finds strength in the rituals, teachings, and shared identity of their belief system.

Others turn to philosophy to make sense of life. Some view life as a test of character; for others, it's an adventure of learning; and still others view it as a random phenomenon requiring us to create our own meaning. Existential philosophers, for example, argue that while life may lack intrinsic meaning, individuals have the power and responsibility to define their purpose through action. Whether guided by sacred texts or inner reflection, the human quest for meaning is universal. It informs how you face suffering, celebrate joy, and plan for the future.

5. Human Behavior Mirrors Natural Ecosystems

Human beings are not separate from nature – we're a very influential part of it. The rhythms, patterns, and principles that govern ecosystems aren't just external realities; they're internal truths reflected in our thoughts, emotions, and social structures. When you look closely, you find that human behavior mirrors the natural world in profound ways. From the flow of energy to the importance of diversity, from emotional storms to power dynamics, nature offers powerful metaphors and lessons for living wisely and sustainably. Understanding these parallels will guide you toward balance, both within yourself and in your relationship with the planet.

Recall - in natural ecosystems, energy flows in a continuous cycle: from the sun to plants, to herbivores, to predators, and finally back to the Earth. This delicate balance maintains life. Similarly, human behavior follows cycles of cause and effect – our thoughts lead to emotions, which drive actions, and those actions bring about consequences. And for the record, consequences are neither good nor bad – they are the situations and circumstances that result from actions. This is the principle of karma: every action creates ripples that return to you in some form. Like nature, human actions must be balanced and thoughtful. What you give and take matters.

For example, overfishing disrupts marine food chains, leading to ecological collapse. In human society, greed, appropriation, and exploitation (of people, resources, or elements) create social imbalances, unrest, and eventual breakdown. Just as nature requires a balanced flow of energy to survive, human behavior must also be sustainable. If not, the result is personal, societal, or environmental collapse.

Biodiversity is a vital indicator of healthy ecosystems. Different species play unique roles, creating systems that are more resilient to change and disruption. In human society, diversity of culture, thought, and perspective serves a similar purpose. It enriches our communities, fuels innovation, and strengthens our ability to adapt in a changing world. Consider

II. Ecosystems

how monoculture farming weakens an ecosystem by reducing genetic diversity, making it vulnerable to disease and collapse. Similarly, societies that suppress diverse voices or rigidly conform to singular ideologies become stagnant and eventually come to an end. Resilience comes from embracing complexity. Just as natural ecosystems depend on biodiversity, human communities thrive on inclusion, cooperation, and openness to different perspectives.

Earth's climate is shaped by natural cycles, but human interference (through pollution, deforestation, and industrialization) has thrown it into imbalance, leading to more intense storms, rising temperatures, and environmental crises. Your inner world functions much the same way. Balance in both the environment and your emotions requires awareness, reflection, and sustainable habits of care. Emotions are natural, but when suppressed or ignored, they can build into destructive "storms." Unchecked anger, fear, or greed disrupts personal relationships, psychological health, and community harmony. Just as deforestation leads to erosion and flooding, internal emotional neglect leads to outbursts and breakdowns.

Sustainable living requires a mindset of giving back, not just taking. Reciprocity, the idea that we must give back to the land that sustains us, is taught in many indigenous traditions as being essential for long-term balance. In contrast, modern consumerism often prioritizes exploitation, appropriation, and the confiscation of resources without regard for replenishment. This leads to environmental degradation, species extinction, and societal decline.

Historically, Indigenous tribes hunted the buffalo with respect and restraint, ensuring the survival of both the species and the culture. European settlers, driven by profit, over-hunted them to near extinction. This stark difference in approach reflects a broader truth: the health and longevity of natural and man-made ecosystems can't be sustained when the sole focus is extraction.

Water is the essence of life on Earth. It connects all living things, nourishes ecosystems, and adapts fluidly (see what I did there, lol) to its surroundings. Your emotions behave in similar ways. When allowed to flow naturally, your emotions cleanse and renew. When blocked like a dam, they build pressure and can erupt destructively. Like water, your emotions must flow freely and cleanly. When your inner realm is in balance, you can nourish the world around you. Just as industrial pollution poisons rivers, repressed or toxic emotions can poison relationships and mental health. Healing requires purification through the reflexive process of honest self-reflection and expression.

Additionally, power – the imposition of your abilities, skills, expectations, will, and desires onto the people, places, and creatures around you – must be exercised responsibly. When it's balanced and ethical, both nature and society thrive. In the wild, predators and prey maintain an ecological equilibrium. If predators overhunt, their food source dwindles, and the predators themselves eventually die out. Human power dynamics work the same way. Leaders who exploit their people or environment may thrive temporarily, but imbalance inevitably leads to societal collapse.

A famous ecological example is the reintroduction of wolves to Yellowstone National Park. After being eradicated, their absence led to overpopulation of deer, which degraded plant life. When wolves returned, the ecosystem repaired itself and balance was slowly restored. In the same way, ethical and balanced leadership will restore order and repair relationships in struggling societies.

In the Christian Bible, it's written *"For everything there is a season, and a time for every matter under heaven..."* (Ecclesiastes 3:1-8) Nature follows the rhythm of seasons – growth in spring, abundance in summer, harvest and decline in autumn, and rest in winter. Human life, too, unfolds in cycles. You experience seasons of energy, success, hardship, healing and rest. Just as a forest regenerates after a fire, you can emerge stronger from loss and struggle. The key is to accept these cycles rather than resist them. Some traditions follow the wisdom that pain and difficulty aren't permanent, they're

II. Ecosystems

simply the "winter" before "spring" returns. With patience and trust, every season brings its own purpose and beauty.

When you study nature, you see yourself reflected in its rhythms. Ecosystems offer powerful metaphors for how you think, feel, lead, and live. Sustainability in ecosystems mirrors self-discipline in human behavior, with biodiversity reflecting the strength of open-mindedness. Storms reveal emotional turbulence, reciprocity highlights the importance of mutual respect, and the seasons teach about patience and trust. By observing and honoring the wisdom of nature, you learn how to live in harmony with the world around you and within yourself. The Earth isn't just your environment – it's your template for how to interact and prosper peacefully (without conflict). Many Indigenous and spiritual traditions remind us that our fate is tied to the Earth: when you harm it, you harm yourself. By respecting nature's balance, you also increase wisdom, maturity, and peace in your own life.

6. C.E.L.L. Development

Cells are the fundamental elements of all living things. Needless to say, it's imperative that cells be exposed, and have access, to beneficial nutrients and conditions that nurture long-term health and optimal development. The human body is fearfully and wonderfully made (Psalm 139:14) – a miracle of interconnected systems, where trillions of cells rely on the right conditions and nutrients to thrive. Without oxygen, water, and nourishment, cells break down, leading to illness, degradation, and eventually death.

Similarly, the man-made economic and social ecosystems of these United States of America function like living organisms. They depend on healthy habitats, equitable resource distribution, and collaborative networks to sustain the health and longevity of society as a whole. Yet, much like a body neglected of its essential needs, the civil fabric that binds the people of these United States of America has been frayed by centuries of institutionalized neglect, exploitation, and exclusion.

C.E.A.S.E. for Equity

I often find myself reflecting on how these United States of America – a nation that prides itself on ideals of freedom and democracy – was built on principles of profound exploitation, exclusion, and murder. To understand where we are today, to make sense of the racialized and financial disparities that persist, you must follow the evolution of our man-made economic and social ecosystems; recognizing and admitting that the dysfunctions emanate from a historical progression that began with colonization, moved through emancipation, and was partially addressed by legislation. However, the ecosystems continue to deteriorate, and remain deeply imbalanced, because the final step of liberation has never been fully embraced.

Liberation, in this context, means not just freedom in name, but the active restoration, empowerment, and healing of those communities that have been marginalized and disenfranchised. Just as living cells require positive conditions and beneficial nutrients, reparative and restorative actions must be manifested in the social and economic ecosystems for true vitality and sustainability to be achieved. The unfinished business of these United States of America is justice. That part….right there…the unfinished business of America is **justice!** To make these United States of America great again requires justice! And IYKYK - justice requires reparations. Not as symbolic gestures but as transformative restorative actions: to heal and empower communities that remain marginalized and disenfranchised due to the legacies of habitual and institutionalized discrimination, oppression, exclusion, and destruction.

Say this part out loud – Colonization wasn't a mere act of settling new lands; it was the original toxin introduced into the social ecosystem of this land. Let that marinate; let that echo in your soul; let that fuel your motivation to cultivate empathy and sustain ecosystems for equity. European settlers established economic practices and policies rooted in the violent displacement of the Indigenous peoples and the enslavement of Africans. The wealth generated from stolen

II. Ecosystems

land and forced labor was not an unfortunate side effect: it was the catalyst for the economic ecosystem as we know it. Colonization created rigid racialized hierarchies, embedding the concept of "white" dominance into the legal, cultural, civic, and financial DNA of the nation.

This initial contamination (aka colonization) had predictable consequences. Much like pollutants in water that poison entire biological systems, colonization poisoned the ideal of equality before it could even take root in these United States of America. Indigenous populations were decimated, abducted Africans and their descendants were commodified, and the very foundation of wealth accumulation was built upon racial exploitation. From the very beginning, the economic and social ecosystems of these United States of America were engineered to serve a select few at the expense of many (i.e., depleting the resources and opportunities of others). The land that now constitutes these United States of America was home to thriving Indigenous civilizations, which had sophisticated social and economic ecosystems that were sustainable, communal, and deeply connected to the land.

European colonizers, driven by greed and imperial ambition, imposed selfish and destructive ideals that valued extraction over sustainability, profit over people. The doctrine of "Manifest Destiny" and the legal fiction of the "Doctrine of Discovery" gave moral cover to acts of genocide and land theft. Indigenous people were forcibly removed from their ancestral homes through violent means, epitomized by events such as the Trail of Tears. Meanwhile, the transatlantic slave trade brought countless Africans to these shores, transforming human beings into commodities for the purpose of fueling an emerging capitalist economy.

This period laid the foundation for the economic might of these United States of America. The wealth generated from stolen land and stolen labor was not incidental nor accidental; it was purposeful and essential. Yet, the dominant narrative painted this violent history as the price of "progress" and "civilization." Oppressive language, from calling Indigenous people "savages" to defining enslaved Africans as "property," dehumanized entire populations and entrenched racialized hierarchies. Thus, colonization strengthened the man-made ecosystems, using the concept of "race" to manipulate and control the socioeconomic legacies of entire cultures. This was codified in law, enforced through violence, and normalized through culture. It wasn't a mistake that "just happened;" instead, it was the blueprint.

The abolition of slavery marked a critical moment, much like stopping the introduction of a toxic substance. However, it was far from a full detoxification. The abolition of slavery in 1865 was a profound moment, but this emancipation without reparations was a hollow victory. Although the 13th Amendment ended the legal ownership of human beings, it didn't transform the economic and social ecosystems which were rooted in their exploitation. There was no redistribution of land or wealth. The promise of "forty acres and a mule" was a broken one. Freed men and women, descendants of enslaved Africans, were left with no resources to build independent lives, while their former enslavers retained their wealth, political power and influence. Emancipation didn't repair the centuries of harm inflicted upon the enslaved; nothing was restructured to correct the severe civic, financial, health, and academic imbalances caused by the slavery.

In biological terms, emancipation was like removing a harmful substance without providing the body with the nutrients needed to heal and regenerate damaged cells. The social ecosystem continued to suffer from institutional and structural inequalities. In fact, new methods and strategies of exploitation emerged almost immediately. Sharecropping replaced slavery as a means of economic control. Despite the 13th, 14th, and 15th Amendments to the Constitution of these United States of America being ratified, "'Black' Codes" and vagrancy laws criminalized the existence of the newly freed people (specifically the men) citizens and fed the convict leasing system, which functioned as slavery by another name. Socially, racialized terrorism through lynching and organized

II. Ecosystems

"white" supremacist groups maintained the racialized caste system, ensuring that newly freed individuals remained financially destitute and socially subjugated.

Thus, while emancipation was a necessary step, it was an insufficient revolution on its own. It offered freedom in name but not in substance. It halted the worst of the abuse but failed to introduce the positive conditions required for recovery and growth. The manufactured ecosystems, influencing the development of these United States of America, remained depleted, with marginalized communities lacking access to the essential resources needed to thrive. The economic ecosystem marginalized Americans whose ancestors were enslaved Africans and Indigenous communities, while the social ecosystem weaponized language and culture to justify their continued oppression and extermination. Phrases like "separate but equal" masked profound inequalities, while stereotypes and racialized caricatures dehumanized people in media and popular discourse based on the amount of melanin they possessed.

The failure to provide reparations after emancipation solidified the racialized disparities that persist to this day. Wealth gaps, educational inequities, healthcare inadequacies, and housing discrimination are not accidents; they're the progeny of policies and practices born out of the post-emancipation betrayal.

The 20th century inspired a new wave of struggle and resistance. The Civil Rights Movement forced America to confront its contradictions. Landmark legislation (e.g., the Civil Rights Act of 1964 and the Voting Rights Act of 1965) were hard-won victories that disrupted the legal architecture of Jim Crow. They concentrated on many of the obvious barriers to racialized equality. These laws were vital interventions, much like administering medication to suppress the symptoms of a chronic illness. They focused on criminalizing overt discrimination and securing essential rights.

Yet, legislative victories, while necessary, proved insufficient. Let's be honest – laws might prohibit explicit acts of discrimination, but they cannot undo centuries of internalized prejudice and inequality. Legislation only treats the visible symptoms of oppression while leaving the underlying structures intact. For every political win, there emerged new, subtler mechanisms of exclusion, terror, and trauma. Redlining by banks and government agencies ensured that families of differing cultures and melanin levels were denied homeownership and the generational wealth it creates. Mass incarceration became a new system of racialized control, driven by policies like the "War on Drugs," which disproportionately targeted immigrant and already disenfranchised communities. Educational and healthcare disparities, along with other social and economic exclusions, persist but in more subtle forms.

Let's also remember that language evolved too! Openly racialized slurs were replaced by coded language that continued to stigmatize marginalized groups – some that come to my mind are "urban," "ethnic," "those people," "thug," and "predator." Media narratives depicted inner-city neighborhoods as inherently criminal, Indigenous reservations as impoverished outposts of failure, and immigrant communities as threats to "American" identity. These narratives justified punitive policies and still shape public opinion to this day.

Legislation addressed symptoms but left the underlying disease untreated. The economic ecosystem continues to attribute positions of wealth, status, influence, and privilege to "whiteness," while the social ecosystem perpetuates stereotypes and biases. Formal equality exists on paper, but the reality is this: inequality persists in our daily language and behaviors. With that said, this brings us to the present; to the unfinished chapter of history in these United States of America. Colonization established the oppressive ecosystems, emancipation granted freedom without repair, and legislation sought to regulate behavior without redistributing power – what remains is the work of liberation.

For any ecosystem (biological or man-made) to truly thrive, it must remove toxins and also introduce positive,

II. Ecosystems

restorative forces. This is where liberation becomes essential – the deliberate process of healing, restoring, and empowering communities that have been historically marginalized and disenfranchised. It goes beyond virtue signaling, symbolic gestures, performative practices, and legislative reforms. It must focus on the recognition of historical harms, the redistribution of resources, and the restructuring of institutions.

Liberation provides the "nutrients" needed for ecosystemic transformation and regeneration. It means investing in communities that have been purposefully deprived of wealth, opportunity, and dignity. Liberation isn't merely the absence of chains or the presence of rights. It's the meticulous process of destroying oppressive ideals, structures, and institutions; the active task of forging equitable alternatives. Central to this process is the actualization of reparations as a comprehensive strategy of restorative justice, not only as a one-time payout.

Reparations have long been a central demand of advocates seeking justice for descendants of enslaved Africans and displaced Indigenous peoples in these United States of America. In this context, they're often dismissed as impractical or controversial. But I'm here to tell you – they aren't a handout to the undeserving, nor a punishment for those implicitly involved in the continued marginalization and disenfranchisement of communities. Reparations are a necessary nutrient infusion for the civic organism we call the United States of America – an overdue compensation for centuries of stolen labor, land, and systemic exclusion.

A comprehensive reparations agenda must go beyond symbolic gestures and concentrate on both historical harms and present-day inequalities through direct restitution, structural reforms, cultural restoration, legislative changes, and community healing initiatives. Reparations must be multifaceted, rectifying the palpable **and** the intangible aspects of discrimination, oppression, exclusion, trauma, terror, and destruction. They must repair the financial damage inflicted on marginalized and disenfranchised communities, challenge the social narratives that devalue their humanity, and restructure the institutions that perpetuate inequality. In light is this revelation, I offer the following restorative actions; reparative approaches I consider as vital for empowering marginalized and disenfranchised communities.

Let's start with a favorite of mine – credit scores. Credit scores, as currently administered by major credit bureaus, have long served as gatekeepers to financial opportunity in these United States of America. However, this approach is inherently flawed, disproportionately harming marginalized and disenfranchised communities because of historical inequities. Practices like redlining, predatory lending, and discriminatory banking have created generational barriers, making it harder for already struggling individuals, and their respective communities, to establish, build, and maintain positive credit profiles.

Reforming the institution of credit scoring will serve as a meaningful form of reparation. This requires redefining creditworthiness to account for structural inequalities, such as adjusting for discriminatory housing practices and expanding alternative data sources like on-time rent, utility, and mobile phone payments. Practical credit repair programs, debt forgiveness initiatives, and transparent oversight of credit bureaus will substantially reverse historic injustices and promote financial inclusion.

Such reforms aren't merely technical adjustments; they're restorative actions that acknowledge and remedy intrinsic biases embedded in financial institutions. By transforming credit scoring into a tool for empowerment rather than exclusion, marginalized communities will be able to access homeownership, entrepreneurship, and improve their financial standing. In doing so, reforming credit scores becomes an essential step toward closing the racialized wealth gap while also sustaining true economic justice.

One of the most publicized and advocated-for forms of reparations is direct financial restitution, as mentioned previously. This includes cash payments to descendants of

II. Ecosystems

enslaved Africans and displaced Indigenous peoples, recognizing this approach as equitable compensation for generations of forced labor and land theft. But reparations must also encompass land restitution and sovereignty, returning land to Indigenous nations and supporting their economic self-determination. Additionally, significant investment and funding for students from marginalized and disenfranchised communities to access higher education and trade school opportunities is essential to ensuring educational equity and preserving cultural heritage (e.g. Historically Black Colleges and Universities aka HBCUs, Tribal Colleges etc.). Debt relief for marginalized communities (e.g. canceling student loan debt, medical debt, and providing zero-interest business loans for entrepreneurs) further removes the economic barriers created by centuries of discrimination, oppression, theft, and murder.

However, reparations cannot be confined to financial measures alone. A vital component of restorative justice involves overhauling the institutional language and behaviors that perpetuate inequality, particularly in the areas of housing, healthcare, education, and criminal justice. Reparative housing policies must prioritize massive investments in affordable housing, end redlining practices, and support homeownership in historically marginalized communities. In the health terrain, universal healthcare policies must be complemented with targeted initiatives to close racialized health disparities. This includes comprehensive psychological health services and community wellness programs, engineered to eliminate intergenerational trauma. Similarly, educational equity measures are crucial to eradicating structural barriers – fully funding public schools, embedding culturally relevant curricula, and providing high-quality resources for impoverished areas. Criminal justice reform must be another priority, necessitating the end of mass incarceration, the abolition of private prisons, and the expansion of restorative justice alternatives.

Media reparations are also essential to reclaiming storytelling power, restoring accurate and authentic cultural narratives, and combating the dehumanizing stereotypes that have long pervaded media and public discourse in these United States of America. Public forums must be established to acknowledge historical atrocities, document personal narratives, and educate the broader public on the legacies of slavery, colonization, and racialized structural oppression. One approach I envision is funding for content to be created by, and for, members of marginalized communities. Moreover, language reform in public policy must eliminate coded, dismissive language in official documents and replace it with terminology that truthfully acknowledges historical and ongoing forms of discrimination and oppression.

Legislative and policy reforms are critical to infusing these restorative actions into our civil society. Reparative tax policies (i.e., progressive taxation aimed at redistributing wealth accumulated through exploitative practices) will help get rid of financial disparities. Furthermore, enforceable anti-discrimination laws must be expanded to protect marginalized communities in employment, housing, education, and healthcare. Safeguarding democracy requires strengthening voting rights protections, including restoring the Voting Rights Act, implementing automatic voter registration, and eliminating voter suppression tactics. Lastly, environmental reparations must fix the disproportionate environmental harms inflicted upon marginalized communities, through targeted clean-up efforts, sustainable development initiatives, and investments in clean air, water, and land restoration.

Beyond the material and legislative approaches, reparations must also encompass psychological and spiritual healing. Providing free, culturally competent psychological health services for communities traumatized by historical and ongoing oppression is essential. Support for community healing spaces, such as cultural centers, spiritual retreats, and wellness initiatives, fosters collective healing and

II. Ecosystems

empowerment, enabling marginalized communities to reclaim their dignity and agency.

As an American descended from enslaved Africans and one of the Indigenous tribes, I often find myself staring at incomplete family trees, fragmented by the brutal realities of slavery and colonization. Every time I attempt to trace my lineage, I run into dead ends – names lost, records destroyed, or never documented in the first place. For descendants of enslaved Africans and Indigenous peoples, this is a common experience. The deliberate erasure of our histories wasn't an accident of time, but a strategy of control, oppression, and dehumanization. This loss of personal and collective memory has left deep scars, severing us from our ancestral roots and cultural identities. Reparations must heal this wound, not only through financial restitution but by investing in the restoration of our historical narratives.

For descendants of enslaved Africans in these United States of America, the institution of slavery was designed to strip us of our humanity; beginning with our names, languages, and family connections. As a result, some of us can only trace our family histories back to the 1870 census (the first in which formerly enslaved people were recorded by name). Before that, there's often nothing but vague plantation records, if they exist at all. Similarly, for Indigenous communities, centuries of displacement, forced assimilation, and cultural genocide have obliterated records and sacred knowledge. Boarding schools and relocation policies deliberately severed tribal connections, leaving many Indigenous descendants struggling to reclaim their heritage.

This loss goes beyond mere genealogy. It affects how I see myself, how I understand my place in history, and how I connect with my living cultures. Without access to my ancestral histories, I'm left with a distorted view of my identity, shaped by the narratives of those who oppressed, terrorized, and tried to erase my ancestors (my people). The psychological impact of this historical amnesia is profound. Personally, I carry a sense of disconnection, alienation, and (at times) invisibility, which I confront almost daily. It's a theft of memory that reverberates throughout generations.

Therefore, reparations must include intentional efforts to restore these lost histories. This means creating well-funded programs dedicated to genealogical research for Americans descended from enslaved Africans and Indigenous tribes, digitizing and preserving existing records, and investing in oral history projects that capture the stories still held within our communities. It also requires opening access to archives held by private institutions, such as churches, universities, and corporations that profited from slavery and colonization. Additionally, reparations must support educational initiatives that embed the true histories of enslaved Africans and Indigenous peoples in these United States of America, centering our voices and perspectives.

Beyond historical documentation, reparations must also include cultural restoration. Language revitalization programs, support for tribal sovereignty, and the preservation of African diasporic traditions are essential to reclaiming what was stolen. These actions go hand in hand with the broader goals of reparations, which are to repair, restore, and empower.

Tracing your ancestry is not simply about knowing who your great-great-grandparents were; it is about reclaiming your dignity, your identity, and your rightful place in history. Reparations that ignore this critical aspect are incomplete. To heal the wounds of the past, you must reconnect with the roots that were deliberately severed. Only then can we begin to restore what was lost and move forward with a sense of welcome, belonging, and unity.

What you just read is so important that it bears repeating. Just as a body can't sustain life without nurturing its cells, a nation can't sustain a healthy society while neglecting vast portions of its population. The progression from colonization to emancipation to legislation has been a journey of partial remedies, each step addressing certain injustices but falling short of holistic healing. Liberation is the essential final phase in this progression.

II. Ecosystems

Liberation requires more than legislative change. It demands a fundamental transformation of our economic and social ecosystems. It requires us to reconcile with the past honestly, redistribute resources equitably, and redefine what it means to be an American citizen. Liberation is the regenerative process that can transform the social and economic ecosystems of these United States of America from practices of exploitation and exclusion into procedures that sustain equity. Only through restorative, and reparative, actions and language can we ensure individuals and communities not only survive but truly thrive in our man-made ecosystems – much like living organisms in healthy and nourishing natural habitats.

Reparations aren't a matter of charity; they're a matter of justice. They're not a singular policy but a holistic approach to justice, encompassing financial restitution, institutional reform, cultural restoration, legislative action, and community healing. Such comprehensive restorative actions are necessary to reverse the deep-rooted inequities that continue to marginalize and disenfranchise communities. They're the necessary final steps in a historical progression that began with colonization and has thus far stopped short of liberation.

Without reparations, the wounds inflicted by centuries of exploitation remain open. Without reparations, discrimination, oppression, exclusion, terror, and murder will continue to be eviscerating elements of our ecosystems. The restorative actions I've presented are the equivalent of oxygen, water, and nutrients for a social ecosystem starved by centuries of intentional neglect. They not only repair past harms but create the conditions necessary for future generations to flourish. Only through a multi-faceted reparations agenda can these United States of America hope to nurture an equitable and thriving society where liberation becomes a reality for all.

As I reflect on the progressive journey of these United States of America, beginning with the first stolen lands to the ongoing fight for justice, I know that the work of liberation is ours to complete. In the end, liberation is more than acts of justice for the marginalized; it's the foundation for the collective health, longevity, and prosperity of the entire nation. Reparations are possible; reparations are imperative. Only through deliberate, restorative action can we build a United States of America that lives up to the ideals that freedom is not a privilege for the few, but a birthright for all.

III. Sammā-sati
(aka The Active, Watchful Mind)
1. Belief
2. Emotions
3. Let's play a game – A Reflexive Exercise
4. The Criticality of Language
5. Your T.E.A.M.

III. Sammā-sati

1. Belief

Belief is the key to what motivates your language and behavior. What you believe determines your decision-making, your motivation to act or speak, your presence/absence, and your understanding/ignorance (the conscious choice to ignore or remain unaware and uninformed). What you believe governs how you monitor, navigate, process, and regulate your responses, and affects your capacity to demonstrate love, empathy, and compassion. Your belief as a human being is what sets you apart from every other species on Earth. It's the most important aspect of your existence, empowering you to determine your own destiny and influence the destinies of those around you.

What you believe fuels your expectations, shapes your intentions, and dictates the manner in which you impact the world around you. What you believe is a mixture of fact and faith. Fact - what you observed, what you can replicate, what you can verify (what ***actually*** happens and why). Faith – your predictions, hopes, and expectations, despite tangible evidence *("Now faith is the substance of things hoped for, the evidence of things not seen"* Hebrews 11:1). The power of belief – in yourself, in nature, in spirits, or in the unseen forces of the universe – is a central theme in many Indigenous and traditional philosophies across cultures.

Many Indigenous tribes believe that thoughts and intentions shape reality. The power of belief can heal, bring abundance, or summon protection. Due to deep belief in spiritual visions, many tribes have traditions where individuals seek guidance through fasting and meditation. True belief in your dreams, even in the face of sacrifice and doubt, leads to transformation and success. The Lakota and Hopi believe in the power of spoken words and thoughts; what you say and believe manifests in the world. The Diné philosophy of Hózhó (pronounced "ho-sho") emphasizes balance, beauty, and harmony. Your belief in positivity and order can bring about well-being.

To illustrate this, there's a story from the Lakota people that tells of a small mouse living in a safe but limited world near a river. One day, the mouse hears about the Far-Off Land, a place of beauty and abundance beyond the great mountains. Despite the disbelief of the other mice, he embarks on a dangerous journey, relying only on his belief that the land exists. Along the way, he sacrifices parts of himself (such as his sight) to help others, including a sick buffalo and a blind wolf. Near the end of his journey, with no vision and feeling hopeless, he believes in his heart that he will succeed. In that moment, he transforms into an eagle, soaring into the sky and reaching the Far-Off Land. From this, we learn that belief in one's vision leads to transformation.

The Taíno people (ancestors to many modern Puerto Ricans) believed in the sacredness of nature, that life's cycles bring abundance and sustenance. Faith in the sacred, such as Zemi spirits (energies that respond to human belief and reverence), brings life. Rituals and ceremonial chanting were done with full faith, as belief was thought to bring protection, prosperity, and healing. Dreams were believed to be messages from the spirit world, and belief in their meaning influenced life decisions.

The story of Yaya, the elemental being of creation and giver of life, highlights this belief. The story says Yaya killed his rebellious son and placed his remains in a sacred gourd. Over time, the people believed the gourd held powerful magic, and soon water and fish appeared inside. One day, the gourd spilled onto the ground, and cassava (aka yuca) began to grow. The people believed this was the spirit of Yaya's son returning to nourish them. This story also explains how yuca became the staple food of the Taíno.

The Ethiopian folktale of the lion's whiskers relays how belief, patience, and persistence can overcome even the toughest obstacles. According to this folktale, a woman named Seble wants to win the love of her stepson, who resents her. She seeks the help of a wise healer, who tells her to bring him a whisker from a living lion as an ingredient for a special

III. Sammā-sati

potion. Terrified but determined, Seble believes she can succeed. Each day, she approaches the lion, offering it food and slowly gaining its trust. After months of patience, the lion allows her to pluck a whisker. When she returns, the healer laughs and tells her, "If you have the patience and courage to get a lion's whisker, you already have the strength to win your stepson's heart!" Seble then applies the same patience and belief in love to her relationship, eventually winning over the boy. As you can see, patience and belief win hearts, changing language and behaviors.

The Ubuntu of Southern Africa believe, "I am because we are." This highlights how community belief shapes individual reality – when others believe in you, you gain strength. The Yoruba of Nigeria, West Africa, emphasize how belief in Orishas (aka deities/forces of nature) means their power manifests in one's life. Rituals, prayers, and affirmations strengthen a person's alignment with destiny (aka *ori*). The Dagara of Burkina Faso believe that a strong reliance on ancestral guidance brings wisdom and protection. Descendants of African traditions believe in the power of thought, faith, and the spoken word in shaping outcomes.

The Taoist philosophy of Wu Wei (effortless action) suggests that by believing and aligning with nature's flow, things will naturally fall into place. According to Zen, the mind creates reality. Through meditation and a strong belief in enlightenment, suffering can be transcended. There's a Buddhist tale that shares how the mind is powerful, how what you believe determines what you can achieve. In this story, a young monk is told to cross a deep canyon by walking over a thin rope bridge. Fear grips him, and he starts shaking. He believes he will fall, and as a result, he does. His master then blindfolds him and tells him to walk across again, believing the bridge is strong. This time, he walks confidently and reaches the other side. When the blindfold is removed, he realizes that there was never a bridge at all – he had walked across the canyon on air. His belief alone had held him up. Vipassana meditation teaches that by observing thoughts, a person can dissolve limiting beliefs and reach enlightenment.

During time I spent in India, I was blessed and fortunate to learn about:
- The power of Sankalpa (intention), which states that strong belief leads to reality. This is why mantras and affirmations are used in spiritual practices.
- Karma & Dharma - Belief in past actions affecting the present (karma) gives people a sense of responsibility and hope for change (dharma).
- Advaita Vedanta (Non-Dualism): Reality is shaped by the mind; belief in separation from the divine is an illusion.
- Bhakti Yoga (Path of Devotion): Pure belief in a deity or higher power brings transformation.
- The Law of Attraction (Modern Interpretation of Hindu Thought): A person's beliefs create their external reality—thinking positively attracts positive experiences.

There's a Hindu Epic about a boy named Ekalavya. It illustrates how true mastery comes not from external validation, but from deep dedication and belief in oneself to overcome barriers. Ekalavya is from a lower caste and wants to learn archery from the great teacher Drona, who refuses to teach him because of his status. Undeterred, Ekalavya carves a statue of Drona out of clay and trains himself every day, believing the statue is his teacher. Through sheer belief and dedication, he becomes an unparalleled archer. When Drona later learns of this, he's amazed and declares Ekalavya the greatest.

As you reflect on the stories from the diverse cultures and traditions, I'm sure you realize how belief isn't simply an exercise of faith; it's an important tool for creating balance, manifesting dreams, and healing, Whether through individual or communal rituals, meditation, spoken word, or patience, these cultures acknowledge how what you hold true in your

III. Sammā-sati

mind and heart can manifest in the world around you. Belief is the force capable of ultimately shaping reality.

You might be familiar with the phrase, "Mind over matter." It emphasizes how what you believe will push you beyond the physical sensations and perceived limitations of the body, to accomplish acts that seem impossible, to control your intricate and complicated structure of muscles, tendons, organs, and joints in fearful and wonderful ways. As a practitioner of the martial arts, I can personally attest to how the body responds to belief (the reality created in my mind), which makes all things possible.

Mind over matter allows some humans to:
- endure high pressures below the water without external breathing equipment (free divers).
- break coconuts, multiple concrete slabs, and very thick blocks of ice with their bare hands (martial artists).
- walk and talk again (stroke survivors).
- lift incredible amounts of weight to save lives.

It goes back to what you believe, which is impacted by the elements of the economic and social ecosystems. "You better check yourself before you wreck yourself"[14] is another phrase that resonates with me. It's both a warning and a reminder that you have the mental capacity to regulate, redirect, and control your responses in situations; the ability to change your own emotional state, by changing your thoughts; you must make the time to process what you observe and hear, before speaking and acting in return; don't be led by your prejudices or biases.

Prejudice is the pre-judgement (typically against a person, situation, or community) before you have all the relevant facts. It's based on pre-meditated/pre-conceived expectations, ideas, and stereotypes that have been shaped by our beliefs and feelings. Your biases are your preferences for or against a person, entity, or idea, based on your prior experiences.

---
14 Ice Cube. *"Check Yo Self."* *The Predator*, Priority Records, 1992.

Your beliefs are malleable. Say that out loud: "My beliefs are malleable!" This means your individual beliefs can be changed, fooled, manipulated, and misdirected – in short, your beliefs can be controlled. Which means the same is true for your emotions. Some of you might be thinking, "Not me!" However, those of you who have ever watched a magician or street hustler at work, understand the truth of my statements. They are masterful in the art of misdirection. Similarly, people who successfully engage in sales, advertising, marketing, politics, and media content production capitalize on their ability to influence your beliefs for their gain – they understand the psychology of the mind and human response to stimuli. Your responses (physical and psychological) can be predicted, which means they can be manipulated, which means you can be controlled if you're not aware and vigilant.

Now let's explore the intricate relationship between beliefs, what we call emotions, and physical sensations, in addition to examining psychological theories, scientific research, and real-world examples to illustrate their dynamic interplay.

2. Emotions

Beliefs, emotions, and sensual (let's keep it clean folks) responses are inseparable, influencing one another in ways that shape human experiences. Your beliefs form the foundation of your perspectives, your emotions serve as responses to those beliefs, and your sensual responses manifest as a result of both. Understanding this correlation provides insight into how thoughts impact all aspects of well-being (psychological and physical health).

Beliefs are cognitive constructs that shape how you interpret the world. They're formed through personal experiences, cultural influences, education, and social interactions. Some are deeply ingrained, while others evolve over time as you gain new knowledge, experiences, and perspectives. They can be rational or irrational, empowering or limiting, and conscious or subconscious. In short, the way you

III. Sammā-sati

perceive reality is largely determined by your belief systems, which influence your psychological and sensual responses to different situations.

For example, if you believe that failure is a reflection of your worth, you might experience anxiety or depression when faced with challenges. Conversely, if you believe that failure is a learning opportunity, you might feel motivated to improve. Research in neuroscience has shown that beliefs are not fixed and that the brain has the ability to rewire itself through neuroplasticity. Psychological theories, such as cognitive-behavioral theory (CBT), emphasize how thoughts influence emotions, reinforcing the connection between beliefs and emotional well-being. When you consciously work to change your negative beliefs, your emotional and physical well-being improves. CBT is one approach that helps individuals identify and restructure harmful beliefs, leading to positive emotional and physiological changes. Meditation, mindfulness, and positive affirmations are also effective tools in rewiring the brain to create healthier thought patterns.

Emotions are not merely mental experiences; they also have physiological consequences. Positive emotions, such as joy and gratitude, trigger the release of endorphins, which promote relaxation and well-being. The mind-body connection is evident in cases of psychosomatic illnesses, where emotional distress manifests as physical symptoms such as headaches, stomach problems, or chronic pain.

Chronic stress is a clear example of how beliefs and emotions affect physical health. If you believe you're constantly under threat or pressure, your emotional state remains heightened and your body releases cortisol and adrenaline, leading to increased heart rate, high blood pressure, muscle tension, and other physical symptoms such as digestive problems . Studies have shown that individuals with high levels of stress issues have weakened immune function, making them more susceptible to illnesses. This highlights the profound impact of mental and emotional states on physical health.

Emotional intelligence plays a crucial role in managing the relationships between beliefs, emotions, and physical sensations. Individuals who are self-aware and able to regulate their emotions are better equipped to manage stress and maintain physical health. Emotional intelligence involves recognizing one's emotions, understanding their triggers, and developing strategies to respond effectively. Practices such as journaling, therapy, and self-reflection help you cultivate emotional intelligence, leading to greater mental and physical resilience.

The placebo effect is another remarkable example of how beliefs influence physical health. Patients who believe they are receiving effective treatment often experience real improvements in their condition, even when given inactive substances. This demonstrates the power of belief in shaping physiological outcomes. Similarly, the nocebo effect occurs when negative expectations lead to adverse physical reactions. These phenomena illustrate the profound impact that beliefs can have on the body's ability to heal and function optimally.

Cultural and social factors shape beliefs, which in turn affect emotional and sensual experiences. Different cultures have varying attitudes toward emotions, stress, and well-being, which influence how individuals respond to challenges. Social norms and expectations also play a role in shaping how people interpret their emotions and physical sensations. For example, collectivist cultures often emphasize communal support and emotional restraint, while individualistic cultures encourage self-expression and personal growth.

Spirituality and mindfulness practices offer valuable insights into the relationship between beliefs, emotions, and physical health. Many spiritual traditions emphasize the mind-body connection, promoting practices such as meditation, prayer, and gratitude to foster emotional and physical well-being. Mindfulness-based interventions have been shown to reduce stress, enhance emotional regulation, and improve overall health. By cultivating awareness of your thoughts and

III. Sammā-sati

emotions, you can develop healthier responses to life's challenges.

Holistic healing approaches recognize the interconnectedness of beliefs, emotions, and physical health. Practices such as acupuncture, yoga, aromatherapy, ayurveda, and energy healing aim to balance the body's systems by addressing mental and emotional well-being. Integrative medicine combines conventional medical treatments with holistic approaches to provide comprehensive care that acknowledges the psychological and emotional dimensions of health.

The intricate correlation between beliefs, emotions, and sensual responses underscores the importance of cultivating positive thought patterns and emotional resilience. By understanding how beliefs shape emotional and physiological experiences, you can take proactive steps to improve your mental and physical health. Practices such as cognitive restructuring, emotional intelligence development, mindfulness, and holistic healing can enhance well-being and promote a healthier, more balanced life. Ultimately, fostering awareness and adaptability in your beliefs and emotional responses can lead to a more fulfilling and harmonious existence.

III. Sammā-sati

3. <u>Let's play a game - A Reflexive Exercise</u>

Before we focus our attention on the criticality of language, let's play a game. Examine each of the images and use the QR code to share your thoughts about the most likely:
- ethnic or cultural background
- gender, and
- age

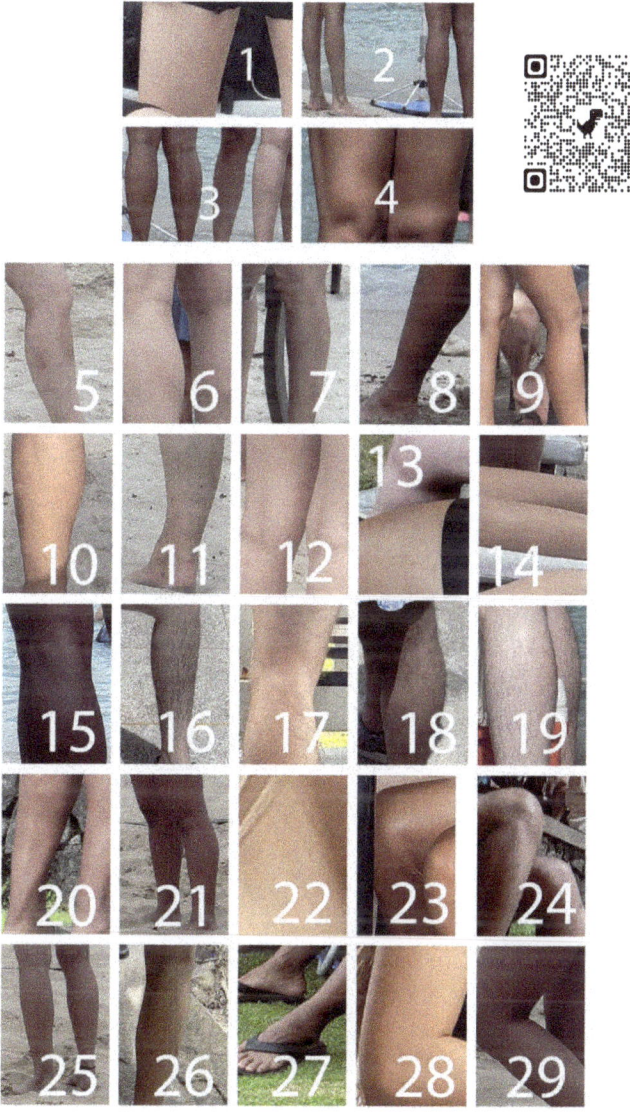

C.E.A.S.E. for Equity

A Reflexive Exercise
This is completely voluntary and no personal information is collected without you providing it.
Thank you for playing.

III. Sammā-sati

I hope you will be able to laugh at yourself when you see the actual answers. At the very least, I hope you will realize an important fact – attempting to determine a person's age, gender, or cultural background based solely on their melanin level is a futile exercise, yet we do it daily. It's a reflection of deeper social conditioning and unconscious bias. With that said, I really appreciate your willingness to play along – thank you. I need you to understand that your compulsion to guess is rooted in a broader cultural habit: one that urges us to categorize and judge based on physical characteristics such as melanin level, body shape, facial features, and posture. These pre-judgments (aka prejudices) are often informed by inherited social scripts, not by objective truth.

We, the people of these United States of America, have been conditioned to pre-judge others through visual markers. From an early age, we learn to associate melanin levels, clothing, facial features, and body type with certain narratives about worth, morality, and intelligence. These associations aren't produced in isolation. They're rooted in historical power structures and reinforced by family values, personal experiences, the media, and education. As such, our perceptions are distorted and cause stereotyping, discrimination, exclusion, exploitation, marginalization, and even erasure of entire communities.

To eliminate or transform these harmful patterns, we must engage in reflexive meditation – the honest, ongoing practice of examining our thoughts and the origins of our biases. This self-awareness helps you recognize how language and behavior, even when subtle, perpetuate oppression. Reflexivity urges you to replace snap judgments with curiosity, compassion, and a commitment to equity.

Cultivating empathy in this way is foundational to actively building inclusive societies; it isn't a passive act. By acknowledging the silliness of judging a person by their legs, we begin to question and eliminate the deeper systems that normalize such judgments. Only through conscious reflection and behavioral changes will we begin to heal and sustain ecosystems that value human dignity in all its forms.

4. <u>The Criticality of Language</u>

Language is humanity's primary method of communicating thoughts, intentions, desires, and feelings. A quote, attributed to the martial arts legend Bruce Lee, warns, *"Don't speak negatively about yourself, even as a joke. Your body doesn't know the difference. Words are energy and they cast spells, that's why it's called spelling. Change the way you speak about yourself, and you can change your life."*

I'm a firm believer that words are powerful tools of creation and transformation. This is why I always stress the importance of critically listening to the words of songs (not the beat) – my wife, my children, and youth that I mentor will probably roll their eyes as they imitate me, lol. Language carries the weight of cultural identity and cosmic harmony. In this context, language becomes an instrument for shaping reality and preserving wisdom. Language is more than a means of communication; in many of the world's oldest and richest philosophies, it is viewed as a sacred force – one that connects the human soul to the divine, the past to the present, and the individual to the cosmos. Spoken words have been revered across cultures as tools of creation and healing, being deeply intertwined with identity and power across different traditions. In the beginning, God said, *"Let there be light: and there was light."* (Gen 1:3)

For many Indigenous tribes, language is not just a tool—it's a living force imbued with spiritual energy. Words carry the power to create, heal, and sustain balance in the world. This belief is embedded in the structure of Native languages themselves. For instance, the Hopi language is built around cycles and continuity rather than linear time, reflecting a worldview where all things are interconnected and time is fluid. You might recall *Hózhó* from the Diné. It teaches that positive thoughts lead to positive emotions, and in turn, to

III. Sammā-sati

peaceful and beautiful actions – speaking positively fosters positive outcomes, while negative words can bring misfortune.

In some African traditions, language functions as a spiritual bridge connecting the present to the past and future. Language is not passive; it's an active, sacred, and living force that connects individuals to their heritage, ancestors, community, and spiritual purpose. The Yoruba concept of *Àṣẹ* (pronounced "ah-SHAY") embodies this belief: it signifies the power to make things happen through words, particularly prayers and blessings. When spoken with conviction, words are believed to shape reality.

West African storytellers and oral historians (called griots) are keepers of this sacred language tradition. They preserve centuries of communal wisdom, moral lessons, and historical memory, often using poetry, music, and metaphor. Proverbs are especially potent in African languages, distilling deep insights into concise expressions. As the saying goes, *"Until the lion learns to write, every story will glorify the hunter"* – a reminder that language defines perspective and power.

Asian philosophies approach language with both reverence and caution. Language can be a guide to truth, but ultimate understanding often lies in silence, contemplation, and transcendence beyond words. In Taoism, for instance, language is seen as inherently limited. Laozi begins the *Tao Te Ching* with the declaration: *"The Tao that can be spoken is not the true Tao."* This paradox emphasizes that ultimate truth cannot be fully expressed in words – true wisdom lies beyond linguistic boundaries.

Buddhism also recognizes the dual nature of language. While teachings, chants, and scriptures can lead seekers toward enlightenment, overattachment to words and concepts can hinder spiritual growth. Zen Buddhism illustrates this through the use of riddles or paradoxes (called koans) which aim to transcend rational thinking and provoke intuitive insight – like *"What is the sound of one hand clapping?"* Even the art of calligraphy in Chinese and Japanese culture is treated as a spiritual exercise, a meditative process where words become embodiments of beauty and insight.

The Taíno people held a worldview in which language was deeply entwined with nature and spirit; language as a vessel of ancestral memory and a channel through which humans connect with nature and spirit. Losing language means losing part of one's soul.

Oral storytelling played a central role in Taíno society, weaving human experience with the natural world – this tradition was especially sacred! It was a critical way for the elders to pass down history, spiritual teachings, and moral codes. These stories were not mere entertainment; they were acts of cultural preservation and spiritual continuity. Myths and legends often attributed voices to rivers, trees, and winds, revealing a belief that nature itself speaks. The tragic loss of the Taíno language due to colonization represents more than the death of words. It marks the erasure of cultural memory, identity, and spiritual worldview. Today, many Puerto Ricans are working to reclaim and revive the Taíno language and traditions as a form of cultural healing.

According to Indian philosophy, language is not merely symbolic. It's a cosmic spiritual force whereby each word, each sound, can shape reality and consciousness. Sanskrit, the liturgical language of Hinduism and Buddhism, is considered the "language of the gods" (aka Devavani). It's believed that the very syllables of Sanskrit resonate with the energies of the universe. This belief is encapsulated in the concept of *Shabda*, or sacred sound, which asserts that vibrations (spoken or unspoken) shape existence itself.

Mantras are perhaps the most recognizable expression of this philosophy. Repeating phrases like *Om Namah Shivaya* or *Gayatri Mantra* is not just devotional but transformational. These sounds are believed to align the practitioner with divine consciousness. Furthermore, both Hindu and Buddhist teachings emphasize that words carry karmic weight. In other words, what you say contributes to your spiritual destiny. The ancient Vedas (meaning "knowledge") of India are believed to

III. Sammā-sati

be among the earliest religious texts. However, they were originally preserved through oral transmission, not writing. This oral tradition highlights the reverence given to the spoken word, where utterance itself was a sacred act.

I implore you to learn from the traditions mentioned above – approach language with respect and mindfulness. Speak with care, listen with reverence, and preserve the words of your ancestors with humility. As such, you'll participate in something much larger than yourself; the sacred dance of creation, connection, and consciousness. Remember, language is more than a means of communication with each other. It's a spiritual tool, a link to identity, a conduit for connecting souls, and a way to shape the world itself.

Language helps with enhancing understanding, deepening connections, developing trust, and cultivating empathy. If I don't understand you – if you don't understand me – there is ignorance and resistance; there is caution and mistrust between us. If you don't feel any connection with me, you're more likely to:
- Pre-judge me.
- Perceive me as a threat.
- Discriminate against me.
- Fortify yourself against potential harm from me, imagined or real.
- Be complicit/silent/absent when I am being mistreated/abused/mutilated/murdered.
- Perpetrate/propagate negative stereotypes and myths about me.

With that said, you're unlikely to sympathize and empathize with me. To sympathize with me, you must understand me and be able to identify with my situation; to empathize with me, you must be willing and able to feel what I feel; to take on my circumstances and feelings as your own. We, as a society, have been fooled/led to believe that we must label everyone and everything by surface-level differences (melanin level, accent, facial features, style of dress, etc.):

- Indigenous, Black, Hispanic, Asian, White, Indian, etc.
- Rasta, Christian, Muslim, Hindu, Buddhist, Jew, etc.
- Conservative, Liberal, Pro-, Anti-, etc.

Labeling causes division, which fuels mistrust (meaning a sense of caution at the very least, a sense of supremacy at its extreme). However, when you look deeper than skin tone, everything is the same:
- Biologically - Muscles, skeletal, organs, etc.
- Sociologically - The human condition

<u>4a. SO! What should be done about the n-word?</u>

A little background about me and my experiences with the n-word growing up. I must warn you that I may switch between past and present tense, but I'm confident you can keep up. My youth was spent in the South End of Bridgeport, CT, during the mid- to late- 1970s. I walked everywhere - to and from school, to the corner stores, the local park, the local mall, and downtown. We took the public bus only when going beyond our local community to visit relatives, see the doctor, or shop for items that couldn't be purchased locally.

I was among Americans whose ancestors were enslaved Africans and Puerto Rican people. I don't recall any other cultural groups living in the projects with me. I heard and saw my fair share of fights and disagreements. I was exposed to music with lyrics that spoke of loving each other, power to the people, having a good time, and hope for deliverance. A derivative of "brother" was used in my community and by recording artists of that era, as a greeting and an acknowledgement of our shared experience. Hearing phrases such as "Hey, my brotha..." and the playful "Brotha, you must be outta your mind!" was affirming, unifying, and empowering.

From what I remember, the n-word was said by "white" folks, "black" comedians, and "black" musical groups – comedians and groups that my mother and some of my family elders reserved for adult gatherings (aka house parties).

III. Sammā-sati

Although I wasn't supposed to watch or listen to these recordings, I would sometimes (sneak to) hear them when my mother hosted a party. But I don't ever recall hearing the n-word being said among the people around me. I sometimes heard "white" folks say it on T.V. – I mean the full word with the "-er" at the end. I am grateful that I was shielded from hearing a "white" person say it in real life. My mother and family elders made it very clear that I was NEVER to say the n-word, EVER!

    There is pain in that word; there is disrespect in that word; there is apathy in that word. That word codifies the extremely oppressive, intimidating, divisive, and destructive language and behaviors employed by "white" folks 1) to suppress, control, and negatively impact the health, wealth, and well-being of "black" communities, 2) to build economic and genealogical legacies from the ideas and contributions of "black" laborers and innovators, 3) to delegitimize and destroy "black" culture. That word symbolizes enslavement, Jim Crow, segregation, strange fruit, civil rights violations, ill-intent, "being put in the back of the car and driven away to never return," subversive tactics, brutality and profiling by law enforcement, and the murder of change agents.

    There is no humor, nor positive intent, nor "wishing you the best," nor "I am praying for your success," nor caring embrace in that word. There is no good thing in that word *nigger*. That word is dehumanizing, aimed at making the target inferior and the perpetrator superior. With that word comes terrorism, psychological trauma, physical harm, imprisonment, and loss of life for no reason. In my youth I didn't say it, my friends didn't say it, and members of my family didn't say it.

    As the 70s transitioned into the 80s, I moved to the East End of Bridgeport as a pre-teen and that's where I began to mature. The new musical art form, known as Rap, was becoming hot! Guys who looked and sounded like they could have been from around my way were combining Disco breakbeats, devices like the TR808, and beatboxing with rhymes that told stories about their experiences, their hopes, their dreams, and their individual and collective visions about life. I identified with their stories; their voices echoed my thoughts and feelings, and their wordplay and rhyming skills inspired me.

Although I heard many other cuss words, I have to admit I don't recall hearing the n-word in rap of the early 80s. My earliest memory of hearing the n-word, with a "ga" ending, used as a term of empowerment and endearment has to be during the late 1980s when a group of young music artists on the West Coast debuted with their first album, calling themselves *niggaz*. And with that, the proverbial floodgates were opened, with my friends and some family members greeting each other with, "Wussup my nigga?" and expressing disbelief (playfully) by saying, "Nigga, you lyin'!" This began the shift from saying "brotha" to "nigga" when referring to "black" men.

Bringing it to the present, I've also heard people use this word to express surprise, joy, support, affirmation, sympathy, anger, and warning. Which brings me to the focus of this particular section. How should we move forward, as a nation and a global community, in coming to grips with the use of the n-word? My insights to the following questions will serve as two suggestive responses:

1. Do we attempt to make it legally unacceptable for anyone to use the word?
2. Who should be allowed to use it?

Let's start with the origins of the word. From what I know, there's agreement among scholars that etymologically the word "nigger" traces its origin to the Latin word "niger", meaning black. Eventually, the word was deliberately weaponized in these United States of America by "white" folks, through legislation and social norms, to dehumanize the enslaved Africans and their descendants. Labeling someone as a "nigger" presumed the inferiority of "black" folks and the superiority of "white" folks. For anyone being called that word, their status was considered to be subhuman, which

III. Sammā-sati

meant they were not due the respect and consideration of "white" adults and children.

I believe there is a shared understanding among many people in these United States of America, regardless of cultural background, that use of the word "nigger" is controversial and offensive, in addition to being divisive, inflammatory, enraging, and murderous. I'm comforted and encouraged to know some jurisdictions have hate crime statutes that enhance penalties for crimes motivated by bias, including racialized bias. Unfortunately, attempts to make it legally unacceptable for anyone to use the n-word, identifying that word as hate speech in these United States of America, have been unsuccessful.

You may be wondering, "How is this possible?" Hate speech law in these United States of America is a complicated intersection of free speech and protection against discrimination. The First Amendment is a protection of most speech, including speech that is offensive or hateful. While hate speech itself may not be criminalized, speech that accompanies or incites criminal conduct can result in enhanced penalties under hate crime laws.

For example, under Title VII of the Civil Rights Act of 1964, racialized epithets used in the workplace can contribute to a hostile work environment, which is a form of employment discrimination. As such, employers are required to take action, to prevent and remedy harassment that creates a hostile work environment based on a person's "race" (i.e. identifiers such as the amount of melanin in their skin, facial features, cultural heritage, and perceived accent/dialect). Schools have some leeway to regulate speech that disrupts the educational environment or infringes on the rights of others. This can include racial epithets that contribute to a hostile educational environment.

Unlike "regular" crimes, where the motivation of the perpetrators might be easily identified and proven, establishing and proving racialized motivation of the perpetrators is not always easy to do. This creates another barrier to criminalizing the use of the n-word. The distinction between a "regular" crime and a hate crime is the motivation of the perpetrator to select a victim based on their characteristics, such as "race." Motivation is the primary factor in hate crimes, but it is the most difficult to prove.

Before I continue with the n-word question, I feel it's important to make a connection between the word *nigger* and the swastika. *The word 'swastika' comes from the Sanskrit svastika, which means "good fortune" or "well-being." The motif (a hooked cross) appears to have first been used in Eurasia, as early as 7000 years ago, perhaps representing the movement of the sun through the sky. To this day, it is a sacred symbol in Hinduism, Buddhism, Jainism, and Odinism. It is a common sight on temples or houses in India or Indonesia. Swastikas also have an ancient history in Europe, appearing on artifacts from pre-Christian European cultures.*[15]
The symbol is known as the Whirling Log of Life by many Indigenous tribes.

However, the swastika, as manipulated, misrepresented, and misappropriated by Hitler, is a painful reminder to people of Jewish heritage. With this in mind, our Hindu, Buddhist, Jain, and Indigenous acquaintances, neighbors, friends, colleagues, family members, and loved ones refrain from using the symbol publicly. They essentially censor themselves, muting an important part of their culture. They demonstrate empathy for our Jewish acquaintances, neighbors, friends, colleagues, family members, and loved ones. To propel us beyond protests, through liberation, and into freedom, non-"black" folks, primarily "white" folks in these United States of America and beyond, must stop asking the question of "Why *can't* I say the n-word?" and start being reflexive about "Why would I *want* to say the n-word?"

You can legislate consequences for language and

---
15 United States Holocaust Memorial Museum. *History of the Swastika.*
https://encyclopedia.ushmm.org/content/en/article/history-of-the-swastika

III. Sammā-sati

behavior, but it's impossible to legislate for character traits such as kindness, compassion, empathy, and love. Considering all that you have just read, in addition to additional readings and research you might be consulting, I'm sure we have arrived at the same conclusion - there doesn't seem to be a proper way of making it legally unacceptable for anyone to use the n-word.

This is an ideal time for my second suggestive response - *Who **should** be allowed to use it?* After all, it's in the music! I hear "black" people say it all the time! In case you haven't figured it out yet, I'm being sarcastic, facetious – I'm just playin' y'all!!

The word "nigga" has been claimed and repurposed by folks who intimately identify with "black" culture, "black" communities, and the "black" experience in these United States of America. As I stated previously, there was a shift from referring to "black" males as "brotha" to "nigga." *This* word is empowering, sympathetic, encouraging, affirming, and celebratory, in addition to being corrective, cautionary, and a way of simply saying, *"I see you."*

The most prevalent use of the n-word I can think of, outside of communities dominated by "black" culture, is in the Hip-Hop music industry. "Does that mean I can say the word if I'm singing along to the music?" Some have argued that you should be able to say it if you intimately identify with "black" culture, "black" communities, and the "black" experience in these United States of America. "So, if I'm 'white' and I do, then you're saying it *is* ok for me to say it, right?" "What about Eminem? Is he allowed to say it?"

As of my writing this book, I've never met Eminem, nor have I ever had a conversation with him. I know of him only through his music, the movie about his struggle to be acknowledged as a rap artist, and interviews. Based on this information and what he has shared about his life, I will say Eminem would be the ONLY "white" person who <u>might</u> get an exception from me to say "nigga" because 1) I believe he intimately identifies as I outlined above and 2) he doesn't seem fixated on why he *can't* say it.

To answer my own suggestive response of *who **should be allowed to use it,*** I encourage you to do your own research into how the media industry thrives and profits from the continued utilization of the word *nigga*, in addition to other negative and stereotypical representations of "black" culture, "black" communities, and the "black" experience. Think about it and research the financial success and popularity of artists who use the n-word and negative connotations of "black" culture, black communities, and the "black" experience, compared to those who don't.

The switch from using the term "brotha" to "nigga" was not accidental or coincidental – it was by design. I've read many articles and watched many documentaries, interviews, and podcasts in which popular, wealthy, and influential entertainers have admitted how their contracts encouraged the continued use of the n-word and other negative and stereotypical representations of "black" culture, "black" communities, and the "black" experience. These "successful" musicians, artists, actors, performers, and writers shared how those in control (e.g. financiers and owners) of their particular area of the media industry (e.g. music, film, television, online, print etc.) expected and demanded the use of the n-word and other negative and stereotypical representations of "black" culture, "black" communities, and the "black" experience to ensure high sales and long-term profitability. Let's take a momentary detour from the question regarding the n-word to examine your T.E.A.M. – Stay with me! I assure you I have an answer :-D.

5. Your T.E.A.M.

I want to redirect your attention back to our objective of cultivating empathy and sustaining ecosystems for equity. Let's shift the focus to your T.E.A.M.
- ***T****houghts* control your
- ***E****motions*, which determine your

III. Sammā-sati

- **A***ctions*, which demonstrate your level of
- **M***aturity*

Being more aware, and in control, of your T.E.A.M. leads to a more healthy, more prosperous, and more peaceful life with everyone and the environment.

Thoughts include
- Self-perception,
- Perception of others, and
- Your assumption of how others perceive you.

Emotions
- Manifest as physical and/or verbal reactions/responses, based on how you remember prior experiences, in familiar or new situations.

Actions
- Attitude is at the core of how you choose to behave and speak.
- The intention of your actions reflects your attitude.

Maturity is
- Controlling the things you can; realizing, recognizing, and acceptance that you can only control your own personal choice of language and behavior,
- Accepting the things you cannot control, and
- Being wise enough to know the difference.

I'll once again lean on how many Indigenous, and some traditional, philosophies around the world view **T**houghts, **E**motions, and **A**ctions as interconnected forces that shape a person's **M**aturity (wisdom, and harmony) with the world. Across Indigenous, African, Asian, Puerto Rican (Taíno), and Asian (specifically Hindu and Buddhist) traditions, these relationships are often seen as part of a natural and spiritual journey toward self-mastery and balance; defining maturity as emotional and mental mastery, self-control, and a harmonious relationship with the world.

Maturity is often mistaken for the passage of time, yet across the world's philosophical traditions, it's defined not by age but by the alignment of thought, emotion, and action. True maturity, as taught from the Indigenous, African, Asian, Taíno, and Indian perspectives, is a state of inner balance that radiates outward, impacting the individual, the community, and the natural world. In these traditions, wisdom isn't simply what one knows – it's how one lives.

Indigenous traditions emphasize that harmony within oneself leads to harmony with the wider world. The mature person is one who has learned to master their thoughts and emotions, who makes choices that bring balance to themselves, their community, and the natural world. The Lakota people describe this principle through the concept of *Wolakota* (WOH-lah-KOH-tah), or "living in balance." For the Lakota, maturity arises when thoughts, emotions, and actions are aligned with values such as respect, humility, and responsibility.

Elders play a crucial role in guiding youth, often through oral storytelling that imparts moral lessons. These stories teach how reckless thoughts give rise to uncontrolled emotions and impulsive actions, while wisdom grows through patience and reflection. Thus, maturity is the inner strength to choose harmony over chaos, emphasizing balance within the self and with nature.

African philosophical systems also place great importance on the interrelationship between thoughts, emotions, and actions. Maturity in African thought is demonstrated through emotional discipline, thoughtful reflection, and actions that serve not just the self, but the greater good. In other words, emotional maturity uplifts the entire community.

The concept of *Ubuntu* teaches that maturity is reflected in how your inner state influences your relationship with others. It's not about personal achievement, but about contributing positively to the community. In section III you read about *Ori,* the Yoruba teaching that refers to the inner consciousness or divine self, which guides one's destiny. When thoughts and emotions are in harmony, right action follows, leading to the fulfillment of one's spiritual purpose. The following African proverb illustrates this wisdom: *"A fool*

III. Sammā-sati

vents all his feelings, but a wise man holds them back."
African griots use storytelling to teach restraint and emotional intelligence, underscoring that true power lies in self-control.

In Asian philosophies, maturity means becoming the master of one's own mind and emotions – only then can one act wisely and live harmoniously within society. Taoism teaches that emotions must flow naturally like water, but wisdom lies in non-attachment. Excessive reaction disrupts one's internal balance and separates the person from the Tao, the natural way of the universe.

Buddhism delves even deeper, explaining that suffering (called *dukkha*) arises when we are ruled by our desires, thoughts, and emotions. Through practices like meditation, one learns to separate impulse from action, thus gaining the clarity needed for wise decisions. Confucianism, meanwhile, emphasizes moral cultivation and self-restraint. The superior person, according to Confucius, is one who refines thought through study, regulates emotion through discipline, and acts with righteousness: *"The superior man thinks before he speaks and acts before he reacts."*

For the Taíno people, thought and emotion were not merely internal experiences – they were seen as forces that could influence the environment itself. Elders taught that emotions like fear and anger polluted the mind, while gratitude and love brought strength, healing, and vitality. Maturity is the art of channeling emotions and thoughts in ways that nurture harmony within oneself, with others, and with the natural world. Your inner world echoes into the environment.

El Coquí, a small sacred frog whose song is ubiquitous on Puerto Rican nights, symbolizes emotional expression. The Taíno believed that just as the frog's song called rain, human emotions influenced the spiritual and physical world. Healing and growth came through ceremonies involving music, storytelling, and introspection – necessary tools for restoring emotional balance and collective well-being.

Indian philosophy, encompassing Hinduism, Buddhism, and Ayurveda, teaches that the soul matures by rising above emotional and mental chaos to act from wisdom and spiritual clarity. In Hinduism, thoughts (*manas*), emotions (*bhava*), and actions (*karma*) are intimately connected, and together they shape one's destiny. The *Bhagavad Gita*, one of Hinduism's central texts, presents the ideal of the wise person who acts from duty, not desire. Krishna teaches: *"When a man surrenders all desires and moves free from attachments, he finds peace"* – detachment and self-control lead to enlightenment and health.

As such, the mature soul is one that has overcome emotional and mental distractions and lives with clarity, compassion, and spiritual purpose. Buddhism's Eightfold Path further instructs that right thought, right speech, and right action are steps toward enlightenment. The goal isn't to repress emotions but to understand and transcend them. Ayurveda adds a physical dimension to this idea, linking emotional imbalances to health issues – anger produces internal heat (*pitta*), while worry creates instability (*vata*), and so on. Healing the body and maturing the mind go hand in hand.

In an increasingly fast-paced and reactive world, these philosophies offer timeless guidance: true maturity is not what you know, but how you live. Maturity comes from emotional discipline, self-reflection, and using thoughts and actions for the greater good. *"Watch your thoughts, they become your words; watch your words, they become your actions; watch your actions, they become your habits; watch your habits, they become your character; watch your character, it becomes your destiny."* - Lao Tzu.

I've found three responses to be highly effective when concentrating on my T.E.A.M.
When someone:
- Threatens me,
- Tries to intimidate me,
- Says or does something that is contrary to my beliefs, or
- Complains about a negative situation, although I already gave them suggestions to avoid or prevent it

III. Sammā-sati

When I want to:
- Say something offensive, or
- Do something that hurts or harms another (physically, psychologically, etc.).

I either
       1) Smile,
       2) Chuckle, or
       3) Stay silent.

It works for me...try it for yourself.

Comedians are masterful at helping us acknowledge, celebrate, highlight, honor, and appreciate aspects of our humanity that are noticeably, and sometimes drastically, different while simultaneously getting us to reflect on how we inevitably experience and share similar circumstances regardless of melanin level, speech patterns, facial features, dialect, traditions, and cultural norms. Let's lean into this approach and agree that it's an immature mind that chooses to:

- hurt rather than heal
- hold a grudge rather than forgive
- destroy rather than cultivate
- separate rather than unify

The following two phrases of wisdom constantly echo through my mind and help me reflect on my T.E.A.M., moment by moment. The first comes from the Christian Bible, in the Book of James Chapter 1, verses 19 and 20: *Know this, my beloved brothers: let every person be quick to hear, slow to speak, slow to anger; for the anger of man does not produce the righteousness of God.* The second is a quote attributed to the martial arts legend, Bruce Lee. *You will continue to suffer if you have an emotional reaction to everything that is said to you. True power is sitting back and observing things with logic. True power is restraint. If words control you that means everyone else can control you. Breathe and allow things to pass."*

C.E.A.S.E. for Equity

At the end of the day, it all comes down to making a serious decision. You have to decide if you're going to let the words of someone else manipulate you into behaving and speaking in ways that are threatening, intimidating, abusive, offensive, dehumanizing, or destructive. During a conversation with my youngest son, I explained how I am not defined by what someone else thinks of me, what someone says about me, or what they choose to call me. I am defined by how my actions align with my words.

Growing up, I had heard the Puerto Rican term "jíbaro" used among friends and their family members, usually followed by laughter. It seemed to be a term of endearment (similar to the n-word among Americans whose ancestors were enslaved Africans). Well, one day I called a close friend a jíbaro, as a joke. Instead of laughing, he immediately stopped what he was doing and glared at me. He looked at me directly, without a trace of amusement in his face or tone, and said, "Don't **ever** call me that! Don't ever call *anyone* that!" He explained he had been taught it was a derogatory term, similar to the n-word. I felt bad and tried to forget the word.

Fast-forward to my adult life, being around my mother-in-love. Although her ability to speak English was very good, she was more comfortable speaking her native language of Spanish. One day, I heard her say that charged word – jíbaro. Everyone either laughed or assented to the use of the word except me. My wife, sensing my confusion, asked what was wrong with me (I'm usually quick with a laugh). I told her about my previous experience with that word. However, she explained that jíbaro wasn't the derogatory, demeaning, or offensive word I had been led to believe it was. Throughout her experience and upbringing, the term was used to describe rural, agricultural workers, especially those living in the mountainous interior of Puerto Rico. Someone from el campo (the field or countryside); someone who had not experienced the city life; someone "stuck in their ways;" someone who doesn't like change.

III. Sammā-sati

The word "jíbaro" is believed to have Indigenous roots, possibly derived from a Taíno or Arawak word referring to "people of the forest" or "mountain people." Traditionally, the term *jíbaro* refers to a rural, working-class Puerto Rican, often a farmer or agricultural laborer who lived a simple and humble life. These individuals were deeply connected to the land and to traditional values, living in the mountainous interior of the island where farming and self-reliance were central to daily existence.

However, the concept of the jíbaro extends beyond occupation or lifestyle. Over time, it evolved into a powerful cultural symbol – embodying the essence of Puerto Rican identity and pride. The jíbaro represents hard work, ingenuity, and a deep sense of cultural authenticity; a figure of resilience and strength; someone who preserved Puerto Rican traditions and values even in the face of economic hardship and foreign influence.

Furthermore, the jíbaro has come to symbolize resistance to colonial domination and external cultural pressures, especially during times when Puerto Rican identity was threatened by assimilation or marginalization. In this way, the jíbaro is not just a figure from the countryside, but a lasting emblem of national spirit and cultural perseverance.

There's a familiar saying – *Sticks and stones might break my bones, but words can never hurt me.* When a loved one or client comes to me for advice about situations in which people are making accusations, I tell them to ask themselves one question – Is it true? I remind them that if it *is* true, then there's no reason to be angry, upset, embarrassed, sad, depressed, worried, aggravated, etc. I remind them that if it *is NOT* true, then there's no reason to be angry, upset, embarrassed, sad, depressed, worried, aggravated, etc.

My approach to the n-word is the same, and it makes me wonder. Do people get upset, offended, angry, and/or ready to fight when they hear the n-word *because they've been told that's how they're supposed to react* OR because they really believe the connotations of that word apply to them? If the attributes associated with being a nigger don't apply to me, why should it matter if someone else says it to me, at me, or around me? Why should I have a reaction? Why should I let it influence how I think about myself?

It makes me think of a something shared by the comedian Dave Chappelle (who I think is brilliant and hilarious, lol). During his *Sticks & Stones* special, Mr. Chappelle recounts a conversation with the woman in charge of the Standards and Practices department. Mr. Chappelle asks, "Why is it that I can say the word 'nigger' with impunity, but I can't say the word 'faggot?'" The woman says, "Because, David. You are not gay." David Chappelle said he responded with, "Well, Reneé, I'm not a nigger either."[16]

Take a moment and find some definitions of the word…yeah, with the hard "-er"…I'll wait…write them below.

---

16 Chappelle, Dave. *Sticks & Stones*. Netflix, 2019

III. Sammā-sati

Some of your definitions probably make reference to "ignorant," "lazy," "inferior," or "uneducated." Other definitions might include terms such as "contempt," "offensive," "derogatory," or "inflammatory." O.k., o.k.…Before you put this book down out of frustration, accusing me of avoiding "The question," let me respond. If you know the words you speak are going to cause hurt, division, PTSD, anger, depression, or death – don't say them. That applies to the n-word, as well as other derogatory words and phrases. "But how will I know if my words will create such severe negative circumstances or put me in potentially harmful situations?" I ask – Are you being for real??? In this day and age of social media, online access, and AI, you should be able to answer that question on your own. Use the next page to reflect, journal, and figure it out.

IV. Consider the "Facts"
(aka The importance of data)
…fair warning - you're being set up ;-)

IV. Consider the "Facts"

Now that you're many, many pages into reading, digesting, questioning, considering, and scrutinizing the contents of this book – while reflecting on your own knowledge, beliefs, feelings, experiences, perspectives, and attitudes – you may have noticed a limited amount of statistical data, charts, graphs, or citations from other organizations, publications, researchers etc. You might be wondering, "Why?" or thinking, "Hmmmm, that *is* a little suspicious!"

I make you aware of this for the sake of transparency and honesty. You see….data is often "cherry picked" and curated to support the claim, point of view, perspective, and/or argument of someone who is trying to "win" or "be right." The quest for liberation, freedom, and peaceful unity is more valuable, critical, precious, and serious than you probably think. When Person A enters a conversation with the intent of "winning," they will go to great lengths to ensure Person B "loses." As Person A strives to maintain a position of being "right," the views, feelings, beliefs, perspective, and experiences of Person B will always be dismissed and seen as "wrong," simply because they're different. This approach to engaging and interacting is exclusionary; it's polarizing; it's what causes fights and quarrels among us; it's what prolongs conflicts; it fuels wars and motivates consumption and appropriation, rather than preservation, conservation, and collaboration.

We live in an era increasingly defined by metrics, algorithms, and evidence-based decisions. Data is often perceived as an objective reflection of reality, a neutral tool for understanding the world. However, the processes of gathering, manipulating, analyzing, and presenting data are far from impartial. At every stage of the cycle – from collection to presentation – data is shaped by human choices, interests, and biases. The discourse of neutrality is promoted to disguise how data is frequently used to reinforce existing power structures, marginalize particular communities, diminish specific voices, and justify institutional inequities; as a means of control by shaping narratives, influencing public perception, and minimizing disparities. Let's explore the subjectivity that's inherent in data collection, manipulation, analysis, and presentation, while also highlighting strategies for resisting the misuse of data in the digital age.

I believe data collection must begin with the careful observation and clear articulation of an issue – because these initial steps to data collection are objectively based on the facts. What follows next, what we mistakenly call the first step in the cycle, is the actual process of data collection. Data collection is far from neutral. I said it, I meant, I'm here to represent it! The decisions of what data to gather, how to gather it, and from whom, are influenced by political, economic, and social factors. One of the most common issues is sampling bias. When data sets are derived from unrepresentative samples, they produce skewed outcomes. A notable example is political polling, which often focuses disproportionately on urban or suburban populations, neglecting rural voices and leading to misguided predictions.

Another layer of subjectivity lies in how terms and categories are constructed. For example, official unemployment statistics often omit discouraged workers who have stopped seeking employment, resulting in an under-reporting of economic hardship. Similarly, responses can be shaped by the way questions are framed during data collection, subtly guiding outcomes. Leading or ambiguously worded questions can steer respondents toward answers that reinforce dominant narratives, rather than uncovering diverse or dissenting perspectives.

Once collected, data may be selectively manipulated to serve specific agendas. As mentioned previously, one tactic is cherry-picking data, where only supportive evidence is presented while contradictory information is ignored. Presenting crime statistics in a way that either inflates or minimizes certain trends, depending on the political message a government or media outlet wishes to convey, is an example of this.

IV. Consider the "Facts"

Statistical distortions also play a powerful role in shaping public perception. The choice between presenting median versus mean income can significantly alter the interpretation of economic well-being. Median income may appear stable, while mean income could reveal extreme wealth disparities skewed by top earners. Similarly, graphs and visuals can be used to exaggerate or obscure trends – through truncated axes, lack of context, or selective highlighting – thereby manipulating your interpretation, misleading conversations, and misguiding decisions without necessarily falsifying the data.

Even when data is accurately collected and transparently presented, biased interpretations can guide its analysis. One pervasive issue is the fallacy of correlation versus causation. Reports that link poverty to crime, for example, may overlook elements of the ecosystem that cause such issues (e.g., underfunded education, lack of economic opportunities, housing discrimination, etc.), and instead place the blame on individuals or communities.

Selective interpretation is another way in which data is weaponized. A single dataset – say, on job growth – can be heralded as evidence of economic prosperity while ignoring stagnant wages or the rise of insecure per diem work. Moreover, expert bias influences how findings are framed. "Expert" analysts bring their own social, political, and economic assumptions to the table, making truly objective interpretation rare.

Take a moment to re-read what I said about making exceptions (the opening paragraphs of this book). Perhaps most troubling is the use of data to justify injustice and inequality. Racialized data, linked to social and economic disparities, reinforce harmful stereotypes if institutional causes are ignored. For example, highlighting academic achievement gaps without acknowledging factors such as unequal funding, insecurities (food, housing, safety), or generational trauma contributes to deficit narratives that blame marginalized communities for their circumstances.

C.E.A.S.E. for Equity

Governments and institutions often utilize data to rationalize policies that perpetuate unfair practices, oppressive tactics, and existing inequalities. For instance, crime statistics are frequently used to justify heightened policing in already over-policed neighborhoods, rather than addressing root causes such as the lack of employment, the lack of social services, and legislation that limits the ability of law-abiding citizens to determine their own health and safety. Similarly, the use of broad economic indicators like GDP growth can obscure deeper issues such as wage stagnation, rising living costs, and wealth concentration.

The digital age has introduced new complexities and dangers in data manipulation, such as algorithmic bias. Artificial intelligence systems, trained using biased datasets, reproduce and amplify those biases. Facial recognition technology, which utilizes AI, has been shown to have significantly higher error rates for people with noticeable melanin levels and particular facial features (nose shape, slant of the eyes, thickness of lips etc.), leading to real-world consequences in law enforcement and surveillance.

In addition to biased algorithms, the rise of data harvesting and surveillance allows corporations and governments to collect vast amounts of personal information, often without informed consent. This data is then used to influence behavior, shape political campaigns, and enforce social control. Be very aware of 1) the apps you're downloading to your mobile devices (giving access to your camera, microphone, contacts etc.) 2) how your "smart" devices are recognizing and storing your voice, dialect, and speech patterns, 3) how smart devices are the gateway for relinquishing your unique personal identifiers (fingerprints, facial and vocal markers, etc.). Also, be hypersensitive about your interactions through social media. You typically "follow" and "like" what aligns with your beliefs and interests, while looking to dispute, debate, and argue with what does not. Social media contributes to the rapid spread of misinformation (also labeled as "fake" news), supported by misleading or

IV. Consider the "Facts"

fabricated statistics which blur the line between fact and fiction.

Understanding the subjectivity of data is a crucial step in resisting its misuse. Several strategies can help promote ethical and transparent data practices. First and foremost, researchers, institutions, and policymakers should clearly articulate their motivation for data collection. Community-driven data initiatives must be part of the data approach. When marginalized communities are provided with the tools to collect and interpret their own data, the result is often a more accurate and empowering portrayal of their realities – one that challenges dominant narratives and supports more equitable policy outcomes. Second, data sources, analytical methods, and potential conflicts of interest must be disclosed to allow for independent verification and accountability. There must be greater transparency in the methodology.

In conjunction with the aforementioned steps, critical media literacy must be widely taught and promoted at every grade level (age appropriate, of course). Individuals must be empowered to question data claims, scrutinize sources, and recognize common forms of statistical manipulation. Only through transparency, accountability, and critical engagement can we re-establish the use of data as a tool for agency, empowerment, and sustaining ecosystems for equity.

#Facts

In the early days of these United States of America, enslaved Africans were brutally violated through abduction, beatings, rape, and murder - #Facts. They were subjected to torment and trauma through physical, sexual, and psychological abuse; separation from loved ones; threats of maiming, crippling, and homicide; willful negligence and malnutrition by their captors…you get the picture. It's my sincere hope that many, if not all of you dear readers, already know that learning to read and write in the language of their captors (historically labeled as "masters") was forbidden for enslaved Africans, and their descendants, in these United

States of America. This was in addition to the prohibition of speaking in, and violent coercion to abandon, their native languages.

Likewise, the people of the diverse Indigenous tribes (including the Taíno and natives of what we call Mexico), were similarly displaced, dishonored, and decimated as a direct result of the planned tactics utilized by early settlers and those put in charge of governing these United States of America - #Facts. Some of you may also be keenly aware of coordinated and consistent approaches to eradicating the original languages of Indigenous people, most notably being the forced attendance of Indigenous youth at "boarding" schools.

Those who governed during the early days of these United States of America instituted a structured plan, still in use today, to spread dis-ease, by way of drugs, alcohol, infectious maladies, and other decomposing agents throughout this land – all for the purpose of eradicating the cultures and communal approaches to living demonstrated by the Indigenous tribes. Intimidation, incendiary strategies (the literal burning of homes and villages), and murder were used to appropriate land and resources for personal gain in the forms of wealth, influence, political position, and dominance. I dare say that the same can be said of those governing today.

Unlike migrants who arrived during the formative years of America, enslaved Africans and people of the Indigenous tribes were forced to relinquish and abandon cultural, historical, communal, and traditional aspects that were detrimental to their identity, survival, heritage, and longevity.

We're oftentimes presented with factors as "facts." Facts are objective – they can be verified by what you see, hear, touch, smell, and taste. Factors are subjective because we attribute our beliefs and past experiences to them; we often lean to our own understanding about the intentions or influences behind them. There are factors that correlate with disparities and opportunities, the widening gaps and, to some degree, the polarization occurring in these United States of America. I encourage every reader, everyone who shares their

IV. Consider the "Facts"

opinion about this book, to investigate the "facts" written in our history books. I'm confident you'll find they're biased to tell the stories from the perspective of the victors (not the victims).

Consider the concepts of "access" and "affordability. Which would you categorize as fact and which as the factor? Keep this in mind as you continue reading. In modern societies, access to essential resources such as healthcare, education, and information is often touted as a marker of progress and equity. Governments, institutions, and private organizations have implemented policies to ensure that individuals can theoretically reach these fundamental services. However, access does not equate to affordability, nor does it guarantee the ability to use these resources in a meaningful way. Despite the increasing availability of services, financial barriers, inequities intentionally designed into each man-made ecosystem, and hidden costs prevent many individuals from the full benefits of what is ostensibly within their reach. To truly liberate and empower marginalized communities, you must understand the distinctions between access and affordability, particularly in healthcare, education, and information.

I categorize access as a fact and view it as a fundamental step toward manifesting and sustaining ecosystems for equity. However, access alone doesn't guarantee the ability to afford or effectively utilize these resources. With that said, I categorize affordability as a factor. Many individuals find themselves in proximity to vital services, yet remain unable to take full advantage of them due to financial constraints, institutional barriers, and hidden costs. This disparity between access and affordability creates an illusion of progress while maintaining deep socioeconomic divisions. As you read, discuss, and re-read, *C.E.A.S.E. for Equity*:
- Acknowledge that access does not equate to affordability,

- Consider how the fabricated ecosystems regulate healthcare, education, criminal justice, information, housing, and food choices,
- Formulate methods for transforming them to ensure freedom and equity.

Access refers to the availability of a resource, meaning that individuals are legally or geographically able to obtain it, whereas affordability determines whether people can actually use and sustain that resource without hardship. While policymakers often measure progress by the expansion of access, the failure to address the cost barriers results in superficial inclusivity that leaves marginalized populations behind. Many individuals may find themselves within physical proximity of a resource – eligible for its benefits or legally entitled to it – yet unable to bear the associated costs that make its use sustainable. Without affordability, access remains a hollow promise, offering opportunities in theory but not in practice. Rectifying the disparities in access and the injustices in affordability requires changes, such as targeted policy reforms, increased subsidies, and community-driven initiatives.

Healthcare is one of the most striking of the habitats in the man-made ecosystems, where the disparity between access and affordability is evident. While medical facilities, health insurance programs, and public health initiatives may exist, financial burdens still prevent many from receiving adequate care. Some nations provide universal or widespread healthcare access, but financial constraints still limit people's ability to receive adequate medical treatment. Insurance premiums, out-of-pocket expenses, and the cost of prescription drugs create barriers even in these circumstances.

In these United States of America, healthcare is accessible in the sense that hospitals and clinics exist and offer services, but affordability remains a severe issue. Expensive treatments, surgeries, and long-term care remain prohibitive for those without sufficient insurance or financial resources. Many individuals delay necessary treatments due to fear of medical

IV. Consider the "Facts"

debt and financial burdens associated with care, leading to worsened health outcomes. Emergency care may be mandated, but follow-up treatments, medication, and specialist consultations often carry prohibitive costs. As a result, patients may delay necessary medical visits, leading to worsened health outcomes.

Even when insurance policies are available, deductibles, co-pays, and uncovered services limit the actual benefits to insured individuals. In some countries with health insurance programs, high deductibles, co-pays, and non-covered procedures make essential treatments unaffordable for many. Health insurance doesn't always mean comprehensive coverage, forcing patients to pay substantial amounts out of pocket.

The growing awareness of issues stemming from psychological wellness has led to expanded access to therapy and psychiatric services. The stigma surrounding mental health has decreased, and therapy services are theoretically accessible. However, the high costs of therapy sessions and psychiatric medications make consistent psychological care unattainable for many individuals, particularly in lower-income communities.

Education is another environment in which access is often confused with affordability. While institutions might offer opportunities for learning, financial obstacles limit the ability of many individuals to fully participate – access does not equate to affordability. Public schools, universities, and online courses offer theoretical accessibility, but associated costs (e.g., transportation, materials, meals, etc.) create significant financial challenges.

Universities and colleges may be physically and legally accessible, but high tuition fees, expensive textbooks, meal plans, and living expenses make higher education an unsustainable option for many students. Those who do enroll often accumulate significant debt, creating long-term financial burdens. Student loan debt further exacerbates these challenges, forcing individuals into long-term financial hardship.

While public education is available to all students, disparities in funding between schools in affluent and low-income areas result in unequal access to quality education. Private schools offer better facilities and programs, but their high costs exclude lower-income scholars. Although public schooling is available in primary and secondary education, funding disparities are clear. Wealthier districts are able to provide more durable, relevant, and up-to-date resources, while lower-income schools struggle with 1) outdated materials, 2) underpaid teachers, 3) inadequate infrastructure, and 4) the targeted removal of courses that liberate students, increase student agency, and provide the "window," "mirror," and "sliding glass door" experiences recommended by Emly Style and Dr. Rudine Sims Bishop.[17]

For example, opportunities to participate in fine and performing arts classes (music, dance, visual art, theater, culinary), "shop" classes (woodworking and auto), and personal hygiene (e.g. estheticians) are absent, or severely impaired, in the lives of lower-income students. It's an aspect of the education that must be transformed or replaced, because these are courses in which students are able to truly express themselves, where they are able to incorporate their cultural experiences and beliefs into their learning, where they can authentically "see" themselves throughout the curriculum.

Access to education needs to extend beyond classroom learning. Opportunities such as study abroad programs and extracurricular activities (e.g. tutoring, sports, community theater, etc.) often carry costs that prevent lower-income students from participating, further widening the opportunity gaps between them and their more affluent peers. Reducing tuition costs, increasing scholarship opportunities, and

---

[17] Style, Emily. "Curriculum as Window and Mirror." Listening for All Voices, edited by Eleanor L. Lee et al., National SEED Project, 1988.
Bishop, Rudine Sims. "Mirrors, Windows, and Sliding Glass Doors." *Perspectives: Choosing and Using Books for the Classroom*, vol. 6, no. 3, Summer 1990, pp. ix–xi.

IV. Consider the "Facts"

improving public school funding can help bridge the gaps in education affordability.

The atmosphere surrounding information experienced a rapid evolution with the proliferation of the internet. With that said, municipalities might implement universal internet coverage to guarantee access to information. Yet the affordability of devices and subscription fees remain barriers to digital equity; without the time required to navigate digital spaces effectively, the access becomes meaningless.

While internet connectivity is available in a multitude of locations (Wi-Fi and public access points), high-speed internet and reliable devices remain expensive. Individuals in low-income communities often struggle with slow connections, outdated hardware, or shared devices, thus limiting their ability to use the internet effectively. Many academic journals, research databases, and even news sources require paid subscriptions, creating barriers to knowledge and preventing economically disadvantaged individuals from accessing critical information that should be universally available.

Even when internet access is available, individuals without proper digital literacy may struggle to utilize it effectively. Training programs, certifications, and workshops cost money, further widening the divide between those who can leverage information and those who cannot. To alleviate this, communities must work to fully fund or subsidize the costs pertaining to high-speed internet access, quality and durable devices, and digital literacy programs to ensure equal access to online resources, which equates to equal access to information.

I'm sure you'll agree that housing is a fundamental human necessity. While shelters, rental units, and homeownership opportunities exist, costs make them unattainable for large segments of the population – affordability remains a crisis worldwide. Every city has options for stable shelter. Subsidized public housing programs exist, but long waitlists, restrictive eligibility requirements, and insufficient funding limit their effectiveness in providing relief and safety. Home ownership requires more than just a mortgage payment – property taxes, maintenance, and insurance costs add to the financial responsibilities, making it out of reach for many. Gentrification further exacerbates the housing problem, pushing vulnerable communities into less desirable areas.

Grocery stores and food sources are widely available, yet food insecurity persists because of rising costs and insufficient wages. Access to organic, fresh, and nutritious food remains a privilege largely determined by wealth. While healthier food choices are available, they're often financially inaccessible to lower-income communities, who must prioritize cheaper, processed foods. You must also consider how many low-income neighborhoods lack local grocery stores that offer fresh produce, making it difficult for residents to access healthy food even if they can afford it. While food assistance programs exist, they often don't provide enough benefits to cover the cost of nutritious, high-quality food.

Employment opportunities might be legally accessible, but factors such as wage stagnation, lack of benefits (health, child care, PTO, etc.), and the cost of career advancement hinder true economic mobility. Employment opportunities may be widely available, but economic stability remains elusive for many workers. Many jobs fail to offer livable wages. The existence of job openings doesn't equate to financial security, forcing individuals to work multiple jobs for survival. Wages haven't kept pace with the rising cost of living, making financial security difficult to attain even for full-time employees.

Many prestigious career paths require unpaid internships, advanced degrees, or expensive certifications, limiting upward mobility for those unable to afford these investments. These, and other networking opportunities required for career growth, often come with financial barriers that further limit upward mobility for lower-income workers. Even when jobs are available, the costs associated with childcare, transportation, and other necessary expenses (e.g.,

IV. Consider the "Facts"

work attire) make it difficult for individuals to sustain a job without additional financial strain.

While individual and collective efforts have resulted in significant strides toward successfully increasing access to essential resources, true equity will remain unattainable and unsustainable without addressing affordability. The illusion of progress created by accessibility masks the deeper economic struggles that prevent millions from utilizing healthcare, education, digital resources, nutritious food, and housing. Policymakers must focus on making these resources not only available, but financially feasible for all individuals; making resources genuinely affordable and sustainable for all. Only then can societies achieve meaningful progress in bridging the gap between opportunity and economic reality.

V. ACTIONABLE STEPS

1. Improve your C.O.R.E.
2. Eradicate H.A.T.E. with L.O.V.E.
3. Be Intentional
4. It's really about R.A.C.E.
5. Desist…
6. …and C.E.A.S.E. for Equity

V. Actionable Steps

1. <u>Improve your C.O.R.E.</u>

Cultivating empathy and sustaining ecosystems for equity requires more than good intentions. It demands deliberate, ongoing improvement of your:

Capacity to
Observe   [honor by not interfering or acting without consent or request]
Respect   [showing regard for the abilities and worth of others – valuing their feelings and views, even if you don't necessarily agree with them; accepting them on an equal basis; giving them the same consideration you would expect for yourself; Respect begins with yourself] &
Empower   [make someone stronger, more confident/competent/capable, especially in controlling their life and claiming their rights; share knowledge – can be transformative; share your story; listen to other peoples' stories; stand up for others; embrace positivity; build support networks]

These actions are foundational for building relationships across cultural differences, addressing structures and institutions of injustice, and creating sustainable environments where all individuals can thrive. By improving your ability to observe deeply, respect fully, and empower authentically, you begin to process of transforming the social and economic ecosystems from the inside out.

Your capacity to observe is the first critical step. Observation goes beyond simply seeing; it requires attention, presence, and an openness to honestly explore what lies deep beneath the surface. It's easy to overlook the daily realities of those most affected; those negatively impacted by inequality in the education, healthcare, housing, finances and wealth, and criminal justice communities of the social and economic ecosystems. When you sharpen our observational awareness, you begin to notice who is excluded from decision-making, whose voices are ignored, where resources are inequitably distributed, and your complicity. By observing with care, you will identify patterns of harm and resilience that might otherwise remain hidden. This awareness is essential for cultivating empathy, as it moves you from assumption to understanding, from indifference to informed engagement.

Observe your own thoughts, beliefs, attitudes, behaviors, and language. Ask yourself the following questions:
1. What do I believe about [insert person, community, culture or concept here]
2. **Why** do I think/feel this way about [insert person, community, culture or concept here]?
3. Where did/does my knowledge and understanding about [insert person, community, culture or concept here] come from?
4. How do I know if my sources about [insert person, community, culture or concept here] are reliable?
5. What do I know to be factual about [insert person, community, culture or concept here]?

These questions are intended as a guide, to help you better understand your perceptions, prejudices, and preferences. When you make adequate time to reflect and respond to each question, you'll gain a better understanding about your 1) capacity to empathize with those who might be noticeably different, 2) ability to identify with, and relate to, the human condition of others, and 3) willingness to speak and behave in ways that liberate, empower, and free those who are negatively impacted by ecosystems of equity. Let me say that again: When YOU make adequate time to reflect *and* respond to each question! As I stated in my opening paragraph – this is self-work. Your daily decisions, actions, and language will determine how efficiently and effectively you will cultivate empathy and sustain ecosystems for equity.

Respect is the next step in the process and builds on observation. To respect others is to acknowledge their inherent worth, regardless of their social status, financial standing,

V. Actionable Steps

cultural background, or experience. Respect means listening without judgment, valuing diverse perspectives, and recognizing lived experience as a source of wisdom. Practicing deep respect is a radical and necessary shift, considering how certain groups are intentionally devalued, dismissed, or destroyed in these United States of America. True respect affirms the dignity of every individual and lays the groundwork for authentic collaboration. Respect opens the door to empathy by helping you see others not as problems to solve but as people to stand with.

Finally, empowerment is where empathy translates into action. Empowerment means creating the conditions for others to lead, contribute, and shape outcomes that affect their lives. It involves sharing power, amplifying underrepresented voices, and nurturing environments where all people can grow and succeed. In ecosystems for equity, leadership isn't concentrated at the top; it's distributed across communities. Improving your ability to empower others requires humility, courage, and a commitment to long-term justice. It means stepping back when needed, making space, and supporting people in finding and using their own voices.

When observation, respect, and empowerment work in concert, they create a powerful atmosphere in which ecosystems for equity to thrive. They equip you to challenge oppressive language and behaviors, while also building structures of care. Empathy, cultivated through this framework, becomes more than a feeling; it becomes a force for transformation. It influences policies, relationships, and practices to prioritize human dignity and shared well-being.

Focusing on your C.O.R.E. helps you examine yourself; it's not about comparing yourself to, diagnosing, or judging what someone else says or does; it's not about detaching from the suffering of others, excusing your actions and language, justifying the damaging words and behaviors of those around you, accusing someone else, or blaming another person or entity.

Ultimately, improving your C.O.R.E. is a social imperative, not just a personal development goal. Your capacity to observe, respect, and empower others helps build bridges in divided communities, redistribute power in unjust systems, and plant the seeds of lasting equity. In choosing to develop them, you take meaningful steps toward manifesting a more just and compassionate world.

While reading this book, some of the following observable attributes may have entered your mind – perhaps you made time to dwell on them:

- melanin level,
- facial features (nose size and shape, eye shape, cheek structure, lip size, etc.)
- accent, dialect, patterns of speech, phrases and colloquialisms,
- country of origin, ethnic background,
- cultural practices, etc.

NOTE: This list is not exhaustive, lol. I challenge you to make time, right now. Pause from reading and reflect on your thinking about each of the attributes – I recommend journaling your observations, thoughts, and feelings in detail. For example, describe the melanin level(s) you're envisioning, using specific colors. (e.g., pale/milky, slightly tan, caramel, brown, shades of wheat, etc.). Write about the type of accent(s) you're hearing in your mind. (Southern, New York, Boston, Hispanic, Asian, African, Irish, Italian, etc.). Write them with unfiltered and unrefined honesty. If you're really feeling like "I got this," discuss your observations with a few thought partners.

2. <u>Eradicate H.A.T.E. with L.O.V.E.</u>

Hate is not merely an emotion; it's a destructive force that manifests in behaviors and language designed to harm, intimidate, and eliminate. I've come to understand hate as a process that begins with **H**arassment, progresses to **A**buse, escalates to **T**errorizing, with the ultimate goal of

V. Actionable Steps

Extinguishing. Keep reading and increase your awareness of how hate operates through these four stages – understand their definitions, recognize their manifestations, and realize their effects on individuals and communities.

Harassment – the onset of hostility – is often the initial expression of hate, involving behaviors that demean, humiliate, or intimidate individuals based on their identifiers. It includes verbal insults, threats, microaggressions, and unwelcome actions that create a hostile environment. Legally, harassment is recognized as a form of discrimination that can nullify a person's rights or impair their ability to benefit from those rights. In Connecticut, harassment is addressed under hate crime statutes, where actions intended to intimidate or harass individuals based on protected characteristics are criminalized.[18]

Abuse is the next step in the progression from harassment, involving repeated and intentional acts that cause physical or psychological harm. It encompasses behaviors such as physical assaults, verbal degradation, and coercive control. Abuse not only affects the immediate victim but also instills fear within the broader community. Connecticut law recognizes various degrees of intimidation based on bigotry or bias, with first-degree intimidation involving physical injury inflicted with the intent to intimidate or harass.[19]

Terrorizing involves actions that instill profound fear, often through threats or acts of violence intended to intimidate individuals or groups. This stage of hate aims to suppress and control through fear, disrupting the sense of safety and security. Under federal law, hate crime acts that involve threats or actual violence based on "race," religion, or other protected characteristics are punishable offenses. These laws acknowledge the terrorizing impact of hate crimes on both individuals and communities.

---

[18] Connecticut General Assembly. *Public Act No. 17-111: An Act Concerning Hate Crimes.* https://cga.ct.gov/2017/SUM/2017SUM00111-R02HB-05743-SUM.htm

[19] Connecticut General Statutes § 53a-181i. *Intimidation Based on Bigotry or Bias in the First Degree.* https://www.cga.ct.gov/current/pub/chap_952.htm#sec_53a-181i

C.E.A.S.E. for Equity

The final and most devastating manifestation of hate is the attempt to extinguish (i.e., eliminate individuals or groups entirely). This can take the form of murder, genocide, or institutional oppression aimed at eradicating a particular identity. Such acts are not only crimes against individuals but also against humanity. U.S. Code § 249 - Hate Crime Act[20] expands federal hate crime laws to include those motivated by a victim's actual or perceived gender, sexual orientation, gender identity, or disability, recognizing the severe consequences of hate-driven actions.

Understanding hate as a process emphasizes the importance of diligent awareness, early intervention, and robust legal frameworks. By recognizing and addressing each stage, you can make comprehensive strategies to combat hate a reality, protect the rights and lives of all individuals, cultivate empathy and sustain ecosystems for equity.

I don't know about you, but I'm disappointed to see how many societies around the world are saturated with hostility, apathy, division, hardship, and the lingering effects of inequality. Unfortunately, the concept of love is often relegated to a sentimental or romantic notion. On the flip side of that coin, true love, as a force for social and economic transformation, is radical and revolutionary. I've reframed love as an acronym that stands for **L**iberate, **O**bserve, **V**alue, and **E**mpower. This turns love into an actionable framework.

This multidimensional approach provides a pathway to empathy, healing, and sustainable change in both individual lives and collective ecosystems for equity. You'll come to view each element of L.O.V.E. as a cornerstone for creating truly inclusive, empathetic, and peacefully thriving societies – moment by moment.

Liberation is the first and most foundational expression of love. Liberation is not only the removal of physical chains but the destruction of barriers that restrict one's ability to live

---

[20] United States, Congress. *U.S. Code Title 18, § 249 - Hate Crime Acts*. https://uscode.house.gov/view.xhtml?req=granuleid:USC-2010-title18-section249&num=0&edition=2010

V. Actionable Steps

fully and authentically. To love is the desire, the intention, and the motivation to work for freedom. It's rooted in the understanding that *you* aren't truly free until *everyone* is free.

Liberating love begins with self-awareness and extends to active resistance against all forms of apathy, oppression, exclusion, terror, and murder. It challenges racialized discrimination, sexism, poverty, ableism, and other methods of domination. Liberation acknowledges the intersections of identity and the ways in which some are marginalized based on multiple identifiers. In this context, love becomes political activism by disrupting the status quo and prioritizing justice.

Historically, liberation movements such as the Civil Rights Movement, the anti-Apartheid struggle, and contemporary efforts for Indigenous sovereignty have been motivated by a deep love for one's people and the belief that all humans deserve dignity. When communities fight to liberate themselves and others, they're exemplifying love in the most courageous and meaningful way.

Liberation also requires internal freedom – from fear, shame, trauma, and limiting beliefs. Practices such as therapy, spiritual routines, and education are some approaches that play a vital role in achieving this internal liberation. When individuals and communities are liberated, they gain the capacity to dream, create, and lead. The love that liberates does not coddle or control; it expands possibilities. To quote Maya Angelou, *"Love recognizes no barriers. It jumps hurdles, leaps fences, penetrates walls to arrive at its destination full of hope."*[21] These words capture the boundless, brave nature of love, showing that it can overcome any obstacle.

Observation, in the context of L.O.V.E., refers to the power of seeing – truly seeing – people as they are. It's about bearing witness without judgment, cultivating empathy, and recognizing the full humanity of others. To observe someone, in love, is to validate their experiences and emotions, especially in a society that often silences, ignores, or distorts marginalized voices.

---

[21] Angelou, Maya. Collected Poems. Random House, 1994.

C.E.A.S.E. for Equity

Observation is also about listening deeply, with compassion. In today's fast-paced and polarized world, people often listen to respond rather than understand. Loving observation shifts this dynamic by fostering active listening to build trust, mitigate conflict, and deepen relationships.

On a societal level, observation leads to awareness; of social injustices, institutional failures, and cultural narratives that perpetuate inequity. Once you observe the financial, political, educational, and civic structures around us clearly, you cannot unsee them. This kind of awareness prompts accountability and drives transformation.

Importantly, observation must be rooted in humility. It's easy to assume that we know what's best for others, especially when trying to help. But true love suspends assumptions and honors each individual's story. It seeks to learn, to hold space, and to affirm. In marginalized communities, simply being seen and heard (without being pitied or judged) is a revolutionary act. **The revolution will not be televised!**[22]

Observation also extends to self-awareness. By carefully and consciously observing your own behaviors, reactions, and thoughts, you uncover unconscious biases, internalized oppression, and attitudes of complicity. Self-observation (aka reflexive thinking) allows for personal growth, while communal observation leads to social progress. To observe, in love, means choosing presence over power and connection over control.

Valuing someone means recognizing their intrinsic worth, independent of their productivity, status, or utility. It means acknowledging that every person is deserving of dignity, respect, and care simply because they exist. Long story short, it means honoring the humanity in everyone – which I experienced and observed during my trips to India and Japan. This is perhaps one of the most radical aspects of love,

---

[22] Scott-Heron, G. *"The Revolution Will Not Be Televised."* On *Pieces of a Man*. Flying Dutchman, 1971.

V. Actionable Steps

particularly in societies that often measure people by what they can produce, how they look, or what they can provide.

Valuing others begins with affirming their identities, cultures, and contributions. It involves challenging stereotypes, celebrating diversity, and fostering inclusion. In relationships, it means expressing appreciation, offering praise, and demonstrating that others are seen and cherished.

At the community level, valuing others translates into practices such as fair wages, safe housing, accessible and affordable healthcare, inclusive education, and representation in decision-making. When entities, organizations, and institutions value people, they invest in their well-being, not as a favor but as a human right.

The practice of valuing is essential for healing and reconciliation. For those who have been historically devalued (due to "race," gender, ability, class, etc.), being genuinely valued can repair generational wounds. Love, when expressed as value, says, "You matter, not because of what you've done, but because of who you are." Self-love is also key in this area. Valuing yourself means setting boundaries, pursuing passions, and rejecting shame. It involves unlearning the internalized messages of unworthiness that often come from oppressive environments. When you value yourself, you're more likely to advocate for your needs and to value others in return. It creates a ripple effect of affirmation and agency. The following Robert A. Heinlein quote highlights the selfless nature of love, emphasizing that true love involves deeply caring about the well-being of others: *"Love is that condition in which the happiness of another person is essential to your own."* [23]

Empowerment is the active process of enabling people to take control of their lives and shape their destinies. It's the natural culmination of love that liberates, observes, and values. To empower someone is to invest in their potential, provide resources, and trust them to lead.

Understand something – Empowerment is not charity! It doesn't view others as helpless, but as powerful agents

---
[23] Heinlein, Robert A. Stranger in a Strange Land. Putnam, 1961.

capable of transformation. It includes education, mentorship, economic opportunities, in addition to access to, and influence within, decision-making spaces. Empowerment breaks cycles of dependency and builds sustainable strength.

In the workplace, empowerment looks like autonomy for employees, listening to their ideas, and recognizing their efforts. In education, it means equipping students with critical thinking skills, cultural knowledge, and a belief in their own brilliance. People have the right to shape their own lives and futures. In communities, it means involving residents in the planning and execution of policies that affect them, thereby increasing buy-in and accountability. Decisions made *with* the people affected are more likely to be effective, fair, and sustainable. To quote Glenn E. Martin (as posted on social media), *"Those closest to the problems are closest to the solutions."*[24]

For marginalized groups, empowerment is especially vital. Generations of disempowerment – through colonization, segregation, disenfranchisement, and poverty – cannot be undone by performative gestures. It requires tangible investments in leadership, infrastructure, and healing. True empowerment is guided by the principle of "nothing about us, without us;" a phrase that has become widely known through disability advocacy; a call for inclusive, participatory decision-making. True empowerment isn't given from the top down – it's built through collaboration, listening, along with shared influence and power.

Empowerment is also about storytelling. When people share their narratives – through art, activism, scholarship, or testimony – they reclaim their agency. Love empowers by amplifying voices, supporting dreams, and nurturing leadership. It selflessly moves beyond intentions to action. Leo Buscaglia captures the essence of selfless love as giving freely without any thought of what we might receive in return – *"Only when we give joyfully, without hesitation or thought of*

---

[24] Martin, Glenn E. X (formerly known as Twitter) post, 2016.

V. Actionable Steps

gain, can we truly know what love means."[25]

When the four elements of LOVE act in synergy, they create a powerful force for change. Liberation without observation can become misguided. Observation without value can feel hollow. Value without empowerment risks becoming patronizing. Empowerment without liberation fails to address root causes. Together, these elements form a holistic framework for personal and collective transformation. This framework can be applied in various contexts:

- Education: LOVE means decolonizing curricula, soliciting and incorporating student input/feedback, affirming their identities, and making tools for success accessible and affordable.
- Healthcare: LOVE means making high-quality healthcare accessible and affordable, respecting patients' stories, affirming their worth, and supporting informed choice.
- Relationships: LOVE means accepting people for who they truly are (e.g. their beliefs, customs, dialect, etc.) freeing loved ones from control, listening deeply, affirming their significance, and supporting their growth.
- Activism: LOVE means fighting injustice with compassion, amplifying community voices, honoring cultural strengths, and building capacity from within.

Love calls us to act, not just to feel; to commit, not just to care. This kind of love doesn't shy away from discomfort; it leans into the work of justice, healing, and collective liberation. The manifestations of LOVE are real, grounded, and practical. They shape how we build institutions, nurture relationships, and envision our future. In the end, active love is the most powerful tool we have for creating a world where everyone can thrive.

---

[25] Buscaglia, Leo. Born for Love: Reflections on Loving. Slack, 1992.

C.E.A.S.E. for Equity

Love is patient, love is kind. It does not envy, it does not boast, it is not proud. It does not dishonor others, it is not self-seeking, it is not easily angered, it keeps no record of wrongs. Love does not delight in evil but rejoices with the truth. It always protects, always trusts, always hopes, always perseveres. Love never fails.   1 Corinthians 13:4-8

3. Be Intentional

When you fail to plan, you plan to fail (attributed to Benjamin Franklin).[26] The following is a slight modification of a plan I created to guide my school district through the process of cultivating empathy and sustaining ecosystems for equity; to successfully transform institutional, educational, legislative, political, housing, criminal justice, and healthcare habitats of the man-made economic and social ecosystems.

Phase I (Years 1 & 2) - RID (focus on current beliefs, behaviors, and language)
1. **R**eflect on how your beliefs, language, and behaviors might exclude or marginalize people.
2. **I**dentify your beliefs, language, and behaviors that exclude or marginalize people.
3. **D**iscard/**D**estroy your beliefs, language, and behaviors that exclude or marginalize people.

Phase II (Years 2 - 4) - APPLY (cultivate a culture of empathy and belonging by changing approaches, practices, and policies)
1. **A**ddress/**A**pplaud present language and behaviors that expand the empathy and equity people experience.
2. **P**ursue authentic relationships, regardless of cultural, political, or academic differences; develop and nurture opportunities where these relationships can grow.
3. **P**ropel your people forward, the eager as well as the hesitant.

---

[26] Franklin, Benjamin. Poor Richard's Almanack, 1748. Various editions.

V. Actionable Steps

4. **L**aunch new opportunities and initiatives that increase agency and understanding (mirrors, windows, sliding glass doors).
5. **Y**ield to programs and activities that acknowledge, celebrate, highlight, honor, and appreciate the contributions and innovations of individuals and communities of historically marginalized groups. Pause "traditional" programs and activities – make time and space for historically marginalized groups to freely express, share, and celebrate their culture.

Phase III (Years 4+) - REFINE (Sustaining ecosystems for equity by improving the ways you continue to move toward inclusion, liberation, and freedom)

1. **R**eview your practices and procedures.
2. **E**xpedite the addition/inclusion of innovative programs, practices, and procedures.
3. **F**ollow-up with stakeholders to gauge the impact of Phases I & II.
4. **I**nvestigate methods, resources, strategies, and programs for empowering stakeholders.
5. i**N**spire stakeholders to engage in this work beyond curated settings.
6. **E**liminate insensitive and ineffective methods, policies, strategies, practices, and programs.

4. It's Really About R.A.C.E.
(**R**eflexive **A**ttitudes **C**ultivating **E**mpathy)

Let's start with an understanding that:
- Your behaviors and language are dictated by your attitude
- Your attitude is shaped by your beliefs
- Your beliefs are formed by your experiences (influenced by culture, economics, mental & physical ability, gender)

With that said, increasing your capacity, and improving your ability, to speak and act in L.O.V.E. really is about R.A.C.E. – Reflexive Attitudes Cultivating Empathy.

Reflexive
> *Reflective means focusing on WHAT you do – your choices, actions and endeavors, reflection makes sense of the experience*

> *Reflexive requires you to question WHY – your beliefs, assumptions, attitudes, and habits*

- Reflective can be thought of as "surface level" and easily observed
- Reflexive can be thought of as "a deeper dive" into what informs who we are as individuals. [adapted from *The Reflexive Teaching Artist* by Kathryn Dawson and Daniel A Kelin II][27]

What are your interactions and relationships with people from cultures, neighborhoods, communities, and/or countries that seem very different from yours?
- Identify your interactions. Are they:
    - Casual or intimate?
    - Formal or familiar?
    - Infrequent or scheduled?
    - Purposeful or unintended?
    - Are you an acquaintance, ally, or accomplice?
    - Co-worker, colleague, friend-outside-of-work (i.e., have you been to their house and have they been to yours)?
- Take accountability
    - Examine your personal biases, prejudices, and preconceived notions about people from said cultures, neighborhoods, communities, and/or countries. *We all grow up with biases and often racism too. Learn to recognize when these come*

---

[27] Dawson, Kathryn, and Daniel A. Kelin II. *The Reflexive Teaching Artist: Collective Wisdom from the Drama/Theatre Field.* Intellect Books, 2014.

V. Actionable Steps

up and correct them in yourself. This is hard and important work of change. You got this.[28]
- Stop viewing any one culture or group of people collectively as dangerous. 'Nuff said!
- Find and meet regularly with a group of thought partners who will challenge you, guide you, be honest with you, and celebrate with you; people to confess, discuss, and correct the conscious and unconscious biases you may have toward those of a seemingly different background, culture, and/or community. Have a few trusted people who will make you aware of when you are complicit to instances of dominance, supremacy, and racialized tactics; usually demonstrated by your silence when offensive/damaging language and behaviors occur in your sphere of influence.
- Learn the accurate history behind the sinister policies and practices that are in place to ensure the healthy development and continuation of dominance, supremacy, and racialized.
- Self-accountability, meaning stop and think about the intent and impact of your words and actions. *Check your language (and your friends). Use anti-racist as well as anti-oppressive language when referring to the marginalized. Speak up and challenge family and friends when they don't do the same. Don't be silent about racist or bigoted jokes. Silence is support. Sometimes you don't have to say the N-word to make us feel like you are calling us one. Phrases like "Those/You people", "You're different", "People like you/them" have a tendency to "other" us in categories that are*

---

[28] Epler, Melinda Briana. "20 Things You Can Do as an Ally Right Now." *Medium*, 6 June 2020

offensive at best and condescending at the very least. [29]

- Work on your personal transformation from becoming an ally to being an accomplice. Do you have a "savior" mentality when working with people from said cultures, neighborhoods, communities, and/or countries, constantly seeking ways to "save" or "help" "them" to do/be "better" or experience circumstances that are "better?" By "better" what you're actually implying is "more like *your* way of living."
- Be quick to listen, slow to speak, and slower to get offended. You can improve by 1) reading books and articles, 2) listening to podcasts, 3) watching documentaries and historic movies, 4) being more aware of how products are marketed and how the diverse groups are depicted in print and video media. Be aware of your ego and resist the urge to 1) become defensive about, 2) find fault with, and/or 3) ignore the perspectives and experiences being shared.

Attitudes
- Be aware of why you avoid/engage with certain people/communities.
- Admit and acknowledge that your attitude determines your language and behavior

Cultivating (developing and nurturing trust)
- Examine the *intent* of your language and behaviors in consideration of the *impact.*
- Plan for consistent opportunities to engage in, and grow from, conversations.
- Pursue authentic relationships with individuals/organizations/communities of historically

---

[29] Reed, Louis L. "Get Your Foot Off My Neck: 16 Ways White America Can Revive Opportunities for Blacks." *Medium,* 4 June 2020

V. Actionable Steps

      marginalized groups.
- Be aware of microaggressions.
- Recognize cultural *appreciation* versus *appropriation*.
- Foster environments that welcome questions, conversations, and cultural exchanges.

Empathy
- Opportunities for "mirror," "window," and "sliding glass door" experiences

Ask yourself, and answer, these questions – Why is it important to reflect on my attitude daily; to cultivate empathy moment by moment? How important is this to me? Probably your best response aligns with, "Because I remember being made to feel 'less than,' unseen, unimportant, or not valued at some point in my life – no one should be made to feel this way."

C.E.A.S.E. for Equity

Each natural ecosystem has specific conditions/habitats, which are critical for living organisms to thrive in harmonious balance. When you successfully nurture habitats of welcome and belonging, it's your responsibility to sustain the conditions in which your fellow humans feel their identity is being acknowledged and accepted, without conditions or preconceived notions.

With that said, let's inspect what we often call our "identity." It's usually the combination of your identifiers. Think about it this way – your identity statements usually start with "I identify as …" or "I am a …," followed by a list of identifiers. These identifiers either represent how you see yourself or how others see you.

For example, some of my identifiers, as I write this book, are: male, father, husband, tall, follically challenged (aka bald, lol), educator, American descended from enslaved Africans ("black"), musician, friend, uncle, elder, brother, son, instructional leader, man, resident director, mentor, presenter, human, advocate, listener, adult, martial artist, trustworthy, motivated, direct. Some of these identifiers are FLUID (what I'm willing and/or able to change) and others which are STATIC (what I'm unwilling and/or unable to change).

My FLUID identifiers are: husband, tall, teacher, musician, friend, instructional leader, resident director, mentor, presenter, advocate, listener, trustworthy, motivated, direct
My STATIC identifiers are: male, father, follically challenged (aka bald), American descended from enslaved Africans ("black"), uncle, elder, brother, son, man, adult, martial artist, human.

Identity is the complex intersection of your identifiers, which might include:
- Physical attributes,
- Behaviors,
- Language, phrases, colloquial expressions,
- Economic condition,
- Education/Achievements,

V. Actionable Steps

- Interactions with, observations by, and opinions of others.

Identity is a mindset that reflects how you're most comfortable behaving and speaking, regardless of affirmation and affiliation; the essence of who you truly are.

Consider this – identity theft involves someone else impersonating you, based on some of your identifiers. The thief does not actually behave and/or speak like you, and would be exposed as a fraud to those who actually know you. Take a moment to list your identifiers – categorize them as FLUID or STATIC. You might even consider comparing and discussing them with thought partners (hint, hint)

I need you to realize something very important – every day there are people working to manipulate you based on your identifiers, for their financial gain, to increase their status/position, or to cause/maintain division and/or discord. These include people within your sphere of influence (e.g., family members, co-workers, social media followers, etc.) and those whom you have never met (social media influencers, news media journalists, advertisers, marketing representatives, etc.).

Explore your biases and how they might influence your perspective about identifiers and identity. For example, experiences throughout my life have reinforced my beliefs about the differences between boys/girls and men/women. I'm biased in my thinking that boys and girls are children, which means they're not yet willing, nor capable of, caring for themselves and/or others (i.e., providing transportation, being employed legally, earning a livable wage, maintaining good health, etc.). However, men and women *are* capable, willing (most of the time, lol), and understand the necessity of doing so.

A sense of welcome and belonging occurs when you feel like your identity is being acknowledged and accepted, without conditions or preconceived notions. YOU determine the sense of inclusion, welcome, and belonging that your

fellow humans perceive when they're around you, based on whether your:
- Tone,
- Language, and
- Behaviors are
  - ❖ Graceful (full of grace),
  - ❖ Sincere, and
  - ❖ Factual (honest without judgement).

V. Actionable Steps

5. Desist…

Desist means to abstain from present *and **future*** actions. It conveys a deliberate choice to stop doing something now, and being mindful and aware of not resuming it in the future – whether those actions are harmful, habitual, or simply no longer desired. Although linguistically simple, the implications of this word become profound when considered in the context of the man-made economic and social ecosystems. To desist is not just a decision for personal benefit. Within the habitats of modern society, it results in significant outcomes, serves as a form of resistance, and catalyzes institutional changes. I've identified the following behaviors and language we must desist, individually and collectively, in order to cultivate empathy and sustain ecosystems for equity:

- Racialization
- The Binary Mindset
- The Survival Mindset
- Using "-isms"
- Weaponizing Information
- Focusing on Civil Rights
- Forced Desegregation
- The Census Process
- The U.S. Tax Codes
- Gaslighting the Homeless
- Federal "Months" and "Days"
- The White Privilege Narrative
- Virtue Signaling about Climate Change
- Victimization Narratives
- The Addiction Narrative
- The Relativity of Truth
- Cultural Appropriation
- Federal Recognition Requirements for Indigenous Tribes
- Reliance on Perpetual Public Assistance Programs
- Efforts to Defund Law Enforcement
- Partitioning the History of these United States of America
- The Narratives of Privilege and Positionality
- Emphasizing a College Degree
- Performative Practices of…
  - Activism
  - Land Acknowledgements
  - ADA Compliance
  - Creating Brave/Safe Spaces
  - Creating "Common Language"
  - Allyship

Desist…Racialization

If a group of "white" people chased and beat up a "black person, would you call that "racist?" How about if a group of Asian people were to do it – would that be considered racist? Now flip the script – what if a group of "black" people chased and beat up a "white" person – would you say they were racist? What if they did this to an Asian person?

I've heard it explained that racism relies on positions of power, influence, or prestige. This hypothesis also argues how "white" people inherently hold such positions because of their "whiteness," therefore making it impossible for "black" people to be racist toward "white" people (because "black" folks are not in those positions). That's ridiculous!!! Tell that to the poor "white" families living in the Hollow…or the struggling Asian families living on the East End…or the "black" political families living on Park Ave.

The concept of "race" has long served as a framework for categorizing human beings based on superficial physical traits such as melanin levels (aka skin "color"), facial features, hair texture, and even speech patterns (including "accents"). Despite its widespread acceptance and institutionalization, the concept of "race" is a construct of the social ecosystem that has no firm grounding in biology or genetics. The classification of people by "race" has historically fueled discrimination, division, exclusion, and violence. In the modern era, where globalization and diversity are increasingly interwoven into the fabric of societies, the continued use of "race" as a defining category undermines efforts to create collaborative and cohesive communities. We must move away from using the concept of "race" altogether. Let that marinate! Simplifying complex human identities into racialized categories impedes empathy and degrades our social and economic ecosystems.

To understand the urgency of discarding the concept of race, it is essential to explore its origins. "Race," as a construct, emerged prominently during what historians call the Age of Exploration and Enlightenment; a time when European powers sought to justify the subjugation and enslavement of non-

V. Actionable Steps

European people. Early pseudo-anthropological studies attempted to categorize humans into distinct racialized groups, often assigning intellectual and moral superiority to those with European features. These ideas were not based on empirical science; they were crafted to rationalize colonialism, slavery, and imperialism.

Modern genetics has thoroughly debunked the notion of biologically distinct races. The Human Genome Project revealed that humans share over 99.9% of their DNA and the genetic variation *within* so-called "racial" groups is often greater than the variation between them.[30] Considering this, "race" must no longer be treated as a legitimate scientific category but as a harmful myth that continues to influence institutional practices, legislative policies, and interpersonal interactions.

The concept of "race" functions as a barrier to empathy by promoting an "us versus them" mentality. When you're taught to view others primarily through a racialized lens, it reinforces a reductive worldview where you flatten the complex human experiences into primitive stereotypes. For example, someone categorized as "black" may be perceived as inherently athletic or dangerous, while someone identified as Asian might be stereotyped as intelligent but socially awkward. These assumptions hinder genuine interpersonal connections and obscure the individuality of the people involved.

Moreover, "race"-based thinking encourages you to interpret suffering and injustice through a filter of racialized identity rather than shared humanity. When the struggles of historically marginalized communities are viewed as "their" problem rather than "our" problem, collective action becomes fragmented and ineffective. Empathy, which is crucial for justice and social cohesion, is stifled when human beings are reduced to categories.

The financial ramifications of racialized thinking are

---

[30] Collins, Francis S., et al. "Initial Sequencing and Analysis of the Human Genome." *Nature*, vol. 409, 2001, pp. 860–921 https://doi.org/10.1038/35057062

extensive and damaging. Racialized categorization often influences discriminatory practices in hiring, promotion, lending, housing, and education. Experiments have shown how employers have favored applicants with "white-sounding" names, landlords have refused to rent to individuals based on racialized appearances, and banks have offered less favorable loan terms to people based on their melanin level.

These patterns of discrimination create financial disparities that are difficult to bridge. They also result in the underutilization of talent, which ultimately hampers healthy growth and development in the economic ecosystem. For instance, when qualified individuals are excluded from opportunities because of racialized prejudice, businesses and institutions miss out on valuable skills and perspectives. This results in the diversion of public resources to address the fallout from such unfair practices, including increased healthcare costs, higher crime rates, and lower educational attainment.

From a macroeconomic perspective, a society that allows racialized biases to shape its economic structures is less efficient and more prone to institutionalized instability. Reducing individuals to racialized categories not only wastes human potential but also sows inefficiency and intergenerational poverty.

Using "race" as a primary identifier also degrades the social ecosystem. Communities built around racialized homogeneity often foster suspicion and hostility toward those who are perceived as outsiders. Segregated neighborhoods, schools, and social circles are artifacts of historical policies, perpetuated by the ongoing insistence of racialized identity.

Diverse communities with inclusive and welcoming attitudes are more innovative, resilient, and prosperous. However, the entrenchment of racialized divisions erodes trust and reduces the willingness of individuals to collaborate across perceived boundaries. This segmentation contributes to political polarization, as people increasingly align with those

V. Actionable Steps

who share their racialized or cultural background, viewing others as competitors or threats.

The fixation on "race" also fuels performative allyship and tokenism, where DEI (Diversity, Equity & Inclusion) efforts become about checking demographic boxes rather than fostering genuine understanding and equality. Instead of destroying oppressive structures, "race"-based initiatives often reinforce them by perpetuating the misguided notion that people must be seen and treated differently based on racialized identifiers.

The cultural impact of racialized categorization is equally damaging, physically and psychologically. It limits the opportunities, techniques, and resources available for people to authentically express their culture, their history and their lived experiences. When individuals are pigeonholed into racialized identities, they're often expected to conform to cultural scripts that may not reflect their lived realities. Can you say, cognitive dissonance?

Consider how media representations frequently rely on racialized tropes: the wise old Asian, the angry "black" woman, the noble Indigenous, or the hardworking Latino. These caricatures aren't only reductive but also harmful, shaping public perceptions in ways that reinforce inequality and limit the scope of cultural expression. Authenticity is sacrificed at the altar of racialized stereotypes, and entire cultures are reduced to consumable products. You don't believe me? Just look at the sports and entertainment industries; look at the music industry; look at the clothing industry.

Moreover, the emphasis on racialized identity obscures the influence of other important factors such as religious beliefs, geographic origin, and individual personality. A low-income "white" child in Appalachia may share more in common with a low-income "black" child in Bridgeport than with affluent individuals of their own so-called "race." Yet, the lens of "race" often prevents these commonalities from being acknowledged, appreciated, or acted upon.

C.E.A.S.E. for Equity

      Educational institutions play a significant role in perpetuating the concept of "race." From a young age, children are taught to categorize, differentiate, and segregate themselves and others based on external characteristics; often racialized (melanin level, facial attributes, hair texture, etc.). Textbooks, curricula, and classroom dynamics often present history and social studies through a racialized lens, which subtly reinforces the notion that "race" is a fixed and meaningful attribute, thereby keeping us from truly connecting with one another.

      This approach distorts historical understanding and impedes critical thinking. Students learn to see history as a series of racialized conflicts rather than the complex interplay of power, financial wealth, geography, and ideology. By framing historical narratives around "race," we limit students' ability to understand the deeper forces that shape human societies and reduce their capacity for nuanced thought and empathy.

      Furthermore, educational gaps often mirror racialized lines, creating a destructive feedback loop where marginalized groups receive lower-quality education. This exacerbates economic and social disadvantages. Breaking this cycle requires a respectful allocation of resources, in addition to a fundamental shift regarding how culture, identity, and history are taught.

      To reverse the harms caused by racialized thinking, we must move toward a post-racialized framework that emphasizes individual humanity and shared experience over superficial categorization. This doesn't mean ignoring the very real consequences of what is called "racism" or pretending that specific characteristics never mattered. To the contrary – it means 1) acknowledging that "race" is a concept that was instituted with destructive intentions, and 2) choosing to build a future where it no longer holds sway.

      Simply put, this involves transforming language, policies, and institutional practices. Surveys and official documents must minimize or eliminate racialized categories, unless absolutely necessary for tracking institutional injustices.

V. Actionable Steps

Education must focus on teaching history, culture, and identity in ways that highlight commonality and complexity rather than division. Media must focus on our shared humanity; representing people as multidimensional individuals rather than racialized archetypes.

Policymakers must pass legislation to close financial gaps, eradicate food and housing insecurity, and correct specific injustices, instead of favoring or targeting racialized categories. Doing so will allow for more precise interventions and reduce the risk of reinforcing the very divisions they aim to remove. At the community level, initiatives that nurture cross-cultural understanding and shared goals will help build solidarity and reduce the focus on "race" as a divisive factor.

The call to abandon the concept of "race" isn't without controversy. Some argue that ignoring "race" risks erasing the lived experiences and ongoing struggles of marginalized groups. People with this line of thinking contend that racialized identity is a source of pride and solidarity in the face of structural oppression. While these concerns have some validity, they're meant to distract and detour you from advocating for a balanced approach. Recognizing the harm that has been done in the name of "race" doesn't require clinging to the construct itself. Instead, you can honor histories of resistance and resilience while working toward a future where such categorization is unnecessary. The goal is not to erase identity but to liberate it from the confines of a flawed and divisive system.

Go ahead...admit it – the continued use of "race" as a foundation for understanding human identity is scientifically baseless and wreaks havoc throughout the social and economic ecosystems! By reducing people to categories based on melanin levels, facial features, and speech patterns, we obscure individuality, hinder empathy, and fortify the structures that support inequality. The deterioration of our social and economic ecosystems can be traced, in part, to the persistence of racialized thinking. To build a more just, cohesive, and prosperous society, you must have the courage to move beyond racialized concepts and embrace the full complexity of human identity. Only then can we cultivate true empathy as a society, unlock collective potential, and sustain ecosystems for equity. All lives matter!

Desist…The Binary Mindset

The binary mindset refers to the belief that individuals must fit into rigid, singular categories. It has long shaped social structures, especially around what we call "race." "Multiracial" individuals, in particular, are often pressured to identify with a single group, erasing the complexity of their identities and magnifying structures of inequity, oppression, and trauma. By forcing individuals into "either/or" frameworks, society reinforces exclusionary practices that perpetuate historical injustices and limit collective progress.

The categorization of the human race into binaries, such as "black" and "white," has deep roots in Western colonialism, slavery, and segregation. Policies like the "one-drop rule" institutionalized the concept of racialized absolutism, treating "race" as a singular and immutable identity to maintain social hierarchies and institutional inequalities. This rigid framework solidified institutions of control and marginalized those who didn't fit neatly into racialized categories, particularly those considered to be "multiracial."

Today, binary thinking persists in identity politics and social movements, compelling individuals to conform to simplified racialized identities. This erasure of nuance reinforces division rather than unity, fosters an "us versus them" mentality, and ignores intersections with class, gender, and ability. Such reductive narratives uphold structural inequalities rather than destroy them.

The effects of binary thinking are far-reaching. Individuals categorized as "multiracial" find themselves excluded from opportunities in education, employment, and healthcare, where rigid racial classifications determine access to resources. In education and the workplace, procedures that

V. Actionable Steps

require individuals to select a single racial identity create barriers and perpetuate marginalization. In healthcare, broad racialized generalizations ignore the diverse experiences within and across racialized groups, resulting in inadequate treatment and poorer health outcomes.

Racialized binaries also serve to sustain power structures that privilege "white" individuals while disadvantaging "black", Indigenous, and other "people of color." Politicians, activists, and media pundits often weaponize racialized categories to deepen divisions by stoking resentment and hindering solidarity across communities. This competition between groups undermines collective efforts toward justice and equity.

There's also a psychological toll of the binary mindset that you must realize. Individuals forced to accept the "multiracial" narrative must deny aspects of their heritage, thereby experiencing identity trauma. This results in feelings of isolation, anxiety, and disconnection from their communities and themselves.

Dismantling the binary mindset requires embracing intersectionality (i.e., a recognition that identities are complex and multifaceted). Institutions must remove the racialization of identities, promote equitable representation, and create policies that reflect lived experiences. Education and the various forms of media must challenge outdated and fabricated notions of "race." Community-building efforts that affirm the fullness of individuals' identities are vital for healing and progress. Moving beyond racialized absolutism is essential to building a just, inclusive society founded on empathy, understanding, and collective empowerment.

Desist…The Survival Mindset

Before diving into approaches for shifting from a survival mindset to a mindset that cultivates empathy and sustains ecosystems for equity, it's critical that we make time to understand deep-seated challenges that hinder the growth and self-sufficiency of disenfranchised communities (which I will refer to as the 'hood). Said communities across the nation struggle with institutional issues that A) hinder economic growth, personal development, prosperity, and communal well-being, and B) manifest in high crime rates, substance abuse, weakened family structures, and deteriorating infrastructure.

While external factors such as historical injustices and economic exclusion have played significant roles, internal community dynamics also contribute to these ongoing struggles. Despite the obvious need for local investment, many members of these communities hesitate to invest in one another and instead prefer to spend their money outside their own neighborhoods.

This phenomenon has far-reaching consequences, including economic stagnation, increased crime, and a lack of community cohesion. To understand this issue, one must consider various perspectives. I'll explore these questions by identifying important social, psychological, and economic barriers while proposing sustainable solutions to encourage investment, trust, and economic circulation within these communities.

I'll incorporate my experiences as an educator, musician, gardener, martial artist, and church elder to examine the following two questions: (1) Why do members of impoverished communities hesitate or refuse to invest in each other? (2) Why do said members prefer to spend their money outside their own neighborhoods?

Once upon a time, I had a videography venture with one of my brothers "from another mother." The fee we charged was miniscule, barely enough to cover the cost of the videotapes and digital media we used. It definitely wasn't adequate compensation for the hours we spent 1) preparing before the event, 2) videoing the event, and 3) editing the footage to the clients' gratitude and satisfaction. We had a passion for the work, and it brought us great joy to meet the clients' specifications. However, we eventually ceased operations because we were losing time with family and loved ones, in addition to money (we operated at a financial loss).

V. Actionable Steps

I share this story to relay how people in struggling communities always seem to want a "hookup." In this instance, they wanted us to supply a high-quality product at a discounted rate because they doubted and disregarded the level of our knowledge, skills, and abilities. They didn't view our locally owned and operated business as a worthwhile investment, sometimes articulating their thoughts with comments like, "I could go to someone else for that price!"

Many 'hoods have long histories of economic exploitation, racial discrimination, and failed initiatives that promised prosperity but delivered little change. Government-led projects, predatory lending, redlining, and corporate disinvestment have led to deep-seated distrust in these aspects of the economic ecosystem. As a result, many community members hesitate to engage in local business ventures for fear of being exploited or let down once again.

One element of this ecosystem, that influences the aforementioned hesitation to invest in each other, comes from a lack of financial literacy and business education. Financial literacy is often lacking in impoverished communities, leading to fear of failure or uncertainty; resulting in a reluctance to invest. Many individuals don't understand investment principles, economic sustainability, or business development. Without access to financial education, aspiring entrepreneurs struggle to secure funding, create sustainable business models, and navigate economic growth opportunities. Likewise, customers, clients, and consumers don't demonstrate an appreciation for the value of some services and goods.

Another element is a psychological and social phenomenon known as the "crabs-in-a-barrel" mentality. This is where individuals, instead of uplifting one another, undermine each other because of jealousy, competition, or ingrained scarcity mindsets. In struggling communities, success is sometimes met with resentment rather than support, discouraging entrepreneurs and potential investors from attempting new ventures.

There's an abundance of innovative ideas and creative approaches to legally providing high-quality goods and services in the 'hood, but the risks associated with starting a business in impoverished areas are high. Limited disposable income, high crime rates, and inconsistent consumer spending create an unpredictable economic landscape. Without strong financial backing or safety nets, community members are less likely to take risks on local investments. Fear of failure, due to economic instability, is an intangible aspect of the ecosystem that impacts the visible success of entrepreneurs and potential business owners. The lack of visible, successful entrepreneurs and investors – those who are able to inspire and mentor others – ripples throughout the community for generations. When individuals don't see people like themselves succeeding in business, they might not believe economic mobility is achievable.

You might be familiar with the saying, "the grass is always greener on the other side of the fence." Likewise, individuals in impoverished communities seem to perceive businesses outside their neighborhoods as offering better quality goods, services, and customer experiences. Contributing factors include inadequate infrastructure (making access to quality goods and services difficult), poorly maintained roads, limited parking, and safety concerns; these further deter individuals from shopping locally, pushing them to seek more convenient options outside their neighborhoods.

And oh yeah, let's not forget about the power of advertising, marketing, and brand recognition! Large corporations are able to spend billions on advertising, creating brand loyalty that often overshadows local businesses. Chain stores, luxury brands, and suburban malls benefit from extensive marketing campaigns that attract consumers, even when similar products or services exist within their own communities. Years of underinvestment have led to local businesses struggling to maintain quality standards, thereby reinforcing the belief that external businesses are superior. The

V. Actionable Steps

result is a preference to spend money outside the community, further weakening the economic ecosystem of the 'hood.

I'm not a psychologist – nor do I play one on television – but I'm going to confidently state there are severe psychological effects to poverty. Based on my personal experiences and direct conversations with friends, mentees, and family members, I have a clear understanding that long-term economic hardship can lead to internalized feelings of inferiority. Lack of community support for local entrepreneurs further amplifies the belief that success, wealth, and high-quality goods are not meant for the 'hood, resulting in money being spent in wealthier areas as a symbol of personal achievement. Without initial consumer buy-in, new businesses fail to gain traction, further discouraging others from pursuing entrepreneurial endeavors.

As an educator, the slogan "Knowledge is power!" echoes in my mind, amidst memories of Saturday morning cartoons. I believe education is a cornerstone of empowerment. Access to financial literacy is often limited in impoverished communities. Many residents haven't been taught the value of investment, savings, and economic circulation within their own neighborhoods. Schools in these areas frequently lack robust financial education programs, leaving students unprepared for wealth management.

Moreover, historical economic exclusion has left a lasting impact. As mentioned previously, institutional procedures related to redlining, discriminatory lending practices, and economic exploitation have created mistrust and fear of financial institutions and investing that ripple throughout generations. The trauma of lost property and businesses in the 'hood has instilled skepticism about economic ventures. When people are repeatedly denied opportunities to build wealth, they develop an ingrained belief that investment is futile.

As a church leader, I know the Bible teaches unity and stewardship. Yet many impoverished communities suffer from division and mistrust. Generations of institutional oppression have sown seeds of self-doubt and internal conflict, leading many to distrust their own people. There's a tendency to view one another as competitors rather than collaborators, weakening the foundation for collective investment. Additionally, historical church abuse and mismanagement of community funds have created skepticism toward community-driven financial efforts.

I'm a witness that spiritual leadership plays a crucial role in rebuilding trust. Teaching principles of Biblical economics, such as communal giving and responsible stewardship, can inspire faith in local reinvestment. However, the challenge remains in overcoming years of cultural conditioning that discourages cooperation.

As a musician, I'm keenly aware of the role that music plays in reinforcing consumerism and how the entertainment industry shapes cultural values and spending habits. Popular culture often glorifies external brands, associating success with foreign luxury rather than local craftsmanship. Many people in impoverished communities measure their worth by their ability to buy products from outside their neighborhoods, believing that name-brand goods elevate their social status. Lyrics and music videos often promote high-end brands while rarely highlighting financial wisdom or community investment.

The recording industry is a powerful habitat for change when musicians use their platforms to promote financial literacy and community pride. Conscious music that uplifts economic self-reliance and community ownership has the capacity to shift perspectives and inspire local investment. My thoughts go to KRS-One, Gang Starr, every artist connected with the Native Tongues, Black Star, Poor Righteous Teachers, Public Enemy, The Roots, and most recently Coast Contra. I submit the notable absence of conscious music as evidence that this messaging is neither valued nor prioritized by lucrative music executives, their representatives, or shareholders. As Coast Contra tries to enlighten us in their song **Legacy** - *"....they want to see us in whips, they want to see us in*

V. Actionable Steps

chains...legacy, legacy, legacy..."[31]

Gardening offers a metaphor for economic self-reliance: cultivating local resources liberates communities from dependence on outsiders, thereby making freedom and independence daily realities. However, gardening requires patience, knowledge, and dedication – qualities that must be nurtured within the community. Without intentional efforts to grow local businesses, impoverished communities will continue to rely on external economies.

Some of you readers have considerable knowledge about nutrition, resulting in a deep understanding about the health benefits of eating fruits and vegetables in their rawest condition. Others understand how our health, our wellness, and our empathy toward each other are intimately linked to our stewardship of earth – we have a responsibility to use the earth's resources for improving the human condition in every part of the globe, not personal gain.

As a vegetable gardener, I'm very familiar with how fresh produce looks and tastes different from what is mass produced for grocery stores. When you consider the amount of produce a package of seeds will yield, the cost is substantially less than the produce purchased at stores. A distinct form of payment, a privilege some might say, is required to grow food in the community, with the currency being time and attention. With that said, it seems more convenient to purchase goods and services externally because residents don't have the privilege of producing food within the community. They're hindered from eating healthy because they're rightfully concerned about paying bills, feeding families, and staying healthy while working at jobs that provide limited wages and/or healthcare benefits – jobs that take them away from the community.

To state the obvious, a portion of land is necessary for growing fresh produce. However, the current infrastructure of the 'hood isn't conducive for growing fresh produce, resulting

---

[31] Coast Contra. *Legacy*. Field Trip Recordings, 2022.

in "food deserts" – another example of why communities spend outside their own neighborhoods. Many inner-city areas lack local grocery stores that have fresh produce and quality goods available, forcing residents to travel to wealthier areas for such things. Consequently, residents become conditioned to consuming external resources. This dependence maintains an environment in which local businesses and community entrepreneurs can't thrive because of a lack of community spending.

I'm disappointed and sad to say that many individuals in the 'hood live in survival mode, where every dollar counts; a survival mindset that's typically been shaped by persistent economic struggles, institutional inequalities, and environmental stressors. In many marginalized communities, generations have endured institutional and legislative barriers such as redlining, employment discrimination, and underfunded schools. These challenges are part of habitats that influence individual, and collective, language and behaviors to prioritize immediate needs over long-term planning. This survival mindset leads to a culture in which competition is prioritized over cooperation; in which scarcity persists; where the thought of investing money in a local business seems too risky when immediate needs like rent, food, and medical bills are pressing.

In impoverished communities, this survival mindset is often coupled with a fear of financial failure and amplified by a lack of mentorship. One of my earliest lessons in the martial arts focused on overcoming fear – fear of failure, fear of pain, and fear of the unknown. As a student of the martial arts, I strive to learn from master practitioners who've walked the path before me. Similarly, communities need business mentors who are willing and able, capable of guiding new entrepreneurs. Such mentorship will reduce the fear of failure and increase the likelihood of success. By nurturing a culture of disciplined risk-taking, communities can break the cycle of scarcity and begin to invest in their own growth.

V. Actionable Steps

The survival mindset has been deeply ingrained in individuals and communities which have faced historical and institutional oppression, economic instability, and social marginalization. While the survival mindset is necessary in times of crisis, it often fosters isolation, competition, and distrust. Said factors hinder long-term growth, empathy, and equity. To build sustainable communities rooted in justice and mutual support, we must transition from mere survival to collaboration, trust, and a deep recognition of each other's humanity.

When communities are forced to operate in habitats shaped by scarcity, instability, or oppression, their collective well-being suffers in deep and lasting ways. Survival mode prioritizes immediate safety and basic needs, but over time, it erodes trust, limits vision, and weakens social bonds. Understanding the effects of this mindset is essential for creating environments where communities not only survive but thrive.

One of the most immediate consequences of a survival mindset is a lack of trust. When resources such as food, housing, safety, or opportunities are limited, individuals begin to see others as threats rather than allies. Cooperation gives way to caution, and people believe that personal gain is the only way to ensure security. This suspicion, often born out of necessity, makes it harder to build relationships and create supportive networks within communities.

Closely tied to this is short-term thinking. In survival mode, long-term planning feels like a luxury. When individuals and families are focused on how to get through the day or week, there's little room for envisioning or investing in the future. This focus on the immediate prevents communities from organizing around lasting goals, such as education reform, economic development, or environmental sustainability. Without the space to dream and strategize, growth is stifled.

A survival mindset also fosters division and conflict. The belief that there is "not enough to go around" puts people against each other, even when they face similar struggles. Instead of uniting around shared challenges, communities devolve into tactics fueled by competition, suspicion, or blame. This conflict weakens the very connections that are needed to build resilience and collective power.

Finally, cultures shaped by survival are often resistant to change. In habitats where people feel vulnerable or exploited, risk becomes dangerous. New ideas, partnerships, or opportunities for collaboration are viewed with skepticism, especially if past experiences have led to disappointment or harm. The fear of failure, or of being taken advantage of, keeps individuals and groups from embracing innovation – they dismiss the potential and promise for positive transformation.

Although the survival mindset is often a rational response to difficult circumstances, it carries heavy costs for communities; the effects of which ripple outward and shape the social landscape. While this mindset is understandable, given the historical contexts, it's not sustainable. To break this cycle, it's essential that we create conditions of safety, abundance, and possibility; nurturing environments in which people are free to imagine, connect, and build a future together. If communities are to be liberated and empowered to thrive, they must embrace a new framework based on trust, cooperation, and our shared humanity.

Desist…Using "-isms"

This modern era is dominated by terms ending in "-ism." Please turn your attention to "racism," elitism, sexism, tokenism, ageism, colorism, ableism, and classism. Each of these concepts attempts to identify and confront a specific form of bias or oppression. I'll assume the original intent behind such terms was to shed light on institutionalized injustice and promote equity. However, their continued and increasingly rigid application in contemporary society has the opposite effect. The use of "-isms" has evolved from tools for increasing awareness into mechanisms of division, resentment, and reductionism.

V. Actionable Steps

Rather than cultivating empathy and nurturing unity, "-isms" pigeonhole individuals into oversimplified identity categories, reinforcing a sense of "us vs. them." In doing so, they impede healthy, restorative, and empowering development in the economic and social ecosystems (the very ecosystems they seek to improve). Society must move away from using "-isms" as primary frameworks for interpreting human behavior and social challenges. Instead, you must adopt more integrative, human-centered approaches that emphasize shared experiences, collective responsibility, and individual dignity.

As part of your work to understand the need to desist in using "-isms," it's important to appreciate why they emerged in the first place. Terms like "racism" and "sexism" were conceived from a desire to describe and combat manifestations of discrimination, oppression, and exclusion. Their purpose was to identify harmful patterns, organize resistance, and uphold justice. In many ways, these terms provided the vocabulary necessary to expose mechanisms of oppression and demand accountability. From the civil rights movement to the feminist waves to disability rights advocacy, naming the "-isms" was crucial to these social justice causes.

However, as the aforementioned terms gained traction, they also became increasingly weaponized, objectified, and detached from their original intent. Rather than encouraging dialogue and shared understanding, they began to act as linguistic boundary lines – terminology used to categorize people as either oppressors or oppressed, enlightened or ignorant, allies or enemies. Over time, the labels became more than descriptors – they became identities. And herein lies the problem: when "-isms" become the lens through which all human interaction is viewed, nuance vanishes, empathy recedes, and mutual understanding becomes nearly impossible.

Spoiler alert! The reductive nature of labels is at the heart of this issue. When you say someone is racist, sexist, ageist, or ableist, you do so to categorize their entire identity, not to enlighten them about their behavior or ideas. This reductionist approach eliminates the possibility of healthy dialogue, growth, or transformation. It shifts the focus from actions and language to fixed personal attributes, turning people into caricatures of whatever "-ism" they're accused of embodying. In order to create atmospheric conditions conducive to cultivating empathy and sustaining ecosystems for equity, you must desist any and all uses of rigid labels that cause defensiveness, guilt, and shame.

Furthermore, "-isms" promote the idea that people belong to mutually exclusive identity groups whose experiences cannot be compared or understood across boundaries. This severely limits your capacity for empathy because it suggests that someone outside a particular identity can't possibly comprehend or relate to the struggles of someone within it. Rather than fostering connections through shared human experience, "-isms" construct silos of identity that discourage cross-cultural dialogue and reinforce division.

I believe empathy is born from curiosity, listening, and your willingness to admit what you don't know, not from categorizing, blaming, and posturing. When you strip away the layers of "-isms" and approach others not as representatives of categories but as individuals with unique stories, you make room for authentic connections. The persistent use "-isms" denies this possibility and instead centers group affiliation as the most significant factor in how people engage with one another.

Another consequence of resorting to the use of "-isms" is what might be called the "analysis paralysis" or "paralysis of perpetual diagnosis." Financial disparities are attributed to classism; gender-based preferences in hiring are chalked up to sexism; interpersonal misunderstandings are explained by "racism" or ableism. While such frameworks may reveal part of the truth, they often ignore the complexity of human motivation, institutional context, and historical nuance. In these United States of America, this practice of diagnosing every issue related to discrimination and injustice through the lens of a corresponding "-ism," is intentionally implemented to distract and delay you from actively working toward

V. Actionable Steps

manifesting "...one nation under God, indivisible, with liberty and justice for all."

This overdiagnosis tends to substitute moral outrage for practical solutions. Instead of addressing institutional problems through actionable reforms, discussions often get stuck in cycles of blame and virtue signaling. It becomes more important to prove one is "anti-racist" or "inclusive" than to understand the root causes of inequality and build coalitions across differences. By naming the problem with an "-ism," many believe their work is done: in reality, it's only the beginning of understanding, not its conclusion. Pause for the cause! Do your own research and acknowledge the effectiveness of "Power to the People!" during the 1960s and 1970s in these United States of America –the most robust example of building coalitions across perceived differences (imho).

Moreover, cancel culture and the diagnostic model of "-isms" create an atmosphere in which individuals, entities, and organizations are hesitant to engage in honest discourse for fear of being boycotted and/or canceled. Academic institutions, workplaces, and political bodies often become paralyzed, afraid that one misstep will result in public censure. This stifles innovation, authentic inquiry, and the kind of policymaking necessary to sustain ecosystems for equity. In other words, the dominance of "-isms" in public discourse contributes to intellectual stagnation and collective decline.

From a financial standpoint, the fragmentation caused by "-isms" impairs productivity and collaboration. The economic ecosystem thrives on cooperation, trust, and diversity of thought. Encouraging people to view each other through identity labels undermines cohesion, creates suspicion, and reduces the capacity for effective problem-solving. Companies that focus excessively on training their employees to recognize microaggressions or implicit biases – without also emphasizing unity, shared goals, and individual potential – create habitats in which hyper-vigilance, alienation, and shame fester.

Moreover, prioritizing "-isms" puts groups against each other, in a zero-sum struggle for recognition and resources, in the social ecosystem. The logic of "-isms" is inherently oppositional: for one group to gain, another must be deprived; for one group to "win," the others must lose. This mentality erodes interest in collective well-being. For instance, discussions about health care disparities, educational inequality, or environmental justice are often derailed by debates over which group is "most marginalized." This ranking of oppression stalls meaningful transformation by replacing collaborative efforts with competition for moral high ground.

The continued use of "-isms" contributes to fragmentation, and confrontational civic engagement, in these United States of America. People become disengaged from institutions and from each other when they believe their voices aren't heard or their identities are misrepresented. Voter apathy, civil distrust, and political extremism are all exacerbated when citizens are encouraged to view each other not as neighbors with shared stakes but as antagonists in a cultural war defined by labels.

To move beyond the limitations of "-isms," you must adopt a new framework; a framework rooted in shared humanity, not in identity politics or categorization. This approach begins with recognizing that all people, regardless of their attributes, are capable of compassion, error, learning, and transformation. It means nurturing spaces where individuals are not reduced to representatives of a group, but are acknowledged in their full complexity as being human.

Education plays a crucial role in this shift. Instead of teaching students primarily about the many "-isms" that separate people, we should prioritize curricula that highlight universal values: cooperation, compassion, justice, courage, empathy, and integrity. This doesn't mean ignoring the existence of historical and current injustices. Rather, it means discussing them through the lens of ethical responsibility and mutual understanding, not categorical blame or identity warfare.

V. Actionable Steps

Our approach to utilizing media and public discourse must also evolve. Journalists, influencers, and public officials must desist from sensationalizing conflict through identity lenses. Instead, they must focus on stories that accentuate common goals and shared struggles. Highlighting human experiences across boundaries (e.g., the need for meaningful work, access to affordable health care, quality education, safe communities, etc.) will create habitats that are more welcoming.

Financially, businesses and institutions must pivot from diversity programs that reinforce identity silos to ones that foster authentic habitats of belonging; where different perspectives are valued not because they tick a demographic box, but because they contribute meaningfully to a shared mission. Performance, collaboration, and innovation should be the benchmarks of success, not compliance with identity quotas.

The continued use of "-isms" as the dominant framework for understanding human interaction is increasingly inadequate, counterproductive, and divisive. While these terms have historically served a valuable purpose in naming injustice and rallying support for transformation, their overuse and misuse now threaten to perpetuate division and obstruct progress. By categorizing individuals into static identity boxes, "-isms" foster resentment, inhibit empathy, and arrest the growth and development that's necessary for collective advancement in the economic and social ecosystems.

You must renew your commitment to improving the human condition for everyone, speaking and behaving with a collaborative mindset that transcends labels and connects to the deeper truths of our shared humanity. Our world is interconnected and complex; therefore, cultivating empathy and sustaining ecosystems for equity requires a richer appreciation of our shared humanity, not precise categorizations of our differences. Making this shift requires courage, humility, commitment, and a willingness to desist in the utilization of rhetorical crutches we have come to rely on.

By doing this you create a pathway to a more unified, compassionate, and dynamic society.

Desist...Weaponizing Information

In these United States of America, information isn't merely a conduit for knowledge but a potent instrument capable of shaping perceptions, reinforcing ideologies, and directing public sentiment. Data, language, and labels are manipulated and transformed from tools of enlightenment into weapons of fear and terror. This weaponization of information has profound implications for the social and economic ecosystems, particularly the erosion of empathy and the degradation of said ecosystems.

Historically, the manipulation of information in these United States of America has roots in colonialism, slavery, and segregation. From the propagation of scientific "racism" to the vilification of civil rights movements, language has long been employed to construct narratives that justify oppression. In contemporary society, media channels, political rhetoric, and digital platforms continue to serve as habitats where information is distorted to evoke fear, delegitimize opposition, and solidify power.

The post-9/11 era provides a poignant example. Terms like "terrorist" were predominantly applied to Muslim individuals, reinforcing xenophobia and justifying policies like the Patriot Act, which curtailed civil liberties in the name of national security. Similarly, during the COVID-19 pandemic, the phrases (which I refuse to immortalize in print) catalyzed anti-Asian hate crimes, demonstrating how labels incite violence and polarize a civil society.

Fear is a primal reaction with profound psychological and neurological implications. It narrows cognitive bandwidth, redirects attention to perceived threats, and reduces the capacity for nuanced thinking. Weaponized information exploits these elements by presenting data and narratives to trigger emotional responses over rational analysis.

V. Actionable Steps

As I wrote previously, crime statistics are often selectively reported; media outlets emphasizing violent crimes committed by marginalized individuals while omitting institutionalized causes or broader contexts. This selective framing activates fear, to support harsh policing and policies for incarcerating individuals, despite evidence that such measures disproportionately affect "black" and "brown" communities.

Empathy is the psychological cornerstone of social cohesion and justice. When fear dominates the informational landscape, empathy suffers. On an individual level, people exposed to fear-inducing narratives become more likely to support punitive policies and less likely to empathize with the suffering of others. On a collective level, communities become polarized, and the moral imagination required to enact inclusive policies diminishes.

The economic ecosystem is profoundly affected by the fear-driven manipulation of information. Policies emphasizing competition, efficiency, and individual responsibility are often justified through narratives that demonize the poor and glorify self-reliance. For instance, welfare recipients are frequently depicted as lazy or fraudulent, despite data showing the contrary. This narrative sustains economic inequity by reducing public support for redistributive policies such as universal healthcare, affordable housing, and the full funding of education.

Politically, the weaponization of information undermines democratic principles by manipulating public opinion and electoral outcomes. Politicians use fear-based language to consolidate power, distract from substantive issues, and suppress voter turnout. Gerrymandering, voter ID laws, and misinformation campaigns disproportionately affect marginalized communities, reducing their political representation.

The portrayal of political protest is another area ripe with information manipulation. Do your research about the formation and purpose of groups such as the Black Panther

Party and the Young Lords; organizations often framed as threats to public safety rather than legitimately working for justice. This framing erodes empathy and justifies repressive responses, including militarized policing and surveillance.

In academic settings, the politicization of information impacts curricula, research funding, and public trust in scholarly institutions. Topics like critical race theory (CRT) have been distorted into cultural boogeymen, despite being legitimate academic frameworks for understanding institutionalized inequity. The backlash against CRT exemplifies how fear can stifle intellectual inquiry and marginalize scholars working on issues of "race", gender, and class.

This tactic discourages students and academics from exploring complex social issues, thereby impeding the development of critical thinking skills necessary for civic engagement and equitable policymaking. When educational content is censored or sanitized, subsequent generations inherit a distorted understanding of history and justice.

Legislation is often a downstream product of public sentiment, which is shaped by informational narratives. Laws that criminalize homelessness, sway reproductive rights, or ban books in schools are frequently justified through fear-based language. By framing certain populations as threats, lawmakers enact policies that perpetuate division while maintaining public support.

Moreover, lobbying efforts and corporate influence exploit information asymmetry to shape legislation that benefits the few at the expense of the many. For instance, debates about climate change persist, in part, due to the strategic dissemination of misleading information, delaying necessary policy interventions and disproportionately affecting vulnerable communities.

The rise of social media and algorithm-driven content has intensified the weaponization of information. Platforms prioritize engagement over accuracy, incentivizing sensationalism and outrage. As a result, misinformation

V. Actionable Steps

spreads rapidly, reinforcing existing prejudices, negative biases, and fears. Digital echo chambers exacerbate polarization, as individuals are less likely to encounter diverse perspectives. This fragmentation of the informational landscape undermines collective empathy and civic dialogue, making it difficult to build consensus around equitable solutions.

 Additionally, the commodification of personal data enables micro-targeted propaganda, further distorting public perception. Political campaigns and interest groups use data analytics to craft fear-inducing messages tailored to specific demographics, manipulating behavior in ways that are both effective and ethically troubling.

 Despite these challenges, there are efforts to resist the weaponization of information. Independent journalism, community-based storytelling, and media literacy education play crucial roles in reclaiming information as a tool for justice and sustaining equity. Organizations that promote data transparency and contextual reporting help counteract fear-based narratives.

 Educational institutions can serve as sites of resistance by fostering critical media literacy and encouraging interdisciplinary approaches to complex social problems. Curricula that highlight diverse voices and lived experiences are critical for cultivating empathy and a more nuanced understanding of institutional issues.

 Policymakers and tech companies must be held accountable for the roles they play in shaping the informational landscape. Regulations that promote algorithmic transparency, protect user privacy, and penalize disinformation campaigns are essential for restoring trust and equity in the digital age.

 In these United States of America, information is a double-edged sword. When wielded responsibly, it can empower, enlighten, unite, and drive progress. But when weaponized, it becomes a tool for inducing fear; corroding empathy and sustaining inequity throughout both of the man-made ecosystems. By examining how data, language, and labels are manipulated to provoke fear and division, we uncover the mechanisms through which the elements in the fabricated ecosystems are shaped and sometimes distorted.

To foster a more just society, we must critically interrogate the information we consume, demand accountability from those who produce and disseminate it, and actively cultivate empathy through inclusive and honest storytelling. Only then can we transform our informational landscape from one of terror to one of truth and equity.

Desist…Focusing on Civil Rights

These United States of America have long been engaged in a struggle for civil rights, focusing on eliminating legal discrimination and ensuring equal treatment under the law. While significant progress has been made, the continued prevalence of inequality suggests that a shift in focus is necessary. By moving from a framework centered on civil rights to one grounded in human rights, the nation can cultivate empathy, nurture a sense of shared humanity, and build ecosystems that sustain equity for all. This transition necessitates broader protections, dismantling institutional inequalities, and manifesting policies that address the root causes of social injustice.

Civil rights protections typically emerge in response to specific injustices. Since this is a reactive approach, new manifestations of discrimination and inequality must be addressed individually, rather than prevented through a one-size-fits-all framework. The civil rights movement in these United States of America is the best example that comes to my mind. It has historically focused on securing legal protections and ensuring equal treatment for marginalized groups. Landmark legislation, such as the Civil Rights Act of 1964 and the Voting Rights Act of 1965, was designed to eliminate racialized segregation and discrimination. However, despite these advancements, severe gaps in economic opportunities, high-quality healthcare, secure housing, education, and criminal justice persist.

V. Actionable Steps

While legislation can impose consequences for discrimination, they cannot fully eliminate the structural disadvantages that marginalized communities face. Gaining civil rights protections often requires lengthy legal battles or the passage of new legislation. This leads to delays in justice and reliance on political good intentions rather than a fundamental commitment to human dignity.

Shifting efforts from civil rights to human rights offers a more holistic approach to addressing inequality. Human rights recognize that every individual has inherent dignity and must be afforded basic needs, protections, and opportunities, regardless of their identity or background. Unlike civil rights, human rights address broader issues related to healthcare, education, housing, criminal justice, nutrition, and employment. By adopting a human rights framework, you can ensure that everyone has access to the necessities for a dignified life.

Human rights are recognized internationally, allowing those who govern within these United States of America to align national policies with global standards. This shift will help the nation learn from, and adopt, best practices from other countries that have successfully transformed their social ecosystem. Rather than waiting for injustices to be challenged in court, a human rights-based approach encourages governments and institutions to proactively create policies that prevent discrimination, inequality, and suffering.

You may have already come to this realization on your own – empathy is the foundation for creating a society that values equity and justice. A human rights approach fosters empathy by emphasizing our shared humanity and collective responsibility to protect one another. By framing healthcare, nutrition, housing, education, criminal justice, and employment as human rights rather than privileges, you shift the conversation from one of entitlement to one of moral obligation. This perspective will encourage and motivate you to support policies that uplift all members of society, instead of viewing assistance programs as handouts.

C.E.A.S.E. for Equity

I'll say it again...Schools and the various forms of media play a vital role in shaping public perception! Including human rights education in curricula and media representation will help instill values of empathy, inclusivity, and social responsibility from an early age. Likewise, engaging in conversations across economic and social lines will help break down prejudices and build mutual understanding. Community programs that bring people together to discuss shared struggles and aspirations will cultivate a greater sense of unity.

Ecosystems for equity can't truly be achieved and sustained through surface-level solutions or isolated policy changes. It requires a comprehensive transmutation of the environments that shape everyday life (education, housing, infrastructure, healthcare, nutrition, and criminal justice); material conditions which perpetuate inequality and social injustice. To create a society where everyone is able to thrive, transformation must occur within the aforementioned environments. These interconnected elements form the backbone of a just society, and focusing on their deep-rooted disparities is essential to sustaining lasting equity.

Education is one of the most powerful tools for social mobility, yet in these United States of America, access to quality education remains largely dependent on socioeconomic status. To destroy institutional inequities, universal access to high-quality education must be a foundational goal. This includes fully funding public schools, particularly those in underserved communities, and ensuring equal access to highly engaged teachers, modern technology, and safe learning environments.

Furthermore, integrating human rights education into school curricula is vital for fostering social awareness and civic responsibility. When students are taught about justice, empathy, and global interdependence, they're more likely to become active participants in creating equitable communities. Devoting your efforts to economic and social gaps in school funding isn't just a matter of fairness: it's a prerequisite for

V. Actionable Steps

breaking cycles of poverty and disempowerment that disproportionately affect marginalized communities.

Say this with me – healthcare is ***not*** a privilege; it's a fundamental human right. Expanding access to affordable healthcare, for all citizens, is essential for achieving and sustaining social equity. Far too often, individuals from low-income and disenfranchised backgrounds face barriers to medical care, resulting in poorer health outcomes and reduced life expectancy.

Intentional work to impact the social determinants (e.g., housing stability, nutrition, and access to clean environments) is crucial for improving public health. Policies must target the disparities in healthcare outcomes that persist among cultural and socioeconomic groups. These include higher rates of chronic illness, maternal mortality, and psychological wellness issues. By committing to healthcare practices that prioritize prevention, accessibility, and affordability, society moves closer to a more humane and just future.

Regarding finances, a just economy is one that provides all individuals with the opportunity and basic skills to earn a living wage, work in safe conditions, and build generational wealth. Ensuring fair wages is more than an economic issue; it's a moral one. Workers shouldn't have to choose between feeding their families, affording medical care, or paying for safe housing.

To protect vulnerable populations, robust social safety nets (e.g. paid family leave) must be implemented. These measures provide stability during times of hardship and promote economic resilience. Supporting small businesses and investing in community development, particularly in historically marginalized areas, will also revitalize local economies and foster economic independence. Empowering communities economically is essential for sustaining ecosystems for equity and destroying the mechanisms that perpetuate the poverty cycle.

The criminal justice system has been a source of inequity since the founding of this country, particularly for communities of non-European descent (Indigenous, enslaved African, Taino, Asian etc.). Ending mass incarceration is a necessary step toward justice. This means shifting from punitive approaches to restorative models that prioritize reformation, psychological wellness support, and community reintegration.

Biases in policing and sentencing practices must also be monitored, investigated, and changed through comprehensive training, oversight, and legislation. Additionally, the criminalization of poverty must be challenged and eradicated. Practices like cash bail and excessive fines for minor infractions disproportionately harm low-income individuals, effectively punishing them for their financial status. By focusing on fairness and transformation, the justice system will move closer to manifesting its intended purpose of serving, protecting, and uplifting all members of society. These changes aren't only possible but they're essential for building a society rooted in shared prosperity and justice. Through intentional, intersectional reform, the concept of equity will evolve from an aspiration into a lived reality for all.

Despite the potential benefits, shifting to a human rights framework faces resistance from various sectors, including political institutions, corporations, and individuals who fear increased oversight and intervention. From ideological divisions in government, to deeply ingrained cultural values and economic self-interests, multiple forces work against the implementation of progressive reforms. Understanding these obstacles is crucial for implementing strategies that will overcome them and move society toward a more equitable future.

One of the most significant challenges to advancing human rights in these United States of America is political resistance. Some policymakers perceive human rights protections – particularly those that involve social welfare, environmental regulations, or expanded civil liberties – as forms of government overreach. Partisan divides further complicate the path toward equity. Progressive policies aimed

V. Actionable Steps

at ensuring fair wages, universal healthcare, or criminal justice reform frequently become mired in political gridlock. In a polarized political climate, bipartisan cooperation is increasingly rare, and legislative efforts that promote equity may be stalled or dismantled, depending on shifts in power. This resistance impedes the development and implementation of policies necessary to correct historical and institutional injustices.

Beyond political resistance, financial concerns of business owners, shareholders, and corporate entities (e.g., boards, trustees, etc.) also play a major role in obstructing equitable reforms. Many businesses resist regulations that prioritize workers' rights (e.g., paid family leave, higher minimum wages, stricter safety standards, etc.) because they fear these measures will reduce profit margins or increase operational costs. While these reforms are intended to promote fairness and protect vulnerable workers, they're often framed by opponents as threats to financial freedom and market efficiency.

Furthermore, restructuring to a more empowering ecosystem requires investment in public infrastructure, healthcare, education, housing, nutrition, and societal safety nets. Critics argue such investments place a heavy burden on taxpayers and government budgets. However, this perspective often ignores the long-term social and economic benefits of a more just society, including reduced poverty, improved public health, and greater economic mobility. Nevertheless, the perception of equity-focused policies as fiscally unsustainable continues to be a roadblock to meaningful change.

Cultural values and deeply held ideologies also influence approaches to human rights, impacting approaches to sustaining ecosystems for equity. American culture places a high premium on individualism, self-reliance, and personal responsibility. While these values are intended to foster innovation and ambition, they also undermine collective efforts to address institutional problems. Policies that promote shared responsibility, such as universal healthcare, may be seen as infringing on individual freedoms or promoting dependency. Without addressing cultural and ideological barriers, even the most well-designed policies may fail to gain public support or achieve their intended impact.

The journey toward human rights, and consequently equity, in these United States of America, is hindered by a complex web of political resistance, financial concerns, and cultural values. These barriers are deeply embedded in the nation's institutions and ideologies, making change simultaneously urgent and difficult. Overcoming these obstacles will require a multi-pronged approach; one that includes policy innovation, public education, and a collective reimagining of what justice and shared responsibility truly mean. Only by confronting these challenges directly can we move closer to a society that honors the dignity and potential of every individual.

The time has come for expanding the focus from civil rights to human rights. By cultivating empathy and transforming the man-made ecosystems to sustain equity, these United States of America can move toward a more just, more inclusive, and more peaceful society. Only through this paradigm shift can we truly guarantee dignity, security, and opportunity for all.

Desist...Forced Desegregation

Forced desegregation, while initially necessary to address institutionalized discrimination and injustice, has also brought about numerous challenges. Implemented through policies such as court-mandated school integration and housing desegregation laws, forced desegregation has often led to resistance, societal unrest, and consequences that have shaped communities in complex ways. While the intention behind these policies was to create equality and opportunity for marginalized groups, they also produced tensions that revealed deep-seated divisions that have been racialized.

The forced desegregation movement in these United States of America gained momentum following landmark

V. Actionable Steps

Supreme Court rulings such as *Brown v. Board of Education,* which declared racial segregation in public schools unconstitutional in 1954. This decision led to widespread efforts to integrate schools, often through busing programs that transported students across districts to achieve a racialized balance (I mentioned *Project Concern* earlier, as part of my history). Similarly, housing policies aimed at breaking down racialized barriers in neighborhoods sought to reduce discrimination in homeownership and renting. However, these efforts were met with resistance from both "white" and disenfranchised communities, leading to challenges that persist to this day.

It's important to highlight how descendants of enslaved Africans, in these United States of America, formed successful communities following landmark legislation. They thrived and experienced success, until being terrorized and ultimately destroyed by those in positions of power and influence (former enslavers, government officials, law enforcement agents, etc.) – something that's often overlooked or excluded from history books.

Following the *Brown v. Board of Education* decision, segregated communities faced both new challenges and opportunities for growth. Despite the ruling's intent to integrate schools, descendants of enslaved Africans retained strong communal bonds and cultural resilience in many neighborhoods, demonstrating significant success in various areas.

Communities formed by descendants of enslaved Africans developed their own institutions, such as churches, businesses, schools, and social organizations. These habitats fostered economic self-sufficiency and cultural pride. After *Brown*, many of these communities continued to thrive by nurturing a strong sense of identity and mutual support. Businesses were established and expanded, providing jobs and services tailored to community needs. Educational institutions, though initially underfunded, became centers for activism and empowerment, pushing for equality while preserving cultural heritage.

Furthermore, said communities became incubators for the Civil Rights Movement, cultivating leaders and strategies that propelled social change nationwide. The shared experience of segregation fostered solidarity and resilience, empowering descendants of enslaved Africans to organize effectively for political representation, economic opportunity, and social justice.

Beyond these United States of America, forced desegregation efforts have also taken place in countries such as South Africa, where apartheid policies enforced strict racialized divisions. When apartheid ended in the early 1990s, efforts to integrate communities faced similar resistance, such as "white" populations relocating to exclusive enclaves – financial disparities continued to dictate mobility and access to resources. These international comparisons highlight the universal complexities involved in implementing desegregation policies and the enduring obstacles they face.

One of the primary issues associated with forced desegregation was community backlash. Looking back in history, many "white" communities openly and publicly resisted integration efforts, leading to protests, verbal assaults, physical violence, and the phenomenon known as "white flight" (i.e., affluent white families moved from urban centers to suburban areas to avoid integration). This exodus exacerbated racialized and financial divides, as resources and funding followed wealthier families into segregated suburban districts. Additionally, disenfranchised communities sometimes opposed forced desegregation due to concerns over losing cultural identity, community schools, and local control over education and resources.

Early resistance to forced desegregation wasn't limited to individuals, as institutions and local governments often worked to undermine integration efforts. Tactics such as redlining, gerrymandering of school districts, and strategic school closures were employed to maintain segregation despite

V. Actionable Steps

federal mandates. These barriers illustrate the deep-rooted opposition that policymakers faced when attempting to enforce desegregation and the enduring impact of institutional resistance on achieving equitable outcomes. The negative, generational, impacts still reverberate throughout the economic and social ecosystems to this day.

Research in educational psychology suggests that students thrive best in environments where they feel a sense of belonging and acceptance. When forced desegregation disrupts established social structures, without adequate support systems in place, the experience will have psychological repercussions for students. Students in the minority experience hostility, discrimination, social isolation, emotional distress, and lower academic performance when integrated into predominantly "white" schools. Feelings of inadequacy and alienation can also be attributed to this, manifesting in behaviors such as code switching and the psychological condition known as imposter syndrome. At the same time, "white" students struggle with resentment, cultural misunderstandings, and other forms of ignorance, creating conditions in which true integration is difficult to achieve.

Peer-group dynamics, cultural differences, and racialized implicit biases contribute to difficulties in fostering genuine connections across boundaries. These factors emphasize the importance of carefully designing and nurturing integration strategies that go beyond mere physical desegregation; actively promote understanding and authentic inclusivity.

While desegregation policies aim to equalize educational opportunities, many schools in disenfranchised communities remain underfunded. The redistribution of students doesn't lead to the redistribution of resources – wealthier communities continue to invest in their schools through private funding and local taxes. This maintains an uneven playing field, one in which underrepresented students still face disadvantages despite attending integrated institutions.

Furthermore, disparities in teacher quality, curriculum offerings, and extracurricular resources continue to reinforce inequities. While integration may have provided access to better facilities for some students, it doesn't always result in improved educational outcomes. The lack of sustained investment in historically underfunded schools perpetuates gaps in achievement and limits the effectiveness of desegregation as a tool for educational equity.

The early days of forced desegregation in housing weren't always beneficial – they led to shifts in urban development that still ripple throughout society to this day. Policies designed to integrate neighborhoods result in increased gentrification, where lower-income residents are displaced due to rising property values and cost of living. Instead of achieving a balanced racial composition, many cities experience continued economic segregation, with marginalized communities pushed further into areas with fewer opportunities and resources.

Housing policies such as the Fair Housing Act of 1968 aimed to address discriminatory practices, but enforcement has been inconsistent. Discriminatory lending practices, landlord biases, and economic barriers still contribute to the persistence of housing segregation despite legal prohibitions. As a result, many low-income families continue to face limited access to quality housing, schools, and employment opportunities, further highlighting the ongoing limitations of forced desegregation in achieving true empowerment.

Despite legal mandates for desegregation, many communities remain segregated due to elements linked to the social and economic ecosystems. Education programs, housing (e.g., district zoning), healthcare, politics, infrastructure, legislation, and cultural norms all contribute to modern forms of segregation where racialized divides persist. The failure to address underlying structural inequalities means that forced desegregation efforts often result in surface-level integration without meaningful changes in social equity.

V. Actionable Steps

In some cases, the consequences of forced desegregation have even led to a re-segregation of schools and neighborhoods. As affluent families opt for private schools, charter schools, or move to exclusive districts, public schools in lower-income areas continue to struggle with funding and resources. This self-segregation reinforces the very divisions that desegregation policies sought to dismantle, raising questions about the long-term effectiveness of these efforts.

Given the challenges associated with forced desegregation, alternative approaches to promoting integration may offer more sustainable solutions. Voluntary desegregation programs, such as magnet schools and controlled-choice policies, allow families to opt into diverse educational environments rather than being forced into them. Community-driven initiatives that address housing affordability, economic development, and equitable resource distribution can help create more organically integrated neighborhoods without the backlash associated with forced measures.

Additionally, fostering cultural competency and inclusive curricula in schools can help bridge racialized divides. Programs that emphasize shared experiences, intergroup dialogue, and collaborative learning can contribute to more meaningful integration efforts that extend beyond physical proximity and promote genuine social cohesion; fostering voluntary integration will be more effective in creating lasting social cohesion. Recognizing the consequences of forced desegregation allows for more informed policymaking that prioritizes inclusivity without exacerbating existing divides.

Ultimately, achieving true integration requires more than legal mandates. It demands sustained efforts to create equitable opportunities, bridge cultural divides, and address the root causes of segregation. By focusing on these broader goals, societies can move toward a more inclusive future without the negative consequences that have historically accompanied forced desegregation efforts.

Desist…The Census Process

The United States Census is often portrayed as a neutral and essential tool for democratic governance, resource distribution, and policymaking. However, beneath its facade of impartiality, it has long functioned as an instrument of institutional oppression, reinforcing inequity, social hierarchies, and institutional barriers that marginalize disadvantaged communities.

Historically, the census served colonial and slaveholding interests, helping to consolidate social and economic power. From its inception, it categorized populations in ways that entrenched racialized hierarchies, disenfranchised and marginalized groups, and legitimized inequality. The infamous "three-fifths compromise," which counted enslaved individuals as only a fraction of a person for political representation, exemplifies how the census manipulated the value of lives to serve ruling elites.

Throughout history in these United States of America, census data has been used to gerrymander districts and skew political representation - perpetuating institutionalized disparities. Under-counting low-income and culturally diverse populations has deprived these communities of vital resources for education, healthcare, housing, and infrastructure, deepening cycles of poverty and limiting opportunities for social mobility.

Census data also shape labor and educational policies. Inaccurate counts lead to policies that overlook wage gaps and employment inequities, further perpetuating financial disparities. Similarly, under-counted schools – often in marginalized communities – suffer from chronic underfunding, thereby contributing to generational poverty. Census data also fuels political manipulation through district redrawing and economic exploitation by corporations that invest disproportionately in wealthier, over-counted communities, leaving marginalized areas neglected.

The census's rigid racialized categorizations impose simplistic labels that erase the complexity of multicultural and

V. Actionable Steps

Indigenous identities, inflicting psychological harm and reinforcing institutional exclusion. Beyond categorization, the census has historically enabled state surveillance and control – from the internment of Japanese Americans during World War II to contemporary fears among immigrant communities about data misuse. This discourages participation and undermines trust.

By understanding its history and impact, and by taking steps to advocate for reform, you can challenge the census's role in sustaining inequitable power structures and work toward a more inclusive and fair society. To create a more just, a more compassionate, and a more liberating society, we must critically examine and reform the census. This includes redesigning data collection to move beyond rigid categories, ensuring culturally sensitive practices, building trust among marginalized communities, and guaranteeing transparency and accountability in how census data is used. Only by correcting these structural flaws can we destroy the institutionalized inequalities the census has long reinforced.

Desist...U.S. Tax Codes

I believe there's an urgent need to reform how we are taxed in these United States of America. The current method of taxing income and wealth in this country is deeply flawed, exacerbating marginalization and perpetuating systemic disparities across all aspects of life (education, healthcare, infrastructure, nutrition, housing, wealth, and justice). Though it's intended to fund public goods and balance economic inequalities, or so we're told, the tax system in these United States of America is designed to disproportionately burden the working- and middle-class while favoring large corporations and the wealthy. This imbalance increases and deepens economic and social divides, in addition to severely limiting your capacity, your willingness, and your ability to cultivate empathy and sustainable ecosystems for equity.

Let's pause for a station identification break, in order to get a better understanding of the significant difference between being rich and being wealthy. In my experience, being rich and being wealthy are often used interchangeably. However, they're fundamentally different concepts. Being rich is an individual mindset for personal and, IMHO, selfish gains. Being rich typically refers to having a high income or possessing enormous sums of money. Rich individuals might own luxury items, drive expensive cars, and live in extravagant homes. However, their financial standing often depends on their active income. If that income stops, their ability to sustain that lifestyle may diminish quickly. Many rich people spend most of what they earn. Without proper financial planning, rich individuals may face financial hardship despite earning significant amounts.

In contrast, being wealthy is a more collaborative lifestyle, focused on long-term financial security and sustainability - for the family and the community. Wealth involves accumulating assets such as investments, real estate, or businesses that generate passive income. A wealthy person may or may not appear outwardly rich, but they have the financial freedom to live comfortably without relying on constant earnings. Wealth allows for financial independence, often extending across generations through inheritance and careful planning.

In essence, being rich is about how much money one makes, while being wealthy is about how much money one keeps and grows. True wealth comes from financial literacy, wise investments, and living within one's means to ensure a stable and prosperous future for subsequent generations, rather than efforts to enjoy temporary luxury in one lifetime.

Now, back to our scheduled program about the need to desist from our current tax code. At the heart of this issue is the regressive nature of certain taxes and the loopholes available to those with wealth. While the federal income tax is progressive in theory, major sources of wealth for the rich (capital gains, dividends, and inheritances) are often taxed at lower rates than earned income. Furthermore, wealth accumulation through stocks, real estate, and offshore accounts often escapes taxation

V. Actionable Steps

entirely. This allows high-net-worth entities to amass and transfer wealth across generations with minimal contribution to the public good, perpetuating the cycles of influence, power, and marginalization.

The current tax structure in these United States of America contributes directly to disparities in education. Public schools are largely funded through local property taxes. This manifests as affluent neighborhoods enjoying well-funded schools with robust resources, while low-income communities face overcrowded classrooms, underpaid teachers, and outdated materials. The consequence is a widening achievement gap that limits upward mobility and entrenches poverty.

Healthcare outcomes are similarly impacted. Tax-funded programs like Medicaid and public health infrastructure are chronically underfunded because of insufficient tax contributions from the wealthiest citizens and corporations. The result - low-income individuals experience limited access to quality care, have shorter life expectancies, and experience higher rates of chronic illness. In contrast, the wealthy are able to afford comprehensive private care, further exacerbating health inequities.

Infrastructure and housing are also affected. Underserved communities frequently suffer from crumbling roads, outdated water systems, and inadequate public transportation due to local and federal funding shortages...potholes in my lawn.[32] These deficiencies directly impact job access, education, and safety. Similarly, the housing crisis - marked by skyrocketing rents, stagnant wages, and tax incentives for real estate investors - forces many families into unstable or substandard living conditions.

Nutrition disparities are yet another symptom of inequitable taxation. Food deserts – areas with limited access to affordable, nutritious food – are prevalent in low-income, marginalized, and disenfranchised communities. Without

---

[32] De La Soul. *Potholes in My Lawn.* Tommy Boy Records, 1989.

proper funding for community grocery stores, food assistance programs, and school meals to make organic foods consistently available and affordable, populations in the aforementioned communities face higher rates of obesity and diet-related diseases due to the prevalence foods which 1) are highly processed (meats, breads, grains, etc.), 2) contain high fructose corn syrup (and similar refined sweeteners), and 3) have been genetically modified or grown using man-made pesticides and herbicides.

Finally, the justice system reflects the consequences of this inequity. Wealthier individuals often avoid severe punishment through expensive legal teams. On the flip side of that coin, low-income individuals typically have to depend on inexperienced, underpaid, and/or overloaded attorneys; in addition to enduring biases of judges and/or jurors, which all result in harsher sentencing. Tax funding for public defenders, rehabilitation programs, and community policing is inadequate, thereby perpetuating cycles of incarceration and disenfranchisement.

To truly cultivate empathy and sustain ecosystems of equity, the approach to taxing income and wealth in these United States of America must be transformed. This includes implementing higher taxes on capital gains and large inheritances, closing tax loopholes, instituting a wealth tax, and reallocating tax revenue to underfunded services. A more equitable tax system will provide the foundation for a society that values shared prosperity, mutual support, and sustainable development across all communities. Transforming it is essential to addressing the root causes of disparity and building a nation where every individual and community is able to thrive.

<u>Desist…Gaslighting the Homeless</u>

Homelessness in these United States of America is another multifaceted issue influenced by the complex interplay of economic and social elements. Identifying legislation, conditions, behaviors, and language, will help you understand

V. Actionable Steps

who becomes homeless and why. Doing so will also equip you to manifest sustainable solutions that honor the dignity and humanity of all individuals.

To me, it seems like there are more homes and apartment buildings going up around me. Cranes dot the skyline, new developments inhabit once-empty lots, and ads promise luxury living spaces. On the surface, this all looks like progress. However, I read reports of people sleeping under bridges and I see them curled up on sidewalks. I've even seen the tents and cardboard shelters tucked away in corners of parks. It makes me sad as I wonder, "How is it that so much housing is being built, yet so many people are still without secure and stable housing?"

In response to my own query, I arrive at one conclusion: homes aren't being built for people in need; they're being built to appease people's greed. Much of the new housing is luxury or market-rate, not designed to provide safe and stable shelter for the homeless. To the contrary, the housing is constructed to generate profits for corporations, developers, and investors. Governments and nonprofits may claim they're tackling the housing crisis, but it seems to me that their actions prioritize financial returns over human lives. It seems like housing has become a commodity, not a human right.

Meanwhile, people are suffering. Some are dying just miles away from empty units they can't afford. Public housing often seems neglected – existing options often come with long waitlists or restrictive criteria. It's disappointing to think about how shelter exists primarily for those who can pay enough to access it. Homes must be made truly affordable, with policies that protect tenants; governed by practices to put people before profits. Until then, every new crib (aka place to live) will be a reminder that we have the resources to end homelessness, but not the will to act on it.

I believe the current term for those who are homeless in these United States of America, "the unhoused," is used to excuse us from our responsibility to care for our fellow humans. The term is strategically used to placate our collective psyche and keep us complicit in this egregious act of negligence. "The unhoused" makes it seem as if humans consciously decide that life would be better without stable, secure, and safe shelter. C'maaan! You don't reeaallly believe a person, or a couple, would willingly choose to put themselves, and possibly children, at the mercy and whim of the natural elements; that they would purposefully rely on the grace of other people to not harm them physically nor psychologically; that they would gladly prefer a nomadic style of living…do ya?

I understand homelessness a very serious issue. With that said, I must admit that "the unhoused" sounds like the title of a low budget horror film to me. There are shelters and sanctuaries, adoptive and fostering agencies, as well as organizations that are funded and equipped to house animals. So, I wonder why there isn't the same financial, political, and philanthropic zeal for humans (especially veterans and our elderly, hmm)?

The homelessness crisis lies at the heart of the economic ecosystem. One of the most pressing issues being reported is an ongoing shortage of affordable housing. As real estate prices continue to climb, many low-income individuals find themselves priced out of the rental market, with few viable alternatives.

In addition to housing costs, income inequality and stagnant wages have further widened the financial divide. While the cost of living continues to rise, many wages, particularly for those in low-skill or service-oriented jobs, haven't kept pace. This imbalance makes it increasingly difficult for individuals and families to achieve or maintain housing stability.

Historical and institutional discrimination has undermined people of Indigenous, enslaved African, Asian, and Latino/Hispanic descent in these United States of America, resulting in disproportionate rates of poverty, unemployment, and, ultimately, homelessness among these populations.

V. Actionable Steps

Addressing homelessness, therefore, requires confronting the racialized disenfranchisement embedded in the nation's economic ecosystem. It requires more than just providing shelter; it demands comprehensive and integrated support services focused on human dignity and opportunity...do you notice a recurring theme yet ;-)? Many individuals experiencing homelessness struggle with psychological wellness issues, unemployment, or a lack of educational opportunities.

Family dynamics also play a role, especially in youth homelessness. Young people aging out of foster care or coming from unstable home environments are particularly vulnerable. Without adequate supports in place, such as transitional housing and life skills training, these individuals often find themselves on the streets with limited resources or guidance.

Environmental factors, natural and constructed, are becoming increasingly influential in shaping patterns of homelessness. Natural disasters such as hurricanes, wildfires, and floods, displace thousands of individuals each year. The 2024 Maui wildfire, for instance, left many residents without homes, contributing to the surge in the local homeless population. Urban planning and the design of public spaces also play a critical role.

Legislation and public policy have a profound impact on both the causes and potential remedies of homelessness. In some jurisdictions, policies aimed at "cleaning up" public areas result in the displacement of homeless encampments, effectively criminalizing homelessness rather than eliminating its root causes. These measures perpetuate instability, often pushing individuals further into the margins without providing tangible solutions or support. Removing these punitive legal frameworks is essential to preventing the further marginalization of homeless individuals. Instead, policies should prioritize supportive interventions that promote transformation, housing stability, and reintegration into society. A justice system rooted in compassion rather than punishment is crucial for sustainable change.

C.E.A.S.E. for Equity

You prioritize what you value – where and how resources are directed reflects what a society holds as precious. Without sufficient funding, even the most well-intentioned programs can't achieve meaningful results. A multifaceted approach is required to reduce, and ultimately eradicate, homelessness. Only through coordinated and compassionate strategies can we hope to break the cycle and create a society where stable housing is affordable for, and accessible to, all. Adequate investment in affordable housing, psychological wellness services, and supportive programs is essential. Likewise, policies that emphasize housing without preconditions are equally important as funding and resource allocation.

Consider how traditional approaches to homelessness often require individuals to meet certain conditions (e.g. sobriety or participation in treatment programs) before gaining access to housing. Innovative models like the "Housing First"[33] approach, pioneered by organizations such as Pathways to Housing, have shown that providing immediate and unconditional housing, in addition to optional supportive services, leads to better health outcomes and long-term stability. By removing the requirement for sobriety or treatment before securing a home, this model prioritizes housing as a fundamental human right and a foundation for recovery.

Public perception plays a significant role in shaping policy and societal responses to homelessness. Misinformation, misconceptions, and stigma often hinder progress by fostering apathy or resistance to supportive programs. Community engagement and public education are therefore essential. Campaigns that humanize those experiencing homelessness, highlight institutional causes, and emphasize the value of inclusive solutions can shift attitudes and encourage collective action. When communities are informed and compassionate, they become powerful advocates and accomplices in the fight

---

[33] Pathways to Housing. "Housing First Model." Pathways Housing First, https://www.pathwayshousingfirst.org/

V. Actionable Steps

to end homelessness.

Desist...Federal "Months" and "Days"

The intent behind "Black History Month," "Hispanic Heritage Month," and "Native American History Month" appears inclusive and celebratory. However, isolating the achievements of specific groups ultimately perpetuates separation and amplifies inequity. Inevitably, some groups are excluded, fostering further division. These United States of America are shaped – literally and figuratively – by the physical, intellectual, and financial contributions of countless cultures, traditions, ideologies, languages, and beliefs.

Our history books offer mere snapshots of the past, often lacking the depth to convey the emotions and experiences of the time. The sufferings of enslaved Africans, displaced Native tribes, abused Chinese migrants, downtrodden Irish, and oppressed Hispanic and Spanish communities are equally significant. Their struggles, resilience, and contributions deserve authentic acknowledgment, not selective exploitation and appropriation.

However, the persistent practice of celebrating "....History/Heritage Month" or ".... Day" reinforces division by focusing on differences rather than the commonalities that unite us. Labeling people by melanin level, beliefs, gender, ability, or age is a long-standing institutional practice. While some claim it fosters recognition and inclusion, it more often promotes stereotyping, discrimination, and a sense of "otherness." Throughout history, labels have been used to 1) justify social hierarchies, 2) racialize classifications to enforce colonial oppression, 3) support gender roles to restrict opportunities, and 4) establish distinctions that perpetuate inequality between the "abled" and "disabled."

Labels also carry stereotypes that shape perceptions and behaviors. Racialized, gender, age, ability assumptions have influenced policing practices, led to wage gaps, and restricted professional advancement. In education and employment, categorizing students and workers by perceived abilities or backgrounds results in lowered expectations and institutional barriers, limiting individual potential.

While proponents argue that labels recognize diverse identities, true inclusion stems from genuine respect and equality, not categorization. Labeling creates the illusion of inclusion while actually increasing division by emphasizing differences over shared humanity. Psychologically, labels alienate individuals and diminish self-esteem. Negative labels may be internalized, leading to reduced motivation, while positive labels can impose limiting expectations that restrict authentic identity exploration.

Labels are frequently exploited in the areas of politics and the media, to increase fear and widen divisions. Politicians often appeal to identity-based groups for support, while biased media coverage reinforces societal stereotypes, increasing polarization and making collective progress harder. Even within social justice movements, an overemphasis on labels creates internal divisions. Feminism and civil rights advocacy, for example, have faced challenges around inclusivity, sometimes alienating potential accomplices because of the narrow focus on specific identifiers. A united society must emphasize the common bonds that connect us, not the categories that separate us.

Desist…The White Privilege Narrative

One of the most pervasive ideas in modern equity discussions is "white privilege." This narrative emphasizes the belief that all "white" individuals benefit from "systemic" advantages, while all "people of color" face disadvantages. While racialized disparities undeniably exist in these United States of America, the misguided assertion that privilege operates solely along racialized lines oversimplifies complex realities such as personal choices and individual effort.

Originally popularized by Peggy McIntosh's 1988 essay *White Privilege: Unpacking the Invisible Knapsack*,[34] the concept of "white privilege" gained traction in academic and activist circles before permeating mainstream culture,

V. Actionable Steps

influencing education, corporate policies, and public discourse. While it helped illuminate certain institutional advantages, its widespread use has also led to controversy. Critics argue it reduces complex socio-economic realities to a binary framework and alienates poor and working-class "white" Americans, further polarizing discussions around "race" and inequality.

If "race" were the sole determinant of success, all "white" people would thrive and all "black" people would struggle. For example, a poor "white" person from Appalachia shares many struggles with a "black" or Latino person from a similarly disadvantaged background. Yet, an exclusive focus on "race" overlooks these shared hardships, alienates potential accomplices, and diminishes the solidarity needed for meaningful social transformation.

Yet reality tells a different story: many "white" individuals face poverty, institutionalized barriers, and lack of opportunity, while many "black" individuals achieve success through perseverance, education, hard work, and community support systems. Reducing societal dynamics to a simple racialized privilege framework is ignorant! It minimizes these nuances and discourages self-determination within "black and brown" communities.

By framing institutionalized inequality primarily in racialized terms, the discourse oversimplifies complex societal challenges and creates a divisive "us versus them" mentality. It risks ignoring the deeper drivers of inequality – such as disparities in education, healthcare, and employment – that cut across racialized lines and require solidarity to address.

Moreover, the singular focus on "white privilege" fosters guilt, rather than meaningful action. Instead of encouraging constructive dialogue about policy reform, it often traps individuals in cycles of guilt or defensiveness, neither of

---

[34] McIntosh, Peggy. "White Privilege: Unpacking the Invisible Knapsack." *Independent School*, vol. 49, no. 2, Winter 1989, pp. 31–36. Also available via National SEED Project, https://www.nationalseedproject.org/key-seed-texts/white-privilege-unpacking-the-invisible-knapsack.

which produces lasting change. That focus also distracts from broader institutionalized issues like wealth inequality, employment barriers, and economic stagnation that affect people across racialized lines. As a result, movements that could unite diverse groups around common goals are weakened by resentment and disengagement. By narrowing activism to issues of racialized guilt and privilege, opportunities for collective action are lost. Successful movements rely on inclusive coalitions.

The emphasis on "white privilege" also fosters resentment by assigning collective guilt based on the amount of melanin in a person's skin, ignoring individual circumstances. Many "white" individuals facing economic hardship feel unfairly vilified, leading to defensiveness rather than openness to dialogue. This framing encourages identity-based tribalism, where people retreat into narrow groups based on identifiers, further deepening societal fragmentation and impeding efforts to build broad-based coalitions.

Moreover, the "white privilege" narrative often devolves into abstract moralizing rather than motivating real-world solutions. Expressions of guilt or virtue signaling, though symbolically powerful, do little to correct the material conditions driving inequality. Organizations and entities promoting this narrative often benefit from maintaining existing structures of power, using racialized discourse to deflect attention from their own roles in perpetuating injustice. While the original intent of highlighting racialized disparities was important, the current use of the "white privilege" narrative often distracts from removing institutionalized inequities that depend on melanin levels.

Growing gaps between the wealthy and the working class have created institutionalized barriers to mobility. Policies that promote living wages, job security, progressive taxation, and expanded access to affordable housing are essential to rectifying these imbalances. Reversing the inequalities that impact wealth must be central to this effort. Equally important are investments in education and healthcare.

V. Actionable Steps

Quality education must be accessible and affordable to all, especially in underfunded communities, and healthcare must be treated as a human right, not a privilege. These foundational supports are critical for fostering upward mobility across racialized lines, throughout the economic and social ecosystems.

Building solidarity across economic and social boundaries requires emphasizing common struggles rather than fixating on differences. Solutions must avoid assigning collective guilt or victimhood based solely on melanin level. Instead, efforts should focus on empowering individuals and communities, addressing institutionalized injustices without perpetuating division or resentment.

While the concept of "white privilege" originally sought to highlight real disparities, its current application often distracts, divides, and derails efforts at institutional reform. Reframing the conversation around shared struggles and common goals offers a more promising foundation for developing into a truly unified society; cultivating empathy and sustaining ecosystems for equity.

Desist…Victimization Narratives

Within the "black" community, the pressure to align with "systemic" oppression narratives is especially intense. Pushing back against victimhood narratives risks accusations of internalized "racism" and betrayal. Those who once supported you might become hostile because your views challenge deeply held beliefs. The emotional toll can be crushing as well. Defending your position amid relentless attacks, risking professional consequences, and enduring social ostracism can cause immense stress and emotional exhaustion. Even the strongest individuals may begin to doubt whether the fight is worth it. You may find yourself questioning your views; not because they're wrong, but because the pressure to conform is overwhelming. Isolation and constant opposition can make even the courageous advocate wonder if silence is safer.

Institutional frameworks have also shifted. Many organizations have adopted anti-racism training, diversity mandates, and implicit bias testing. Expressing skepticism or refusing to participate may invite disciplinary action or accusations of violating institutional values. In extreme cases, dissenters have faced lawsuits, harassment, and threats to their personal safety. The legal landscape increasingly favors those who uphold equity narratives, exposing critics to defamation, exclusion, and loss of opportunities.

Even if your views are rooted in logic, history, and fact, real change won't happen without significant influence. Recent ideological movements are deeply embedded and amplified by major institutions and media outlets. Challenging them requires extraordinary resilience. When people are conditioned to view the world through a lens of oppression and racial division, challenging that view often triggers defensive reactions. Instead of persuading, you may be further alienated and your words twisted against you.

Given these realities, you must ask yourself: Is speaking out worth the cost? Am I prepared for backlash, career losses, and strained relationships? Can I accept that my message might be ignored or misrepresented? If you answer "Yes!" and move forward, prepare for a long battle that may feel lonely at times. Build resilience, find accomplices, and understand that the opposition will not relent. Transforming the man-made ecosystems demands patience, observation, and strategy.

Challenging current practices, policies, and ideologies is not just an intellectual debate. It's a direct confrontation against beliefs that have been deeply woven into discussions of "race" and justice in these United States of America. The risks are real: professional consequences, social alienation, psychological strain, and legal battles. Yet the question remains: Is the cost too high? History shows that standing against dominant ideologies demands great sacrifice. The choice is yours; know that the path will test your resolve at every turn.

V. Actionable Steps

With all that said, some have called me brave. As a "black" man, educator, and leader for equity and inclusion, I have dedicated my career to creating environments where all students are empowered to succeed. My commitment to true equity remains firm. Yet today, I find myself at odds with dominant narratives around "race," privilege, and inclusion.

While the intentions behind modern equity movements may be noble, their emphasis on "white privilege," "black" victimization, racialized fear, and perpetual oppression ultimately hinders progress. Challenging these ideas isn't an act of betrayal but of courage. True equity demands honesty, and real inclusion requires rejecting divisive rhetoric in favor of empowering solutions.

Initially, equity and inclusion efforts sought to dismantle real institutional barriers. The Civil Rights Movement and policies like affirmative action were about expanding opportunity and ensuring justice. However, the focus has shifted. Instead of empowering individuals, today's ideology categorizes people into rigid groups of oppressors and oppressed. This shift reinforces division. The constant emphasis on "white privilege" suggests success is granted, not earned. On the flip side of that coin, the narrative of "black" victimization discourages agency and resilience; rather than building confidence, it fosters a mindset of defeat.

Today's equity discourse prioritizes grievance over growth, thereby encouraging dependency and fueling resentment. The idea that "systemic" oppression is still the defining force in "black and brown" lives ignores decades of progress. It breeds fatalism and discourages ambition, replacing it with a sense of hopelessness. By defining "black and brown" individuals as perpetual victims, this narrative ignores the innovations and contributions of "black and brown" inventors and entrepreneurs of the past, it strips us of present-day self-determination, and diminishes our potential for future peace and prosperity.

Instead of dwelling on barriers, we should highlight stories of triumph, perseverance, and self-reliance. Fear-based narratives *disempower*; messages of empowerment inspire. Despite obvious and ongoing flaws, the present opportunities for success in these United States of America are unparalleled in history – regardless of melanin level. Professionals, entrepreneurs, and leaders, of various skin shades and cultural backgrounds, have risen in both of the man-made ecosystems. These are not anomalies but evidence that "race" no longer defines destiny – it's determined by the capabilities and the content of a person's character, not the color of their skin (to paraphrase Dr. Martin Luther King, Jr.).

    Now, I'll admit that these United States of America were founded on racist principles and beliefs, because of the misconception that one "race" was superior to other "races." To those who say, "These United States of America are still fundamentally racist!" I say, you're dismissing the lived experiences of millions who have succeeded. Conversations I've had with rideshare drivers, grocery store workers, food service employees, small business owners, managers, supervisors, and executives of various melanin levels and countries of origin all point to this critical revelation - cultural values, work ethic, and personal choices matter. Claiming that these United States of America are irredeemably racist discourages young individuals from striving for influence, agency, liberation, financial prosperity, and self-sufficiency. As I stated earlier, this outlook promotes a culture of grievance rather than growth.

    I have a very good friend – a brother from another mother. He was literally born on a banana boat, as his mother immigrated from Cuba to these United States of America. He grew up in Bridgeport, went to the same high school as me. I recall how he was homeless for a time after graduating high school, living in his car while studying to become a Certified Public Accountant (C.P.A.) Long story short, he surpassed his initial goal. He went from being the lead accountant for a top construction firm, to the C.F.O. of Fortune 500 companies, to having his own successful businesses. He's amassed wealth and secured a financial legacy for his children. He's successful

V. Actionable Steps

because he's able to determine how he's spends his time; how he spends his time isn't dictated or controlled by obligations to work.

Now, he could have done what was easiest while he was in high school – turned to selling drugs. Likewise, he could have resorted to crime while he was homeless. He could've viewed himself as a victim, blaming "white" folks, "racism," and the "system" for the circumstances that seemed to place barriers and obstacles in his way. But he didn't!! He recognized that it was within his ability, and primarily his responsibility, to change his situation. He made sacrifices, he stayed focused, he read and studied – he had a vision, made a plan, and worked hard to achieve his dream.

Sustaining true equity must focus on creating opportunities for all, not reinforcing divisions based on melanin levels, physical features, perceived accents, or cultural traditions. It must prioritize education, financial empowerment, health and wellness, and community agency, not ideological battles that deepen resentment.

As an educator, I focus on real solutions like mentorship, academic accountability, financial literacy, and critical thinking. I refuse to lower expectations under the guise of equity. I challenge every student to rise above barriers, take ownership of their future, and reject victimhood. Challenging dominant equity narratives is an act of courage. It demands that you reject divisive ideas and instead build a future defined by unity, opportunity, and success for all.

If you're sincere about cultivating genuine empathy and sustaining inclusive ecosystems for equity, seriously consider the behaviors and language that you must change. Work alongside those within your sphere of influence (e.g. colleagues, friends, family, allies, accomplices) to make meaningful progress, for today and for generations to come.

<u>Desist…The Addiction Narrative</u>

In these United States of America, addiction is often framed narrowly as a personal dependency on substances like narcotics and alcohol, or behaviors like gambling and pornography. This prevailing definition distorts public understanding and stifles the implementation of compassionate, sustainable solutions. I challenge you to research and understand addiction as a profound, often extreme, manifestation of trauma, instead of a chemical dependency or impulsive behavior; that addiction, at its core, is conceived and nurtured in habitats where individuals feel unseen, unwelcome, unvalued, disempowered, and disconnected. To cultivate empathy and sustain ecosystems for equity in these United States of America, we must move beyond the limited pathology of addiction and instead recognize its roots are intricately linked to psychological and physiological exclusion in the social and economic ecosystems.

When addiction is viewed only through the lens of dependency, it individualizes what is fundamentally a collective and societal failure. Similar to depression, substance abuse and behavioral addictions don't arise in isolation. They're often responses to chronic emotional pain, social alienation, and structural inequalities. For example, people who grow up in underfunded neighborhoods with failing schools, inadequate healthcare, and housing instability are more likely to experience trauma that's never adequately addressed. These environmental stressors contribute significantly to mental health deterioration and feelings of powerlessness. Addiction becomes an attempt to feel something, anything, in a world that has made them feel invisible, unimportant, powerless, and worthless – a coping mechanism.

The habitats in which we operate (education, housing, healthcare, justice, infrastructure, nutrition, and employment) either nurture or neglect human potential. In these United States of America, these areas are deeply stratified by race, class, and geography, thus creating conditions where trauma festers for those at the margins. Consider education: under-resourced schools often lack mental essential supports that buffer trauma and foster belonging (thriving Arts programs, health counselors, nutritious meals, and extracurricular

V. Actionable Steps

programs). Similarly, the lack of affordable housing leaves people unsheltered, eroding the sense of safety and stability that is critical to psychological well-being. Without access to equitable healthcare, physical ailments and mental health issues go untreated, compounding cycles of pain and dependency.

Consider how the justice system has a punitive rather than restorative approach. Instead of addressing the underlying trauma that precipitates substance use, incarceration is frequently the default response to addiction, especially for marginalized and disenfranchised communities. Prisons are not healing environments; they're extensions of exclusion and dehumanization. By criminalizing addiction, our society amplifies disconnection and reinforces the very conditions that cause addiction to flourish.

To cultivate empathy and sustain equity in these United States, we must confront the emotional and structural roots of addiction. Empathy begins with recognizing, acknowledging, and admitting that addiction isn't a moral failure or a character flaw – addiction is a symptom of complicit neglect and abandonment. Adjusting your perspective in this way invites policies that are trauma-informed and healing-centered. It calls for investments in public schools that prioritize emotional intelligence alongside academics. It demands healthcare systems that integrate mental health and addiction recovery into primary care. It necessitates affordable, dignified housing as a foundation for recovery and empowerment. And it compels us to reimagine justice not as punishment, but as accountability, restoration, and reconnection.

Ultimately, addiction thrives in environments of exclusion, and it heals in environments of welcome and belonging. Reclaiming empathy means replacing stigma with understanding, and isolation with community. Only when we shift our lens, from dependency to disconnection, can we build systems that reduce addiction and nurture resilience, dignity, and equity for all.

Desist…The Relativity of Truth

Truth has long been debated philosophically. Some argue it is absolute and unchanging; others claim it is relative, shaped by culture and experience. However, in its purest form, truth does not bend to perception. It remains constant, independent of belief or interpretation. Absolute truth refers to facts that are universal and unchanging, unaffected by societal norms or individual viewpoints.

Ancient Egyptian philosophy embodies this distinction through the principle of Maat, representing truth, balance, and cosmic order; it governs the universe. In Egyptian mythology, a soul's heart is weighed against Maat's feather after death. If the heart is lighter, the soul ascends; if heavier, it's devoured. Here, righteousness is an absolute, not a relative, standard. Similarly, across other African communities, moral customs may vary, but the principle that justice exists beyond human perception remains constant. What one community finds acceptable, another may reject, but this cultural variation does not alter the existence of universal moral truth.

Among the Lakota people, the sacred figure – White Buffalo Calf Woman – emphasized that truth governs all relationships between humans and nature. Though interpretations of ceremonies may differ across generations or groups, the core principle of spiritual unity remains an absolute truth.

In Chinese philosophy, Confucius taught that virtues like respect and righteousness were not open to debate; they were necessary for societal harmony. Daoism speaks of the Dao, the way of nature; an absolute order that persists regardless of human recognition. Yet while the underlying truths are constant, their practical application has varied across cultures and eras.

Latin American folklore offers another example in the form of La Llorona, the Weeping Woman. Though interpretations differ, with some viewing her story as a cautionary tale for children and others as a symbol of colonial

V. Actionable Steps

grief, the fundamental message remains the same – the absolute truth that actions have consequences.

While human cultures shape interpretations of truth, they don't alter the existence of absolute truths. Recognizing this difference is critical to understanding justice, morality, and the universal principles that govern human life.

I shared all of that to highlight how truth is not relative. The equity narrative often promotes a deceptive phrase: "Speak your truth." However, "my truth" is a product of my personal experiences, beliefs, and opinions, not based on immutable absolutes. As you examined and confessed earlier, your beliefs are malleable, shaped by your experiences (past and present) and future expectations.

"Speaking my truth" has gained traction as a form of personal empowerment and authenticity; rooted in my personal beliefs and cultural perspectives, thus making truth relative. While it can validate individual experiences, its inherently subjective nature renders it a relative truth rather than an objective one. This relativity is debilitating to sustaining ecosystems for equity, which require shared understanding, accountability, and collective action grounded in factual and structural realities.

Transforming the economic and social ecosystems to sustain equity depends on truth that transcends personal perspective. When "my truth" is treated as sacrosanct, it dismisses others' experiences, thus undermining cohesion and mutual progress. For example, when one person's truth minimizes the trauma experienced by another, it disrupts the solidarity required for equity work, prioritizes individual comfort over structural change, and allows select voices to dominate under the guise of personal authenticity.

Furthermore, relativistic truths lead to competing narratives that stall critical dialogue and policy development. Equity demands a commitment to rigorous truth-telling rooted in evidence, historical context, and empathy. While personal stories are vital, they must be integrated into a collective narrative that pursues justice; moving beyond "my truth" toward "**the**" truth" is essential for building lasting, equitable systems.

Desist...Cultural Appropriation

Cultural exchange has long been a cornerstone of human history, resulting in shared traditions, knowledge, and artistic inspiration. However, in contemporary discourse, distinguishing between cultural appreciation and cultural appropriation has become increasingly important. There's a fine line between appreciation and appropriation – the act of observation. Both start with your observation of a cultural practice, behavior, word or phrase, tradition, or ritual that you admire (or at the very least, one that you're curious about). This leads to an interest in learning about, and participating in, said cultural expressions.

Both have the potential to influence mainstream culture in these United States of America. When elements of a culture are adopted, they often gain visibility; bringing awareness to behaviors and language that may not have been widely recognized. However, the way these elements are integrated into society determines whether the act is appropriation or appreciation.

Throughout history, cultures have borrowed from one another. The Silk Road, for example, facilitated the exchange of goods, ideas, and cultural practices across Asia, the Middle East, and Europe. Similarly, the influence of African, Indigenous, and Asian traditions on Western art, music, and fashion is undeniable. However, these exchanges haven't always been equitable. Colonialism and imperialism often resulted in the forced assimilation and exploitation of marginalized cultures, leading to resentment and calls for cultural preservation. By understanding the historical context of cultural interactions, we can better discern when cultural borrowing crosses the line into appropriation.

To understand the differences between cultural appropriation and appreciation, it's essential to understand these terms better. Cultural appreciation refers to the respectful

V. Actionable Steps

engagement with another culture, which involves learning about, acknowledging, and actively participating in its traditions. This includes studying a culture's history, collaborating with its members, and ensuring that representation is accurate and respectful. Cultural appreciation sometimes includes an invitation, or approval, to celebrate alongside the people of that cultural. Think of Indigenous ceremonies such as the Sun Dance, the Green Corn Ceremony, and the Vision Quest. While it's ok to appreciate the sacred nature and cultural significance of these ceremonies by learning more about them on your own, it would be insensitive to organize or take part in your own version of them.

Cultural appropriation, on the other hand, occurs when aspects of a culture are adopted without permission, understanding, or proper context. Cultural appropriation is the ignorant imitation and exploitation of cultural aspects, typically based on stereotypes, for an increase in personal wealth, fame, influence, or status. Appropriation involves the commercialization or commodification of cultural elements, stripping them of their original meaning.

The most significant difference between cultural appropriation and cultural appreciation has to do with intent and impact. Cultural appreciation involves respectful learning and engagement with another culture, often done with permission, understanding, and acknowledgment of its origins. It seeks to honor traditions and foster cross-cultural understanding. On the other hand, cultural appropriation occurs when elements of a culture are taken out of context, commodified, or used without proper acknowledgment. It often disregards the historical or communal significance of those cultural elements, sometimes reducing sacred or meaningful traditions to trends or entertainment. Appropriation is harmful because it involves a dominant culture exploiting aspects of a marginalized culture without recognizing the struggles associated with it.

Another significant difference is the role of power dynamics. Cultural appropriation typically involves an imbalance of power, where a dominant culture adopts aspects of a historically oppressed culture without understanding or addressing the historical oppression tied to those cultural elements. Appreciation, however, involves conscious efforts to respect, credit, and support the culture being engaged with, often by learning from its members and ensuring that their voices are heard.

There have been numerous instances of cultural appropriation throughout history, particularly in the areas of fashion, music, and entertainment. For example, the use of Indigenous headdresses as fashion statements or festival accessories disregards the deep spiritual and cultural significance of these items. Similarly, the adoption of traditional African hairstyles, such as cornrows and dreadlocks, by individuals who do not acknowledge their cultural roots can lead to controversy, especially when the same styles are stigmatized when worn by members of the originating culture.

Another notable example is the commercialization of yoga. Originally a spiritual practice deeply rooted in Indian philosophy, yoga has been commodified in Western societies, often stripped of its spiritual and cultural significance. This raises questions about whether the practice is being respected or merely used for profit.

In contrast, there are many ways individuals and organizations can engage with other cultures respectfully. For instance, when non-Japanese individuals study the Japanese tea ceremony with a trained sensei, learning about its history and cultural importance, they are engaging in cultural appreciation. Similarly, collaborations between artists from different cultural backgrounds that acknowledge and celebrate each contributor's traditions foster mutual respect and understanding.

Supporting Indigenous artisans by purchasing authentic handmade crafts rather than mass-produced imitations is another example of practicing cultural appreciation. By giving credit and financial support to the communities that create cultural products, individuals contribute to the preservation and celebration of diverse traditions.

V. Actionable Steps

Media and popular culture play a significant role in shaping perceptions of cultural exchange. The portrayal of cultures in movies, television, and music either perpetuates stereotypes or fosters appreciation and understanding. When Hollywood casts non-Asian actors to play Asian roles (a practice known as whitewashing), it diminishes opportunities for authentic representation and reinforces cultural appropriation. Conversely, films and media that engage consultants and creators from the cultures they represent lead to more authentic and respectful portrayals.

Music is another realm where cultural exchange occurs frequently. Genres like jazz, rock, and hip-hop have roots in "African American" culture but have been widely adopted worldwide. The key to appreciating these genres lies in acknowledging their origins and supporting the communities that created them rather than erasing their historical significance.

To avoid cultural appropriation and promote cultural appreciation, you must take intentional, informed steps. This begins with learning about the cultural elements you wish to engage with, including their historical and social significance. Consulting members of that culture will provide meaningful guidance and help ensure respectful engagement. Acknowledging the origins of cultural practices and supporting the artists, businesses, and communities behind them is also crucial. Recognizing power imbalances will foster more thoughtful and ethical cultural interactions.

While both appropriation and appreciation involve cultural exchange, their differences lie in intent, respect, and awareness of power dynamics. Appreciation seeks to honor and understand, while appropriation exploits and/or misrepresents. By making conscious, respectful choices, you will cultivate empathy and sustain ecosystems for equity to thrive.

APPRECIATION / APPROPRIATION

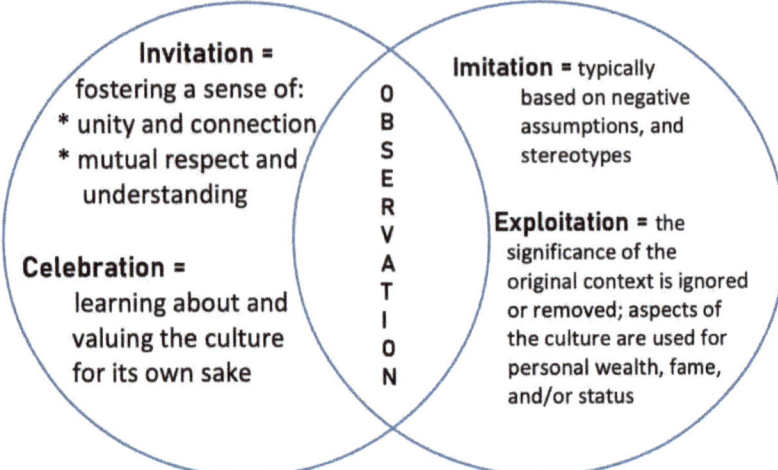

Desist...Reliance on Perpetual Public Assistance Programs

Public assistance programs (aka welfare) are designed to offer temporary relief and basic necessities to individuals facing economic hardship. However, their structure often produces consequences that hinder rather than help the long-term development and liberation of disenfranchised communities. Instead of fostering self-sufficiency, prolonged reliance on public assistance can create cycles of dependency, destabilize families, and weaken community structures.

These programs have been linked to broader social challenges, including gentrification, single-parent households, crime, increased incarceration rates, and homelessness. Moreover, the welfare system often unintentionally encourages fraud and penalizes recipients for pursuing financial independence, better health, family stability, and safer communities. Modest increases in income can trigger sharp reductions or the loss of essential benefits (e.g., food assistance, housing subsidies, healthcare, etc.), thus dis-incentivizing ambition.

V. Actionable Steps

The COVID-19 pandemic highlighted some of these structural flaws. Many individuals delayed returning to work because enhanced unemployment benefits exceeded wages from low-paying jobs, demonstrating how well-intentioned relief efforts can discourage workforce reentry; thereby harming businesses struggling to reopen and further weakening communities.

Over time, this dynamic can numb the recipient's desire for education, entrepreneurship, and mobility, particularly when generations of families experience welfare as a primary means of survival. Children raised in such environments may lack role models for financial autonomy, reinforcing cycles of poverty and diminishing community vitality. I'm grateful my mother didn't let a reliance on short-term public assistance become long-term bondage. She's my role model for what can be done when you trust God, have a vision, make a plan, and work hard to liberate yourself – she refused to let it become a cycle that her heirs would have to break.

The psychological and physical impacts of long-term welfare dependency cannot be overlooked. I can attest to how reliance on welfare takes a toll on personal identity and self-worth. I deeply understand how individuals in these mechanisms often internalize stigma and experience chronic stress, anxiety, and health disparities, conditions that further limit the recipients' ability to achieve economic and social mobility. Without clear pathways for transitioning out of public assistance, recipients are left navigating complex bureaucracies that punish progress rather than reward it.

As mentioned previously, welfare programs also stifle entrepreneurship. Strict income thresholds discourage recipients from pursuing self-employment or starting businesses, as temporary income spikes can result in benefit loss. This disincentivization, combined with a lack of financial literacy education, perpetuates generational dependency and stifles economic innovation within marginalized communities.

Similarly, government-subsidized housing initiatives, while improving neighborhood conditions, can lead to rising property values and gentrification. Low-income residents are displaced as rents outpace assistance levels, severing them from critical support systems and eroding community cohesion.

Welfare policies have also been criticized for inadvertently discouraging marriage and family stability. Programs that reduce or eliminate benefits when a second income is introduced can financially penalize low-income couples for marrying, contributing to the rise of single-parent households. I believe this was an intentional design to influence family structures – to undermine long-term family stability, particularly in communities already grappling with limited employment opportunities.

Efforts to support marriage and family formation must focus on removing financial deterrents, promoting educational and economic opportunities, and strengthening community ties without stigmatizing single parents. Revitalizing male employment, addressing mass incarceration, and supporting father involvement through targeted programs are critical steps toward restoring family cohesion.

I'm aware of families where 1) the father is fully able and capable of working but refuses to do so, or 2) evidence of the father's existence is erased from the home (although he secretly lives with the family). This behavior takes a psychological toll on recipients – sometimes manifesting as abuse and crime – in addition to a financial toll on tax-paying citizens. Fraud, though committed by a minority of recipients, undermines public trust in welfare systems. Attempts to combat fraud often introduce cumbersome bureaucratic obstacles that disproportionately burden honest recipients. Additionally, many welfare programs inadvertently penalize savings and modest income growth, trapping individuals in subsistence rather than facilitating empowerment.

High concentrations of welfare dependency often intersect with elevated crime rates and incarceration, particularly in marginalized communities. Economic despair and limited legitimate opportunities often push individuals

V. Actionable Steps

toward illicit activities. Generational poverty exacerbates this trend, as youth lacking stable housing, education, and role models are more vulnerable to criminal behavior. Incarceration then further fragments families and diminishes economic potential, perpetuating cycles of poverty and instability.

True transformation requires a reimagining of welfare programs as platforms for long-term empowerment rather than permanent support. Policies should reward progress with transitional assistance models that gradually reduce benefits as income rises. Integrating work requirements, education incentives, financial literacy education, and entrepreneurship support will create realistic pathways to independence.

Strengthening family structures through marriage incentives, counseling services, and tax benefits, in addition to investing in youth development and community-based support networks, is vital. Deliberate investment in vocational education, job training, and small business development – especially in high-demand industries – will produce economic resilience.

Access to affordable childcare and transportation must also be prioritized; removing logistical barriers to employment and education. Transforming welfare to promote independence, family stability, and community strength will reform public assistance from a mechanism of dependency into a bridge to opportunity, empowering individuals and communities to thrive. By framing public assistance policies to encourage economic empowerment, strengthen family structures, and foster community-driven support networks, society will shift from a structure of dependency to one that promotes true liberation, self-sufficiency, and long-term prosperity for all individuals.

<u>Desist…Efforts to Defund Law Enforcement</u>

In recent years, the call to "defund the police" has emerged as a widely publicized demand, in response to ongoing incidents of police violence, "systemic racism," and a general distrust that members of marginalized communities exhibit toward law enforcement. While the urgency behind these calls is rooted in genuine pain and legitimate concerns, the slogan itself is often misunderstood. When this clarion call is interpreted literally, it leads to detrimental consequences for both social cohesion and economic stability.

Rather than stripping resources away from law enforcement agencies, a more effective and restorative approach involves reallocating and increasing funding to emphasize 1) psychological wellness, 2) de-escalation training, and 3) advanced physical preparedness rooted in situational awareness and restraint. Such an approach acknowledges the need for reform while recognizing the essential role law enforcement plays in a functioning, peaceful, and fair society. Strategic investment in law enforcement is necessary for transforming the social and economic ecosystems in these United States of America.

"Defunding the police" has come to mean the removal or severe reduction of funding for law enforcement agencies. Such actions result in significant risks to public safety and societal stability. A sudden or substantial reduction in police resources results in slower emergency response times, increased crime rates, and decreased morale among officers. These consequences disproportionately affect vulnerable communities, which often rely more heavily on public safety services. The erosion of public trust in law enforcement is a problem, but removing resources exacerbates the issue rather than solving it.

Much like educators, law enforcement agents are often burdened with responsibilities far beyond their expected duties. They're called upon to address mental health crises, domestic violence, homelessness, negligence, and abuse (substance, psychological, and physical) – issues that require multidisciplinary and humane responses. Without the proper resources, officers are ill-equipped to manage these challenges effectively, increasing the likelihood of tragic outcomes.

V. Actionable Steps

Rather than removing the police presence, we should be transforming it.

A foundational pillar of effective policing is the psychological well-being of the officers themselves. High-stress environments, traumatic experiences, and the constant threat of violence take a significant toll on law enforcement personnel. The effects of this stress manifest as burnout, poor decision-making, and, in the worst cases, unnecessary use of force.

By allocating more funds to routine and consistent psychological wellness checks, departments will create a culture that prioritizes social and emotional well-being. These checks shouldn't be punitive but supportive, allowing officers to seek help without fear of stigma or reprisal. Embedded psychological health professionals, peer support programs, and mandatory counseling sessions after critical incidents will significantly improve both officer well-being and public interactions.

Increased funding must also support action research into officer wellness and its correlation with community outcomes. Understanding the psychological dynamics at play will help shape policy and training, thereby increasing the compassion and competence demonstrated by law enforcement agencies and their respective agents.

I believe one of the most direct ways to reduce violent encounters with law enforcement agents, and improve public trust, is through comprehensive de-escalation training. Such training will transform attitudes, while equipping law enforcement agents with the language and skills to defuse potentially volatile situations without resorting to force. Focusing on communication skills, emotional intelligence, conflict resolution, and decision-making under stress will improve how law enforcement agents are perceived in the community.

It must be noted that de-escalation isn't an innate ability; it must be taught, practiced, and refined. Funding is necessary to provide this training early and regularly, not just as a one-time workshop. Scenarios should be realistic and incorporate feedback mechanisms, such as video review, self-reflection, and peer assessment. Law enforcement agents must also be evaluated on their de-escalation performance, making it a core component of their professional development and promotion.

Moreover, de-escalation techniques must be tailored to diverse communities. Cultural competency training, including immersive experiences, will enhance the effectiveness of de-escalation strategies by ensuring officers understand the cultural contexts and communication styles of the communities they serve. This nuanced understanding will significantly reduce misunderstandings that escalate into physical confrontations.

Another transformative investment must concentrate on physical preparedness rooted in martial arts training. Traditional law enforcement training often focuses on intimidation, brute strength, and firearms, neglecting the nuanced, disciplined physicality that martial arts emphasize. Disciplines such as Krav Maga, Soo Bahk Do, Brazilian Jiu-Jitsu, Judo, and Aikido teach not only self-defense but also restraint, control, and situational awareness.

Martial arts training will condition law enforcement agents to remain calm under pressure, assess threats accurately, and use the least amount of force necessary to subdue a suspect. It nurtures respect, discipline, and a non-aggressive mindset. Regular training in these disciplines will reduce reliance on lethal force and build public confidence in the professionalism and self-control of agents.

Agencies that incorporate martial arts into their training programs will notice fewer injuries to both officers and suspects, realizing a practical benefit to this investment. Adopting a martial arts approach aligns with community expectations for safer and more humane law enforcement practices.

Funding must be part of a broader commitment to holistic community policing; supporting programs that place

V. Actionable Steps

officers in schools, community centers, and neighborhood events to build relationships, not to police the people. Community policing requires training, time, and personnel for nurturing trusting relationships; resources that only adequate funding can provide. Contrary to what their sole function seems to be – reactive and violent responders after a crime occurs – law enforcement agencies must become proactive and visible participants within the communities they serve. This means creating opportunities, through collaborative planning, for officers to be seen outside of crisis situations (walking through neighborhoods, attending local events, engaging in community meetings, and building rapport with residents).

When law enforcement agents are known members of the community, trust increases, and the need for force decreases. Officers who understand local dynamics, youth culture, and community history are more likely to engage empathetically, thereby making them more effective. This proximity and familiarity will also enhance the efficacy of de-escalation and mental health interventions.

Proactive engagement is about presence, not intimidation. It's about demonstrating a commitment to community well-being and signaling to residents that law enforcement is invested in their safety and prosperity. When officers are consistently visible in a non-enforcement capacity, they become approachable, trusted, and integrated members of the community. This visibility also serves as a deterrent to crime, as a known and trusted presence of law enforcement will reduce opportunities for criminal activity. Furthermore, community members are more likely to cooperate with officers whom they see as allies rather than adversaries. This cooperation leads to more effective crime prevention and resolution, further strengthening the bonds throughout the community.

When people feel secure, they're more likely to invest in their neighborhoods, start businesses, and build vibrant social networks. Conversely, communities plagued by violence and instability often experience economic stagnation, an exodus of capital, and social fragmentation.

Reimagining law enforcement as a guardian of community well-being plays a critical role in transforming the social and economic ecosystems in these United States of America. With adequate funding and thoughtful implementation, law enforcement can evolve into a force that heals communities as well as enforcing laws. The changes needed to make law enforcement more humane, effective, and just will only be possible, and sustainable, through intentional investment: designed to rebuild the trust and safety that are essential for a just and thriving society.

Desist…Partitioning the History of these United States of America

There are great conversations about the disparities being experienced in some communities (e.g., inner cities, migrant communities, etc.). The conversations are typically hosted by, and include, political leaders, heads of social and civic organizations, in addition to those deemed to be experts and thought leaders. Terms and concepts such as "minority," "marginalized," "intention," "impact," "displaced," "privileged," "diversity," "inclusion," "disenfranchised," "equity," "belonging," "race," "discrimination," "impoverished," "marginalized," and "equality" are examined and used as part of these conversations. These conversations (sometimes called conventions, summits, etc.) are usually "by invitation" only, to discuss topics such as:

- The "racist" history of these United States of America,
- The unequal treatment of specific ethnic and cultural groups,
- The disparities in education,
- The disadvantages associated with being from and/or part of a particular community,
- The disproportionate distribution of wealth and resources,

V. Actionable Steps

- The poverty crisis,
- The homeless epidemic,
- The inadequacies in healthcare for [insert group identifier here],
- The unfair sentences and incarceration rates of [insert group identifier here] etc.

The participants of said conversations, their subordinates, and their designees come away with a resolve to do something, to make an "impact." They organize committees and focus groups to gather data about the tangible effects, research possible solutions, and make recommendations for policies and programs. What's interesting to me is…these conversations rarely (if ever) examine, explore, or expose the causes. Likewise, they rarely (if ever) involve those directly affected by the aforementioned issues – those closest to the problems are closest to the solution.[23]

Writing this makes me think of my great-grandmother and the time period in which she grew up. More specifically, the importance of covering wounds. Inserting this memory might seem strange to some of you, but stay with me. My great-grandmother referred to the covering as "dressing," which would need to be checked and changed regularly, to prevent infection and aid the healing process. I share this story from my life to say the aforementioned entities and their representatives develop agendas, programs, and legislation to address the symptoms without ever treating the cause. They "add dressing" (i.e., cover the obvious and visible manifestations) without ever treating the dis-ease.

I'm going to state the obvious - the causes of the dis-ease must be appropriately, adequately, and immediately treated or removed. If not, the dis-ease will fester and eventually spread to epidemic proportions. So, what's my point? That the causes of poverty, unequal treatment, disparities in education, healthcare inadequacies, disproportionate distributions of wealth and resources, unfair sentencing etc. haven't been exposed and eradicated, therefore the dis-ease continues to plague the people of these United States of America. We're in an epidemic!

The way history is taught in these United States of America has long been a subject of controversy. Beyond mere debates over curriculum content, the structure and delivery of historical education play a significant role in shaping national identity, civic engagement, and social cohesion. At its core, U.S. history education often reflects dominant cultural narratives, selectively including events and figures that uphold a particular vision of American exceptionalism.

This approach not only distorts historical accuracy but also marginalizes the experiences and contributions of disenfranchised communities. By sanitizing uncomfortable truths and omitting or trivializing the voices of disenfranchised, marginalized, and individuals and others, traditional U.S. history instruction fosters polarization, recycles institutional injustices, and perpetuates exclusionary behaviors and language.

The dominant narrative of U.S. history has historically been written by and for those in positions of power – "white," male, landowning citizens. This perspective has framed the history of these United States of America as a linear progression toward freedom and democracy, often overlooking the complex and contradictory realities faced by many communities. The mythologizing of the Founding Fathers, the glorification of westward expansion, and the underrepresentation of institutional oppression serve to uphold a particular national identity rooted in Eurocentric colonizing ideals.

Textbooks, which often act as the primary source of historical content in classrooms, play a significant role in perpetuating this narrative. U.S. history textbooks downplay the enslavement of Africans and their descendants, colonialism, and racialized violence while elevating stories of "white" heroism and ingenuity. For instance, the institution of slavery is often discussed as a peripheral issue rather than a foundational component of the economy and social order in

V. Actionable Steps

these United States of America. Similarly, Indigenous genocide is frequently glossed over or framed as an unfortunate consequence of progress.

This selective storytelling isn't accidental but reflects broader political and cultural battles over who gets to define the nation's past. Curriculum standards are often influenced by state legislatures and education boards, leading to significant regional differences in how history is taught. In states with more conservative political leadership, there's a tendency to resist inclusive curricula that critically inspect issues of "race," gender, and inequality. This resistance has been exacerbated by recent efforts to ban discussions of "critical 'race' theory," a term often misused to describe any critical examination of racialized institutional practices.

The exclusion of marginalized voices in U.S. history education isn't merely a matter of representation but of justice and truth. When the histories of displaced, discarded, disenfranchised, and marginalized cultures are omitted or misrepresented, students receive an incomplete and misleading picture of the nation's development; students remain ignorant.

For "African American" history, coverage often begins with the enslavement of African people and ends with the Civil Rights Movement, with little discussion of contemporary issues such as mass incarceration, voter suppression, and economic disparities. This limited scope fails to convey the ongoing struggle for justice and reinforces the notion that racialized discrimination, intimidation, injustice, oppression, and exclusion are relics of the past.

Indigenous histories are similarly marginalized; their civilizations frequently introduced only in the context of European colonization; their cultures depicted as static or vanishing rather than dynamic and resilient. There is little acknowledgment of treaty violations, forced removals, or the contemporary challenges faced by Indigenous communities. Where are the acknowledgements, celebrations, highlights, honors, and appreciations for the resilience and achievements demonstrated by Indigenous descendants (despite efforts to eradicate them)? Chirp chirp...chirp chirp...crickets. Silence is complicity.

Latin/Hispanic and Asian American histories are also underrepresented. The labor contributions, civil rights struggles, and cultural influences of these communities are often sidelined or omitted entirely. Furthermore, discussions of xenophobia, such as the Chinese Exclusion Act or Japanese American internment, are typically brief and lack sufficient context.

The exclusionary nature of history education not only marginalizes certain communities but also contributes to national polarization. By presenting a singular, sanitized version of past actions, language, and legislation in these United States of America, educational institutions alienate students whose lived experiences contradict these narratives. This alienation leads to disengagement from civic life and skepticism toward democratic institutions.

Moreover, students from dominant cultural backgrounds may internalize a distorted sense of national identity, one that's uncritical and resistant to acknowledging injustice. I've been told by such students – who encounter alternative perspectives in higher education, the media, or interpersonal relationships – that they experience defensiveness, cognitive dissonance, and distrust. These reactions are fueled by ideological polarization and resistance to social change.

The politicization of history education further amplifies these divides. Efforts to introduce more inclusive curricula are often met with accusations of indoctrination or anti-American sentiment. Debates over how to teach history have become proxies for larger cultural conflicts, turning classrooms into battlegrounds in the so-called "culture wars." This contentious environment hinders the development of critical thinking skills and discourages open dialogue.

For students from marginalized backgrounds, the current approach to history education can be deeply harmful. With their communities excluded from the narrative, these

V. Actionable Steps

students may feel invisible or devalued. This lack of representation negatively impacts self-esteem, academic engagement, and a sense of belonging. This is a recurring complaint of students and young adults I counsel.

Research in educational psychology has shown that culturally inclusive curricula improve student outcomes by validating students' identities and experiences. In contrast, curricula that ignore or misrepresent marginalized communities contribute to achievement gaps and disciplinary disparities. Furthermore, the absence of diverse historical perspectives limits all students' ability to understand complex social dynamics. Without exposure to the realities of institutionalized oppression and racialized injustices, students are ill-equipped to engage in meaningful conversations about "race," inequality, and justice. This gap in understanding perpetuates ignorance and hinders efforts toward social progress. It minimizes your capacity for empathy and represses your willingness to sustain ecosystems for equity.

Addressing the shortcomings of U.S. history education requires a fundamental shift in both content and pedagogy. First and foremost, curricula must be expanded to include the histories of all communities that have shaped the nation. This means integrating "Black," Indigenous, Latino/Hispanic, Asian American, and other marginalized voices into the core narrative rather than relegating them to special topics or elective courses.

Culturally inclusive history education for these United States of America should also embrace a critical lens, encouraging students to examine historical events from multiple perspectives and to question dominant narratives. This approach fosters critical thinking, empathy, and a more nuanced understanding of the past. Teacher training is a crucial component of this transformation. Educators must be equipped with the knowledge and tools to facilitate complex discussions about identity, power, and injustice. Professional development programs must emphasize cultural competency, reflexive bias pedagogy, and trauma-informed teaching practices.

Community involvement is another key factor. Schools must collaborate with local historians, cultural organizations, and community leaders to ensure that curricula reflect the diverse experiences of students and their families. This partnership will help bridge gaps between classroom learning and lived reality.

Policy changes at the state and federal levels are necessary as well. Education standards must mandate the inclusion of diverse histories and protect educators' ability to teach about institutional inequality without fear of censorship. Courses like African American/Latin American studies should be required, not an elective, honors, or advanced placement option. Investment in curriculum development, teacher training, and classroom resources is essential to support these goals.

Transforming history education isn't a panacea for all social ills, but it's a critical step toward acknowledging past wrongs, honoring diverse contributions, and fostering a more equitable future. Our only hope of understanding the full story of these United States of America is by honestly 1) telling where we've been, where we are, and where we must go, and 2) admitting what was done, what's still being done, and what we must do to liberate, free, and empower those who are disenfranchised, displaced, discarded, and marginalized.

To build a more inclusive and unified nation, we must reimagine history education as a tool for empowerment, critical inquiry, and collective healing. The sacrifices, contributions, struggles, and innovations of the hidden figures must be infused into the daily teaching and learning, uplifted and highlighted as integral to the foundation, formation, development, and prosperity of these United States of America.

We'll never cultivate empathy and sustain ecosystems for equity without 1) acknowledging the past, 2) truthfully, honestly, openly identifying and defining the beliefs, values, language, and behaviors that got us here, and 3) critically implementing approaches, strategies, and methods that will

V. Actionable Steps

result in better future outcomes for all. True equity is admitting and understanding that history matters.

<u>Desist…The Narratives of
Privilege and Positionality</u>

The concepts of privilege and positionality are central to contemporary social discourse, particularly in relation to "race," gender, class, and other identifiers. Though originally intended to promote awareness and equity, they're often used in ways that reinforce mechanisms of disparity and oppression.

Privilege refers to unearned advantages tied to aspects of identifiers such as "race," gender, social status, and financial standing. Positionality reflects how social and political contexts shape individual perspectives. Although these concepts aim to highlight inequalities and institutional disparities, their application often rigidly categorizes people into privileged or oppressed groups, deepening divisions rather than fostering understanding.

Recent discussions around privilege, particularly racialized privilege, focus on exposing inequality but often have contrary consequences. By assigning individuals static labels, based on identifiers rather than actions or character, discourse around privilege alienates groups, discourages dialogue, and promotes a narrow view of individuals that overlooks personal complexity and potential for growth.

This binary framing also leads to the weaponization of guilt. Constant reminders of privilege burden individuals with guilt that rarely translates into meaningful action. Instead of fostering authentic engagement, guilt often results in performative gestures, without correcting deeper institutional issues. Over time, the binary mindset fosters resentment and disengagement, undermining genuine efforts toward cultivating empathy and sustaining ecosystems for equity.

Institutional responses to the privilege discourse widen disparities while creating additional barriers. While attempting to redress past injustices, policies that prioritize identifiers over merit – "color" of skin over capability and content of character

– risk cementing identity-based hierarchies. Instead of disrupting and dismantling inequality, such approaches simply reverse its direction, reinforcing exclusion and undermining fairness. A singular focus on identifiers often overlooks broader institutionalized factors, such as class, that contribute to persistent inequity.

The focus on positionality also leads individuals to internalize narratives of victimhood, which limits personal agency and resilience. Constant emphasis on oppression risks defining individuals by their disadvantages, which hinders empowerment and advancement. Furthermore, attempts to dismantle supremacy through identity-based frameworks sometimes establish new dominance structures rather than eliminating oppression entirely. This approach reshuffles power structures instead of eradicating them.

Prioritizing identity politics over shared struggles exacerbates social fragmentation. When issues, common to our shared humanity (e.g., education, employment, housing, and healthcare), are overshadowed by identity-based grievances, opportunities for collective action diminish. Divisions deepen, social trust erodes, and progress stalls as institutionalized challenges affecting all groups are sidelined.

A more effective approach centers on liberation and empowerment, rather than guilt. Providing marginalized communities with resources for self-determination promotes resilience and long-term change. Liberation and empowerment foster agency, allowing individuals to overcome institutionalized barriers without being confined to narratives of victimhood.

Focusing on our shared humanity also builds solidarity. Recognizing common struggles across diverse groups strengthens coalitions capable of driving meaningful change. I witnessed this firsthand – the focus on our shared humanity – throughout my entire time in India, particularly while touring the Gurdwara Bangla Sahib Sikh temple in New Delhi. Issues like workers' rights, healthcare access, and economic reform transcend identity divisions and offer opportunities for united

V. Actionable Steps

action. The rallying cry, "Power to the People," referred to all people, regardless of skin "color", class, or status.

True equity is rooted in freedom that's fertilized with resources and opportunities. A just society offers individuals the chance to succeed based on ability and effort, rather than privileging one group over another in response to historical wrongs. Our approach to sustaining ecosystems for equity should focus on balancing the scales, not on assigning blame or perpetuating guilt. By shifting the focus from blame to collaboration, we'll foster greater social cohesion and collective progress.

<u>Desist...Emphasizing a College Degree</u>

In these United States, a cultural narrative persists that a four-year college degree is the singular path to success. This emphasis is often fueled by institutions and societal expectations. It has overshadowed the value of skilled trades such as electricians, bakers, welders, chefs, carpenters, farmers, plumbers, and other hands-on professions that form the backbone of the nation's infrastructure. I believe prioritizing college degrees over skilled trades perpetuates inequality and retards healthy development within the economic and social ecosystems.

In my work as an educator, I've witnessed how emphasis on a college degree manifests as anxiety, depression, risky behavior, disrespectful language, defiance to authority, and mental break-down in students; how it frustrates and saddens parents; how it negatively affects siblings. To cultivate empathy and sustain ecosystems for equity in these United States of America, we must shift our focus toward embracing and elevating skilled trades as viable, respectable, and empowering career paths.

The overwhelming push toward college education disproportionately affects marginalized communities. Many individuals from low-income, marginalized, and disenfranchised communities face incredible barriers to accessing and affording college. Student loan debt, lack of generational wealth, and institutionalized exclusion make higher education a physical, financial and psychological burden. Devaluing trades and presenting college as the only legitimate option traps people into cycles of debt and disappointment. This narrow emphasis on academic prestige contributes to a kind of educational elitism that exacerbates insecurity and stifles mobility.

In the economic ecosystem, the growing shortage of skilled tradespeople causes an imbalance in national productivity, infrastructure maintenance, and local economies. Jobs in the trades often offer strong starting wages, job security, and upward mobility without the burden of debt. However, these paths are frequently overlooked in public school systems and career counseling, which continue to steer students away from trades under the misguided assumption that such work is less valuable or honorable. By failing to promote these professions, we limit the labor force and slow economic equity efforts, further marginalizing those already on the periphery.

The social ecosystem is similarly strained by the devaluation of skilled labor. When an entire segment of the workforce is viewed as inferior because a college degree is lacking, social stratification is reinforced. This perception creates a psychological hierarchy that divides communities and contributes to classism. It also discourages empathy, as those in academic or professional spheres fail to recognize the intelligence, creativity, and problem-solving required in trade work. Fostering respect for skilled labor will dismantle these barriers while cultivating a more inclusive and empathetic society.

Promoting skilled trades as a pathway to empowerment and liberation is essential. Trade schools are often more accessible, less expensive, and shorter in duration than traditional four-year colleges. They provide hands-on experience, immediate employment opportunities, and a sense of purpose. For marginalized individuals, learning a trade can lead to financial independence, community leadership, and

V. Actionable Steps

self-determination. Owning a trade-based business, for example, allows individuals to build wealth, mentor others, and contribute meaningfully to their neighborhoods – acts that are foundational to sustainable equity.

True freedom rests in the power to choose a path that aligns with one's strengths, interests, and needs without societal stigma. By valuing all forms of labor and learning – eliminating the false hierarchy between academic and vocational learning – we strengthen the collective well-being of our society and create ecosystems where everyone, not just the credentialed few, can flourish; we open the door for more American citizens to thrive. The liberation that comes from mastering a trade (being valued for one's skills, building generational wealth, and contributing to one's community) is profound. It fosters stability, dignity, and a sense of making a positive difference in the lives of others – qualities that every person deserves.

Desist…Virtue Signaling about Climate Change

In recent years, "climate change" has become a central issue in political, academic, and entertainment conversations. While raising awareness and taking action are critical, the rise of virtue signaling has distorted policy priorities and hindered progress throughout the social and economic ecosystems.

Virtue signaling, at its core, is the act of expressing opinions or sentiments to demonstrate one's good character or moral correctness, often without corresponding actions. It appears, at surface level, that societies across these United States of America are uniting to combat a threat to human existence. The virtue signaling I want to highlight relates to "climate change." News flash – the climate is *always* changing.

The economic ecosystem, particularly in these United States of America, is predicated on the relentless consumption of natural resources. It was formed through centuries of colonization, slavery, land theft, and the strategic devaluation of Indigenous and marginalized populations. Forests have been clear-cut for urban expansion, lands have been stripped of minerals, wetlands drained for real estate development, and rivers dammed or diverted to meet industrial needs. These actions destroy nature's natural defenses. Forests, for example, regulate rainfall and reduce soil erosion, while wetlands absorb floodwaters and buffer storm surges. When these ecosystems are disrupted or eliminated, communities are left vulnerable to the full force of hurricanes, floods, wildfires, and droughts.

The core motivator – an insatiable desire to expand capital; an expansion that requires a constant input of raw materials and energy (regardless of environmental cost). Consequently, what's being called a climate crisis isn't merely nature's unpredictability – it's a direct correlation to human activity. It's the inevitable outcome of language and behaviors that prioritize profit over sustainability, competition over cooperation, and consumption over conservation.

This reality is rarely acknowledged in mainstream discussions about "climate change." Instead, narratives center on individual responsibility (i.e., drive less, recycle more, etc.), thereby shifting focus away from the transformation that is truly needed to cultivate empathy and sustain ecosystems for equity. Framing discussions of "climate change" in this way unfairly blames the consumer; it implies the frequency and severity of natural "disasters" will be corrected only when consumers make better choices. In truth, the scale of environmental degradation demands structural reforms, not merely behavioral adjustments.

When virtue signaling replaces evidence-based approaches to reforming behaviors, it adversely affects crucial sectors such as housing, healthcare, education, nutrition, and infrastructure, particularly for marginalized populations. Virtue signaling often leads to performative policies that favor symbolic gestures over practical outcomes; surface level solutions which aren't inherently transformative. Instead of challenging the patterns of exploitation that cause "climate change," the proposed solutions perpetuate them with new tools – enabling the same entities, organizations, and

V. Actionable Steps

institutions to retain influence, control, and dominance over resources and communities.

In housing, for instance, mandates for "green" construction and materials, though environmentally sound in theory, increase costs and restrict affordable housing development. Policies that prioritize carbon neutrality, without considering affordability, displace low-income communities and exacerbate housing shortages. Rather than alleviating inequality, these initiatives amplify it, turning environmental progress into a luxury for the affluent rather than a fundamental human right.

In healthcare, virtue signaling in this area shifts attention from direct patient needs to symbolic sustainability targets. Hospitals and clinics may invest in expensive "green" certifications or carbon offset programs, diverting funds from critical services like preventive care or psychological support. While environmental responsibility is important, prioritizing optics over outcomes reduces access to care for the underserved and strain already limited resources.

Similarly, in education, more and more schools seem to be adopting environmental policies that are more performative than impactful. While admirable on the surface, switching to biodegradable materials, collecting recyclable materials and composting, or promoting meatless days often mask the deeper issue of underfunded schools. These measures become distractions from more pressing needs such as curriculum development, teacher training, and equal access to educational technology. Moreover, schools in disadvantaged areas struggle to implement such policies, further widening gaps.

Nutrition initiatives also suffer from misguided virtue signaling. Emphasis on carbon-conscious diets, such as plant-based eating, overlooks food security and affordability. Low-income families typically don't have the means to participate in these dietary shifts, especially in areas with limited or no access to fresh produce. Imposing such ideals, without reforming structural disparities in food distribution and pricing, undermines both health and environmental goals.

Infrastructure also bears the burden of symbolic advocacy over substance. While building bike lanes and promoting electric vehicles are valuable, these efforts overlook more urgent needs like repairing decaying public transport systems, updating water pipelines, or improving energy access in rural areas. Infrastructure must be built with resilience and equity in mind, not merely as a canvas for climate messaging.

To counteract the negative effects of virtue signaling, we must cultivate empathy in order to sustain ecosystems for equity. Policymakers must engage with diverse communities to understand their needs, thus ensuring that climate action is inclusive and grounded in real-life contexts. Environmental policies must prioritize practical, scalable interventions such as retrofitting existing buildings, expanding community health clinics with sustainable designs, and investing in reliable public transportation.

Education on environmental reform must be integrated into policy planning, to foster a more holistic understanding of sustainability. As highlighted earlier in this text, true environmental stewardship requires recognizing the interconnectedness of ecological and human systems. Only by aligning environmental goals with civic responsibilities can we sustain the ecosystems (both natural and manmade) on which humanity depends for health, wisdom, peace, prosperity, and longevity.

The fundamental driver of the increasing frequency and severity of weather-related tragedies isn't ignorance or apathy. It's the deliberate preservation of practices that sustain economic and social disparities; behaviors and language that require those from marginalized and disenfranchised communities to labor in mines, factories, and fields while a small elite reaps the benefits. The increasing frequency and severity of natural disasters is a byproduct of this imbalance, as those in positions of wealth, influence, and power exploit both human and natural resources with impunity.

What underlies degradation within the natural and man-made ecosystems isn't just economic greed, but a fundamental

V. Actionable Steps

lack of empathy for each other and for the planet that sustains us. The disconnection from nature augments policies and industries that prioritize short-term profit over long-term resilience. Exploiting landscapes for fossil fuel extraction, deforestation, and unsustainable agriculture all contribute to a warming planet, which in turn fuels stronger and more frequent natural disasters. Until humanity cultivates a deeper respect for the earth and for one another, we will continue to suffer the consequences of our own ecological negligence.

We must be honest about the individuals, institutions and entities that govern these United States of America, in addition to admitting our own involvement in putting them in these positions of power and influence. The current discourse on "climate change," dominated by virtue signaling and symbolic gestures, serves to protect those who have the most to lose from genuine transformation.

True climate justice requires acknowledging that sustaining ecosystems for equity is incompatible with unchecked capitalism. I'm jus' sayin'…A society that incentivizes growth without limit will always find new ways to extract, pollute, and exploit. Reducing the severity and frequency of weather-related catastrophes therefore means 1) confronting entrenched power dynamics, 2) redistributing wealth, and 3) amplifying Indigenous, localized, and regenerative models of land stewardship.

If the goal is to genuinely minimize "climate change" and reduce the impact on the social and economic ecosystems, then conversations must shift away from virtue signaling and toward structural accountability. This path is undoubtedly more difficult than advocating for electric vehicles or planting trees, but it's the only path that concentrates on the causes. "Climate change" isn't a technological problem; it's a civic and political one. Until we confront the institutions, organizations, and entities that benefit from ecological destruction, any "solution" will be temporary, inadequate, or performative.

C.E.A.S.E. for Equity

Desist...Federal Recognition Requirements for Indigenous Tribes

The federal recognition of Indigenous tribes in the United States is often portrayed as a necessary gateway to sovereignty, rights, and access to vital resources. While recognition can offer crucial benefits like as access to healthcare, education, and legal standing, I want to point out a fundamental issue with this. The process of deciding which Indigenous groups qualify for recognition (being upheld by those governing these United States of America) was conceived, and remains rooted, in colonial logic and bureaucratic control – it undermines Indigenous autonomy and identity. At its nucleus, the concept of federal recognition rests on the assumption that the government of these United States of America has the authority to determine the legitimacy of Indigenous nations.

Why should Indigenous peoples, whose existence on the land predates these United States of America, need validation from the very government that displaced, dispossessed, and attempted to assimilate them? Rather than honoring Indigenous sovereignty as inherent, the recognition process is a conditional status, granted by an external power. This dynamic deeply erodes the principle of self-determination and reinforces a hierarchical relationship in which the federal government sits above Indigenous nations.

From what I understand, the process of obtaining federal recognition is notoriously slow, complex, and costly. Tribes must apply through the Bureau of Indian Affairs (BIA) and submit extensive documentation showing historical continuity, political authority, and community existence dating back centuries. I think back to news stories informing us how the Eastern Pequot, Golden Hill Paugussett, and the Schaghticoke tribes in Connecticut were denied recognition by the BIA. What the what?!? I bet these very tribes interacted with, and even helped, the early colonists who would later become governors, legislators, and political leaders in these lands. Yet, they now have to ask for permission to be a

V. Actionable Steps

recognized tribe?!? Get outta here!! Do you honestly believe this wasn't part of a premeditated plan to engineer ecosystems that diminish, dismiss, exclude, oppress, and erase specific cultures?

Adding insult to injury are the criteria for recognition – daunting barriers for Indigenous communities, especially those unable to maintain or recover written records destroyed at the urging of government, public, and private entities. Many tribes must hire legal experts and researchers at significant cost, making recognition inaccessible for those lacking financial resources. It's not uncommon for petitions to take decades to be reviewed, leaving entire generations in limbo.

Some of the federal recognition requirements include 1) a tribe must show their historical continuity, 2) there must be evidence a tribe is a distinct community, and 3) a tribe must provide evidence of its uninterrupted existence since contact with non-Indigenous settlers or explorers. I'm not a cussin' man, but this is some…ridiculous nonsense! The people governing these United States of America have historically done everything in their power to disrupt and destroy the very continuity that's required. Policies of forced removal, boarding schools, and assimilation campaigns fractured Indigenous families, erased cultural practices and dismantled native structures of sovereignty and governance. Now, tribes are penalized for the very losses inflicted upon them by colonial patterns of exploitation, extermination, and erasure. In some cases, communities that adapted or went underground to survive are disqualified from recognition because they no longer fit the government's narrow criteria for what a tribe should look like. Ain't *that* a kick in the head!

The recognition process is also marked by inconsistency and subjectivity. Tribes with similar histories may receive vastly different outcomes depending on the political climate, lobbying capacity, and public perception. Some tribes have successfully obtained recognition through legislation or administrative rulings, while others with equally compelling evidence have been denied. This inconsistency undermines the integrity of the process and reveals how recognition can be influenced by political considerations rather than objective standards.

For unrecognized tribes, the consequences are severe. They're excluded from accessing federal programs connected to health, education, housing, and economic development funding. Without recognition, tribes lack the legal status to reclaim ancestral lands, exercise self-governance, or participate in nation-to-nation negotiations with the federal government. These exclusions exacerbate disenfranchisement in the economic and social ecosystems.

Beyond legal and material consequences, the denial of recognition has significant cultural and psychological effects. It delegitimizes Indigenous identities in the public eye and creates painful divisions between those who are federally recognized and those who are not. Federal recognition, as a marker of legitimacy, affects how Indigenous people are perceived by outsiders and by each other.

Ultimately, the very concept of federal recognition perpetuates the logic of settler colonialism. It treats Indigenous sovereignty not as a pre-existing fact but as a status to be earned or granted by the colonizing state. Tribes are often expected to conform to Western models of governance and documentation in order to be recognized, further marginalizing traditional practices and approaches to knowledge.

Rather than supporting Indigenous self-determination, the recognition system in these United States of America reinforces dominance over Indigenous lives. It forces Indigenous nations to prove their existence to a colonial power structure that has long sought to erase them. It imposes impossible bureaucratic burdens and perpetuates a model of control rather than partnership. True justice requires the acknowledgement of Indigenous sovereignty as inherent, supporting the self-recognition of tribes, while shifting power away from federal gatekeeping and toward Indigenous self-determination. Until then, the current recognition framework

V. Actionable Steps

will remain a symbol of both historical erasure and ongoing inequality.

<u>Desist…Performative Practices of…</u>
<u>…*Activism*</u>

In recent years, diversity and inclusion have taken center stage in corporate and institutional discourse. Yet much of this focus has been criticized as performative; the gestures appear progressive but lack the substance needed to reform deeper institutional issues. A prime example is corporate responses to "white privilege." Many companies publicly commit to inclusivity through diversity workshops and inclusive language, while ignoring the structural inequalities embedded within their operations.

For instance, organizations may implement implicit bias training to raise awareness of unconscious prejudices. While such programs encourage personal reflection, they often fail to eradicate the organizational systems that sustain inequality. Companies continue to exploit workers with low wages and poor conditions, even as they promote a progressive image. These symbolic actions project an illusion of change while the root causes of wealth inequality, labor exploitation, and racialized injustice remain untouched.

Performative activism allows institutions to maintain the status quo under the guise of social progress. Diversity programs offer a sense of progress for those seeking to appear socially conscious, but without structural transformation, they offer little to marginalized communities. This superficial focus not only obscures real issues but also undermines the broader fight for justice and equality.

The concept of allyship is similarly compromised. Many self-identified allies engage in visible acts (i.e., posting on social media, attending protests, using inclusive language, etc.), without committing to the long-term work of eradicating oppression. These actions often elevate the ally's social standing without effecting tangible change. True allyship demands more than public performance; it requires sustained engagement, a willingness to listen, and direct support for marginalized communities.

To transition from symbolic to meaningful action, the focus must shift from rhetorical displays of privilege to concrete steps that resolve institutional inequality. This means moving beyond token efforts and advocating for real policy reforms, such as equitable hiring practices, fair wages, and inclusive workplace policies. Real change demands eliminating power structures, not just adopting socially accepted language.

Another facet of performative activism is what can be called performative empathy. This means using the language of compassion without truly engaging with the experiences of others. When individuals adopt such language without understanding the issues, empathy becomes shallow and ineffective. Genuine empathy requires active listening, humility, and a commitment to respond meaningfully to others' realities.

Reducing activism to performative language and posturing diverts attention from the transformative work required to confront injustice. In a nut shell, performative activism fails to confront the structures that perpetuate injustice. It simply offers the illusion of progress while reinforcing inequality. To create lasting change, individuals and institutions must replace symbolic gestures with sustained, purposeful action. Only through honest engagement, meaningful reform, and deep empathy can we build a more just and equitable society.

...Land Acknowledgements

Land acknowledgments are rooted in Indigenous traditions, where recognizing the land and its history are an integral part of cultural practices. Indigenous peoples have long expressed reverence for the land, acknowledging their connection to it through ceremonies and oral traditions. Land acknowledgments have become increasingly common in these United States of America, particularly in public and private academic institutions, nonprofit organizations, and political

V. Actionable Steps

entities. These statements recognize that the land on which events take place was originally inhabited by Indigenous peoples before colonization.

The increased use of land acknowledgments is largely driven by a desire to demonstrate an awareness of historical injustices. I must applaud this desire. In some cases, these statements are meant to signal solidarity with Indigenous tribes and acknowledge the ongoing impact of colonization. While land acknowledgments are intended to show respect, I argue that they often serve as performative gestures, lacking substantive action to support Indigenous communities. Some of my key criticisms include:

1. Lack of Actionable Change: Institutions issue land acknowledgments without taking concrete steps to support Indigenous communities. Recognizing the land's history without making efforts to return land, invest in Indigenous-led initiatives, or challenge structural inequalities reduces these statements to symbolic gestures.
2. Institutional Hypocrisy: Some organizations that perform land acknowledgments actively participate in institutional practices that harm Indigenous communities. For example, universities that acknowledge Indigenous land may continue to profit from endowments tied to land expropriation or fail to support Indigenous students through scholarships or cultural initiatives.
3. Tokenization of Indigenous Communities: Some land acknowledgments become a routine part of events without meaningful engagement with Indigenous voices. Rather than fostering genuine relationships with Indigenous communities, these acknowledgments become empty words recited for the sake of appearances.
4. Colonial Guilt Without Accountability: Land acknowledgments serve as a means for non-Indigenous

individuals, organizations, and institutions to ease guilt without addressing ongoing injustices. Acknowledging historical harm isn't equivalent to addressing contemporary issues such as land rights, environmental justice, or Indigenous sovereignty.

Another concern I have is the commodification of land acknowledgments. Some corporations and organizations use these statements as public relations tools, rather than making genuine efforts to support Indigenous communities. By incorporating land acknowledgments into branding and marketing strategies, companies appear socially conscious while continuing practices that contribute to Indigenous marginalization. Furthermore, I'm sure organizations and institutions consult Indigenous communities for land acknowledgment language, without providing proper and adequate compensation for said knowledge and labor. This exploitative practice further undermines the authenticity of these statements.

For land acknowledgments to be meaningful, they must be accompanied by action. Alright, alright…I'm jus' gonna come out 'n say it – Give the land back! Although there are some who might exclaim, "That's ridiculous; that's outrageous; how dare you suggest such a thing?" To you I say, "It ain't…get over yourself! Returning land to Indigenous peoples is a necessary act of justice. Long before the formation of these United States of America, Indigenous nations stewarded this land with intimate knowledge, respect, and reverence, focused on peaceful co-existence and sustainability. Colonization violently dispossessed them of their homelands through reneged treaties, forced removals, imposed addictions, targeted sickness, and warfare. The present-day call to give the land back isn't just about reconciling historical wrongs. It's about restoring sovereignty, ecological stewardship, and cultural survival for the original inhabitants of this land.

I know, I know…some are mentally picketing, protesting, and posturing, adamantly screaming, "That's

V. Actionable Steps

impossible!" (No, it's not.) "Where would the companies go?" (They have the money and resources to figure it out.) "That wouldn't be fair to the homeowners?" (Was it fair to displace the Indigenous people?) "Do you realize entire communities would have to be moved and restructured?" (Yup, I do!) Relocation, when planned ethically and equitably, is not impossible. This country, known as the United States of America, is a collection of creative, ingenious, and innovative problem solvers; citizens who are more than capable of figuring out ways to make this happen.

Governments and business entities have long track records of displacing communities for infrastructure, environmental restoration, or commercial development. Entire towns have been relocated for highways, airports, dams, etc. The same commitment and resources can be mobilized to facilitate reparative relocation. Municipalities and businesses occupying land, identified for return, can be offered federal or state-supported transitions to alternative spaces, especially on underutilized public land.

For homeowners, relocation doesn't have to be punitive. Fair buyouts, replacement housing, and support for moving costs can ensure families are relocated with dignity and security. Programs like these already exist for flood zones and eminent domain projects. The difference is that this would be done for justice and not profit. Hmmmm…imagine that!

Returning land to Indigenous nations allows for the reestablishment of cultural and spiritual ties, protection of sacred sites, and restoration of land-based knowledge systems. Indigenous governance and land management align with sustainability and environmental healing. If you're being honest with yourself, these are practices our modern world urgently needs.

Let me be clear, I'm not talking about the removal of every non-Indigenous person. Instead, I'm advocating for the reconfiguring of land ownership and stewardship through consent, compensation, and cooperation. As a society, we must accept and admit that Indigenous nations should rightfully, and legally, own the land. By returning the land, we acknowledge Indigenous sovereignty, challenge settler-colonial systems, and take tangible steps toward a more equitable future.

Think about it - Relocation may be inconvenient, but dispossession was catastrophic! With vision, political will, and a genuine commitment to justice, land return is possible. Carefully consider the following as actions that must also be taken to make progress radiate beyond performative gestures:

1. Institutions must explore ways to compensate Indigenous communities, whether through direct financial support, land repatriation, or funding for Indigenous-led programs. Some universities offer tuition waivers for Indigenous students, but more substantial commitments are necessary.
2. Organizations must work with Indigenous leaders to ensure that land acknowledgments are accurate and aligned with the needs and priorities of Indigenous communities. Providing platforms for Indigenous voices and leadership is essential.
3. Institutions that issue land acknowledgments must also advocate for policies that support Indigenous sovereignty, land rights, and financial empowerment. This includes supporting legal battles for land reclamation and opposing projects that threaten Indigenous land and resources.
4. Schools and universities must incorporate Indigenous history and contemporary issues into their curricula. A land acknowledgment without a broader commitment to education on Indigenous struggles and contributions is insufficient.
5. Businesses and institutions must create opportunities for Indigenous artists, entrepreneurs, and professionals. Hiring Indigenous people, contracting Indigenous-owned businesses, and investing in Indigenous-led initiatives are concrete ways to support Indigenous liberation, financial prosperity, and cultural influence.

V. Actionable Steps

Land acknowledgments have the potential to raise awareness about historical injustices and honor Indigenous communities. However, without substantive actions, they risk becoming hollow performances. To avoid performative activism, institutions and individuals must move beyond acknowledgment and commit to tangible support for Indigenous communities. Only through meaningful actions can land acknowledgments contribute to genuine reconciliation and justice.

...ADA Compliance

In these United States of America, performative practices have come to define many civic, political, corporate, and academic interactions. Performative allyship, corporate virtue signaling, and surface-level inclusivity often substitute for meaningful action, creating an illusion of progress. These practices fail to eradicate institutional injustice and reinforce barriers that continue to marginalize physically and neurologically challenged individuals.

From corporate campaigns to institutional policies, the disability rights movement has increasingly encountered symbolic gestures as compliance with the American with Disabilities Act (ADA). Companies post supportive messages without enacting real change, while entities and organizations implement minimal accessibility measures that fail to undo deeper structural inequities.

In education, performative inclusion appears through gestures like Disability Awareness Month, yet schools often lack individualized resources, proper infrastructure, or inclusive pedagogy. Schools I these United States of America tend to treat inclusivity as a performance rather than an integral part of the learning environment. In the realm of entertainment, exclusion still prevails as well. Many venues remain inaccessible, and physically and neurologically challenged artists are often tokenized rather than genuinely included. In these United States of America, physically and neurologically challenged performing artists are typically included only when convenient, rather than meaningfully integrated into the creative space.

Many Indigenous communities recognize every member's value as essential to communal survival. Individuals with physical and neurological challenges aren't viewed as a burden but as contributors with unique strengths. In contrast, institutions in these United States of America often offer symbolic roles to physically and neurologically challenged individuals while denying them real leadership opportunities.

In Confucian and Buddhist traditions, people with physical and neurological challenges are cared for within the family and honored, similar to the elderly (who are respected as holders of wisdom). Yet in these United States of America, they're frequently isolated or institutionalized, acknowledged only when politically or socially expedient. Puerto Rican culture, rooted in African and Indigenous traditions, emphasizes communal care. This contrasts with the emphasis on independence in these United States of America, which often leaves physically and neurologically challenged individuals to navigate bureaucratic systems with little to no guidance, prioritizing efficiency over dignity.

Across sectors like employment and healthcare, performative inclusion normalizes exclusion. As a gardener, I know that planting seeds without nurturing the soil results in shallow growth. Likewise, showcasing individuals with physical and neurological challenges, without changing the institutions that marginalize them, is superficial progress.

The martial arts – Shotokan karate from Japan, Soo Bahk Do from Korea, and Kalaripayattu from India – teach harmony, discipline, and internal strength. Yet in the narrative throughout these United States of America, physically and neurologically challenged individuals are often reduced to either being "inspirational" or "pitiful," thereby denying their complexity, capabilities, and humanity.

Even religious institutions are complicit. Many preach inclusivity but fail to provide accessible spaces or meaningful opportunities for leadership and influence. To build a society

V. Actionable Steps

that genuinely supports physically and neurologically challenged individuals, we must move beyond symbolic actions and embrace institutional change. Lessons from global cultures and diverse professional fields show that real inclusion is rooted in action, not appearance. Equity requires restructuring the very policies and practices that govern our institutions, ensuring that physically and neurologically challenged individuals are seen, valued, and fully empowered to thrive.

...Creating Brave/Safe Spaces

The ideas that "we must create brave spaces...," that "we must create safe spaces...," along with encouragements to "speak your truth," are misleading at best. The "creation" of the aforementioned spaces keeps control in the hands of those already in positions of power, dominance, and influence. This performative gesture is scripted by those who have the most to lose and the least to gain.

Let me start by defining bravery: it's when you do what's right and for the greater good of the community (i.e., you do what is just aka justice), in opposition to challenges, threats, adversity, and potentially death – remember this. Adjacent to bravery is your sense of safety: it's a state of mind, a confidence in yourself that combines 1) your awareness of the environment and surroundings, 2) your awareness of what the people around you are doing, and 3) your ability to enter, move through, and exit (i.e. your ability to navigate) situations, circumstances, and relationships.

Situations are based on your personal decisions, choices, language, and behavior. You have complete control over your situations. Circumstances are based on 1) the decisions, choices, language, and behavior of others, and 2) natural environmental patterns beyond your knowledge or ability to control.

Your sense of safety is proportional to your confidence in the knowledge, abilities, and resources you have access to.

You are responsible for your sense of safety. ***You*** determine your level of bravery.

For example, when I walk into a room filled with my middle school students, I feel safe (although I am clearly outnumbered). I feel safe because of the knowledge I possess about adolescent psychological development, conflict resolution, the school policies and codes of conduct, and classroom management. I feel safe because I'm very confident in my ability to 1) establish meaningful connections through conversations and humor, 2) demonstrate kindness, compassion, and empathy, and 3) develop a sincere rapport and respectful relationships. I feel safe because I'm confident that the equipment, instruments, and technology at my disposal are appropriate and adequate for gaining the students' interest, keeping the students actively engaged, and encouraging the students to express joy as they demonstrate their learning and understanding during our time together.

Suppose I knew, prior to entering the class, that the students might revolt and become violent toward me. This begs the question, "Would I still feel safe?" My answer is still a firm "yes." I'd still feel safe because I'm confident in my knowledge of the layout of the room, the location of the exits, and my physical strength. I'm confident in the skills and abilities I possess to defend myself against multiple attackers (especially those who possess a fraction of my size, strength, and fighting experience). I'm confident in my resolve to use the equipment, instruments, and technology both offensively and defensively, until help arrives, until I can exit the situation, or until the threat has stopped.

To say we must create "brave" spaces means we are intentionally creating environments that are inherently challenging, hostile, aggressive, terrorizing, intimidating, damaging, and traumatizing to the very people who we are expecting to be "brave." Why would we want to do this? Why would we want to create spaces in which a person or group of people has to struggle? Why would we see this as a way of

V. Actionable Steps

"being supportive" or "empowering" them? I'm just going to come right out and say it – That makes NO sense!

Some of you are probably thinking, and might say to me, *Brother Gordon, you're oversimplifying it.* To you, my reply is – Not at all. Those in positions of influence, dominance, and decision-making power are purposefully overcomplicating this sector of the fabricated ecosystems, to keep us distracted, disorganized, divided, and detached from one another.

...*Creating "Common Language"*

Earlier, I discussed the importance of language. As humans, we have fundamental methods of communication, both verbally and nonverbally. Despite the wide variety of spoken languages and dialects throughout the globe, we share facial expressions to indicate joy, sadness, angry, frustration; our body language conveys acceptance, rejection. With that said, attempts are consistently being made to "normalize" certain language and behaviors. Let's pause for a brief look at the process of normalizing. At its foundation, normalizing is based on "norms" which advance the agenda, goals, ideology, and objectives of a particular group, organization, or entity (typically those in positions of dominance, power, and influence).

In these United States of America, the need for a "common language" is frequently promoted in discussions of social justice and equity. Advocates argue that establishing standardized terminology fosters greater awareness and strengthens our collaborative efforts; equipping us to better identify, scrutinize, understand, and eliminate injustices. However, while the intention may be to create unity, the actual impact of enforcing a "common language" is detrimental to cultivating empathy and sustaining ecosystems for equity. This approach often imposes a single perspective that fails to capture the complexities of individual experiences, especially for marginalized groups. Additionally, an overemphasis on linguistic compliance shifts the focus away from genuine dialogue and hinders meaningful connections.

The concept of a "common language" is often driven by entities that already hold power, such as academic circles, media outlets, and corporate human resources departments. When language is reduced to a rigid framework dictated by the aforementioned entities, it minimizes complex, deeply personal experiences into simplified, pre-approved narratives. For instance, the use of generalized terms like "privilege" or "oppression" may fail to convey the multifaceted struggles of marginalized communities, leading to oversimplifications that don't reflect the lived realities of those most affected by these issues. As a result, language frameworks imposed by these elite entities may fail to resonate with, or reflect, the perspectives of those directly affected by social injustice.

Another strategic purpose for enforcing a "common language" relates to reinforcing a culture of linguistic policing rather than open listening and engagement. When linguistic compliance becomes a priority, individuals focus more on avoiding "incorrect" language than on engaging in meaningful conversations about the underlying issues. This shift leads to fear-based interactions, where people become hesitant to ask questions, admit gaps in knowledge, or discuss difficult topics openly.

I firmly believe that my students are genuinely curious about cultures – about people who have different ideas, beliefs, customs, traditions, speech patterns, dialects, accents, melanin levels, and lived experiences than they do. I believe said students honestly have good intentions in their desire to know more about these cultures; they want to ask questions in order to appreciate (not appropriate) these cultures; they're motivated by an admiration and respect for the cultures. I also believe, wholeheartedly, that they're afraid of saying the "wrong" thing. This fear stifles curiosity and the potential for growth. In settings where individuals are preoccupied with adhering to an approved script or vocabulary, the rich, nuanced

V. Actionable Steps

dialogue necessary for genuine understanding and empathy becomes compromised.

While language is undeniably important in shaping social discourse, it is ultimately a tool for communication, not a solution to institutional problems. The fixation on terminology diverts attention from the structural changes that are needed to achieve equity. For example, many corporations and organizations adopt inclusive language to project a progressive image, yet fail to implement the type of policy changes that substantively correct issues like financial disparity, underfunded education, unstable housing, unjust incarceration, inappropriate and inadequate healthcare, or racialized discrimination.

The focus on language serves as a smokescreen, a superficial commitment to equity and social justice, while continuing exploitative practices. When language becomes a substitute for action, the actual issues of inequality and injustice are left to fester. Rigid language requirements alienate potential accomplices who are genuinely interested in supporting social justice but might not be familiar with evolving terminology. For many, the complexity of language used in social justice and equity discussions creates barriers to entry. This makes it difficult for participants to engage with patience, grace and empathy.

I've had many friends and colleagues say to me, "I wasn't sure if I should have said something; I'm afraid of saying the wrong thing," after being in the presence of racialized, discriminatory, abusive, and traumatizing behaviors and language. I trust they have a sincere desire to confront, disrupt, and discourage such words and actions. However, they're afraid of using the "wrong" words. I believe any words and actions that support, edify, empower, strengthen, encourage, liberate, and free the oppressed, the enslaved, the intimidated, the marginalized, the discarded, the ignored, and the unappreciated are "right."

When individuals are shamed or dismissed for using outdated or unfamiliar language, they may feel discouraged from participating in discussions or taking action. Rather than fostering a welcoming environment for growth, this kind of linguistic exclusion creates an "in-group" mentality that limits the reach and impact of social movements; it contributes to creating an "us vs. them" dynamic rather than fostering collaboration and unity. Those who are adept at using approved terminology are exalted as morally superior, while those who struggle or reject these linguistic norms are unfairly labeled as indifferent, hostile, insensitive, "phobic," or traitors to the cause. This dynamic undermines the potential for collective action by creating atmospheres of judgment and exclusion rather than empathy and understanding.

Moreover, the over-reliance on specialized language creates echo chambers (insular spaces where only those with the same linguistic background feel comfortable participating). This limits the cross-cultural and cross-class communication that is crucial for the healthy transformation, and sustenance, of robust ecosystems. By restricting the flow of ideas and perspectives to a select group, we become disconnected from the broader society and less effective in our advocacy for change.

Another consequence of a rigid "common language" is the potential to detach activism from the everyday realities of those most affected by social injustices. People who face economic hardship, incarceration, or lack access to higher education may not have the time or resources to engage with complex academic or corporate terminology. By prioritizing linguistic conformity, advocates for justice and equity risk becoming disconnected from the very communities they aim to serve. Efforts that are more concerned with the "correct" language, than with practical action, alienate the very individuals whose lives need the most immediate attention.

To create a more inclusive and effective approach to cultivating empathy and sustaining ecosystems for equity, it's essential to prioritize lived experiences, open dialogue, and tangible action over terminology. Discussions must focus on understanding individuals' personal stories and lived

V. Actionable Steps

experiences, as much as the concrete actions required to correct institutional issues. Instead of policing language, activists, educators, accomplices, and advocates must encourage people to speak in their own words (using culturally familiar terms and phrases), allowing for more organic and meaningful dialogue.

We must inspire interactions that promote understanding, growth, and collective responsibility; opportunities for individuals to ask questions, make mistakes, and grow in their understanding of the issues. Instead of shaming people for using the "wrong" words, activists, educators, accomplices, and advocates must guide discussions with patience and empathy, recognizing that learning and growth are ongoing processes.

While language is a crucial tool for communication, the true measure of commitment to cultivating empathy and sustaining ecosystems for equity lies in policy changes, economic support, and community initiatives; advocacy, service, and education that fosters deeper and more meaningful engagement.

It's important that you consider how language is dynamic – it will naturally evolve in response to cultural and social shifts. As such, rigid definitions become outdated and exclusionary as our work to expand human rights progresses. By allowing language to evolve organically, prioritizing empathy, and encouraging open dialogue, you'll help sustain a more inclusive and equitable society that is responsive to the needs of all communities. You'll guide meaningful change where all voices are heard, all cultures are seen, and all perspectives are valued.

...Allyship

One of the core issues I see with the concept of allyship is this – it inherently focuses more on the individual or entity offering support, instead of the people or communities in need of said support. The term "ally" positions said figure as a supportive figure who can distance themselves from the struggles of marginalized communities. This positioning allows allies to express solidarity without significant risk to their own comfort, security, status, influence, or wealth. Instead of actively working to eliminate the structures of oppression, many allies operate within them.

Allies actually benefit (economically and/or socially), while offering occasional acts of sympathy or outrage. This makes their language and behaviors performative, ineffective, and ultimately deceptive. Beneath the surface of well-meaning gestures and public declarations, allyship fails to bring about real structural change. The narrative of allyship allows individuals to claim a moral high ground without requiring any meaningful actions, institutional changes, or risks. The framework of allyship prioritizes comfort over commitment and optics over outcomes. True equity, liberation, and freedom cannot be achieved through passive or symbolic gestures.

For example, there were allies who supported the colonies during the Revolutionary War, with financial backing, food, equipment, and other resources. However, they did so in secret, without revealing their identities until the war had been won. Likewise, the allies who helped to liberate enslaved Africans, and their descendants, were not publicly known until they chose to disclose their support. There were no signs posted to state "Underground railroad stops at this location." In this modern era, allies attend protests or share social media posts, calling for justice, without significantly disrupting their own daily lives or challenging the structures that grant them privileges and advantages. As such, the ally's role remains passive, perpetuating the idea that equity and justice is to be achieved through performative gestures rather than transformative action. In each instance, these allies could claim and maintain plausible deniability.

What's needed is a shift from being allies to being accomplices – individuals and entities that actively eliminate structures of oppression, discrimination; working alongside marginalized groups with shared risk, responsibility, and accountability. Exploring the limitations and failures of

V. Actionable Steps

allyship will emphasize the need for true accomplices; those with "skin in the game," committed to cultivating empathy and sustaining ecosystems for equity.

Unlike accomplices, who are held accountable for their actions and are willing to face the consequences of their involvement, allies often lack accountability. Allies can choose when to participate in activism and when to disengage, without facing the daily institutionalized consequences that marginalized communities endure. For example, an individual might champion anti-racism on social media but return to their routine, unaffected by the structural inequalities that persist. This lack of accountability enables individuals to engage with social justice superficially, often with the primary motivation of appearing "woke" or socially conscious, rather than enacting actual change.

The ease with which allies can step in and out of movements perpetuates the cycle where social justice becomes an aesthetic or a trend, rather than a sustained effort to confront and eliminate oppression, discrimination, and exclusion. To borrow a phrase from one of my brothers…this prevents moments from becoming movements. Consequently, allyship becomes more about gaining social capital than making actual contributions toward structural change. In this framework, the interests of marginalized communities are often sidelined in favor of maintaining a sense of personal moral superiority for the ally. Allyship often falls short of manifesting true institutional change and actively harms the very movements it supposedly to support. This occurs in several ways, including co-opting struggles without creating meaningful shifts in power, tokenizing marginalized individuals, and gatekeeping narratives.

Throughout history, movements for equity and social justice have been weakened by allies who, despite professing support for the cause, ultimately upheld the existing power structures. A clear example can be seen in the Civil Rights Movement, where "white" citizens, who saw themselves as allies to "black" Americans, often resisted more radical demands for institutional changes. These allies were willing to support changes that didn't challenge the deeply entrenched racialized hierarchies, thus ensuring that the status quo remained intact.

Similarly, modern corporate and political allyship has manifested as diversity statements, awareness campaigns, and symbolic gestures such as "Awareness" and "History" month celebrations. While these actions might raise awareness, they do little to address the underlying power imbalances in society. This type of allyship fails to redistribute power and resources, instead allowing institutions to maintain the structures that perpetuate inequality and disparity. Without concrete policy changes or institutional reforms, such symbolic acts ultimately offer little more than a veneer of progress.

Allyship also amplifies the practice of elevating a few individuals from marginalized groups to serve as representatives while leaving the structural causes untouched (aka tokenism). This process creates the illusion of equity and inclusion but doesn't concentrate on rectifying the root causes of oppression, inequality, and unfair treatment. Although companies, organizations, and entities showcase diverse individuals in leadership positions, the underlying disparities in wealth, opportunity, and justice remain. Token representation in leadership or the media often serves as a superficial response to reform the economic and social ecosystems for equity; it distracts from the deeper, more uncomfortable work of eliminating the languages and behaviors that cause oppression, exclusion, and destruction.

Another flaw in allyship is the tendency for allies to position themselves as gatekeepers. As such, they decide which voices will be amplified and which forms of resistance are acceptable, effectively controlling the narrative. This gatekeeping leads to the silencing of more radical voices that call for profound transformation. The insistence on maintaining respectability and acceptability stifles innovative solutions to injustice and alienates those pushing for more transformative changes. When allies control the dialogue, they perpetuate the

V. Actionable Steps

structures of power they claim to oppose, ensuring that no fundamental challenge to existing systems occurs.

Transitioning from an allyship perspective to an accomplice mindset is important for cultivating empathy and sustaining ecosystems for equity. While allies express support, accomplices go further by actively working to disrupt and destroy oppressive behaviors and language, even at personal cost. An accomplice isn't merely a supportive bystander but an active participant in the fight for liberation. This role demands a deep commitment to justice for all, to seeing the humanity in everyone, and to recognizing that liberation is a shared struggle.

Accomplices understand that true solidarity requires personal risk and sacrifice, as their efforts must directly confront the structures that support and maintain discrimination, oppression, inequality, and disparity. For example, accomplices openly organize protests, boldly confront discriminatory practices within their own communities, or publicly provide financial and logistical support to grassroots movements. An accomplice's commitment requires a willingness to challenge the very structures that elevate their own status, influence, and wealth, rather than simply offering passive support.

The key difference between allies and accomplices is their approach to power. While allies often focus on symbolic gestures, accomplices work to dismantle and eradicate existing power structures by redistributing resources, empowering marginalized communities, and amplifying disenfranchised voices. Accomplices don't merely benefit from status, influence, and wealth; they leverage it to actively challenge injustice.

An accomplice's role involves risk, demonstrated by engaging in direct action, refusing to comply with discriminatory or dismissive policies, or facing potential professional or personal repercussions. True accomplices bravely accept the consequences of their actions; they understand that cultivating empathy and sustaining ecosystems for equity requires standing up to intimidation, exploitation, appropriation, and eradication at great personal cost. This willingness to face adversity underscores their deep commitment to the liberation of marginalized communities.

True liberation is a collective effort that cannot be achieved through individual action alone. Accomplices work to build community-based networks of resistance that are interconnected and sustainable. They focus on grassroots movements, mutual aid, and transforming structures to empower marginalized groups. By rejecting the politics of respectability, accomplices advocate for radical, transformative change rather than conforming to mainstream norms.

Accomplices also commit to continuous self-education and reflection. They recognize that their role is not to "save" marginalized communities (known as the "white savior" complex) but to stand alongside them and listen. This process of learning and evolving ensures that your activism remains relevant and aligned with the needs of the movement. Accomplices are open to critique, able and willing to acknowledge mistakes, actively engaged in adapting approaches to ensure consistent support. Long-lasting, transformative progress can only be achieved by shifting from allyship to becoming accomplices.

6. …and C.E.A.S.E. for Equity

I'd be buggin' (aka fooling myself aka crazy) if I thought everyone reading this was thinking, "Yeah, you're right…that's exactly what we need to do!" I'm sure there are more than a few who are thinking, "Come on, Michael! You expect us to just stop doing things that have been done for years…decades…centuries even? We can't just cease all of these destructive and disingenuous behaviors immediately; we can't, all of a sudden, desist from the language and behaviors that are now imbedded into who we are as a nation!" My response (as my youngest son might say) – That's cap (in other words, that's a lie)!!

V. Actionable Steps

To prove my point, that you and I can stop the language and behaviors that cause the deterioration of the natural and man-made, ecosystems, think of a diet fad…any of them. People immediately change their eating habits for a desired result (e.g. more energy, weight loss, medical requirements etc.). This mindset to change started with a drop (an idea), increased to a ripple (a localized community of people developed), and (many times) flooded theses United States of America as a nationwide phenomenon (impacting the social and economic ecosystems). Accountability groups formed, in person and on social media, with participants eager to share the work they're "putting in," the progress they're making, the positive impact of their choices, and persuasive reasons for others to do the same.

So don't tell me that you can't choose to immediately disrupt the offensive, abusive, traumatizing, violent, and destructive words and actions that occur around you. I'm directing this at the man in the mirror first - *can't* really means *won't*. An amazing and wonderful aspect of being human is your ability to adapt and change for the better – to desist and cease from the behaviors and language that polarize us, weaken us, and destroy us as a human race.

Unlike "desist," which often implies your voluntary or moral refusal to continue, "cease" may result from internal decisions, external pressures, natural exhaustion, or forceful imposition. In both of the man-made ecosystems (economic and social), the act of ceasing has profound implications – it means immediately ending unsustainable practices and social norms (elimination), redistributing wealth and resources (reformation), and precipitating structural shifts (transformation). Let your ceasing signal 1) your commitment to rethinking your language, behaviors, and relationships, 2) your willingness to support and apply innovative approaches, 3) and your moral turning point.

It's my hope that you now have a more sympathetic realization about how life for residents of impoverished communities has long been defined by the struggle for survival, due to melanin levels, cultural backgrounds, and/or religious/communal beliefs. Financial instability, institutional oppression, discriminatory procedures, and historical injustices have fostered a mindset of mistrust, fear, scarcity, competition, and self-preservation. While these instincts may have been necessary in times of hardship, they're traumatizing. They ultimately become barriers to progress, preventing people from forming the connections and collaborations necessary for long-term health, peace, and prosperity.

To build thriving communities, we must transform the fabricated ecosystems – transition from a survival mindset to one focused on collective empowerment; prioritizing trust, cooperation, mutual respect; sincerely acting and speaking in ways that acknowledge, celebrate, highlight, honor, and appreciate (not appropriate) the humanity in each person. The remainder of this book is dedicated to steps for making the shift to positively impact the liberation, freedom, and empowerment experienced by future generations.

Build Trust and Strengthen Social Bonds

Trust is the foundation of collaboration; the foundation of any strong, resilient communities. Without it, individuals hesitate to invest in their communities, fearing exploitation or disappointment. Trust emboldens individuals to take collective risks, and nurture environments that serve the common good. In environments shaped by uncertainty, inequality, or past harm, rebuilding trust becomes essential. Cultivating trust requires intentional effort, grounded in transparency, relationship-building, and consistent, ethical leadership. When these elements come together, they strengthen the social fabric and create opportunities for collective success.

The first step toward cultivating trust is establishing transparency. Open communication about shared goals, available resources, and current challenges helps reduce suspicion and prevent misinformation. When individuals and organizations are clear about their intentions and processes, it invites participation and reinforces mutual respect.

V. Actionable Steps

Transparency builds confidence, especially when people feel seen, heard, and included in influencing decisions that affect their lives.

Next, it's essential to prioritize relationship-building. Communities thrive when people know and support one another. Investing in social connections through mentorship programs, community events, and networking opportunities develops a sense of belonging and shared responsibility. These bonds become especially important in times of stress or uncertainty, instances when trust in institutions wavers. In such times, intimate interpersonal relationships remain a powerful force for cohesion.

Trust is also reinforced through demonstrated consistency and integrity. Leaders, whether formal or informal, must uphold ethical standards and follow through on commitments. Reliability signals accountability and builds credibility over time. Inconsistent actions or broken promises, by contrast, quickly unravel the trust that takes so long to build. These principles come to life through practical community initiatives that increase opportunities, not lengthy legislation that employs complex and specialized language (aimed at making it difficult for the general public to comprehend).

For example, community investment groups, where members pool resources to support local businesses, encourage collaboration and financial empowerment rooted in mutual benefit. Mentorship programs offer guidance and support, especially for young entrepreneurs or emerging leaders, providing the benefit of established wisdom and encouragement. Additionally, hosting regular community forums, to discuss economic development or local issues, informs residents while reinforcing their role as active participants in shaping their shared future.

Cultivating trust is not a one-time effort, but a continuous practice rooted in openness, connection, and accountability. As communities 1) engage in transparent communication, 2) deepen relationships, and 3) model ethical leadership, they create conditions where collaboration will flourish and collective visions become a daily reality.

Emphasize Collective Success Over Individual Gain

A collaborative mindset shifts the focus from "I must succeed alone" to "We can succeed together – Sí, se puede!" By working together, individuals can access resources, skills, and opportunities that would be unattainable in isolation. Transforming the economic ecosystem, to liberate and empower marginalized communities, requires more than isolated programs – it demands a holistic, grassroots approach that integrates education, investment, infrastructure, and cultural transformation. When communities are equipped with the tools to understand and navigate financial systems, support their own businesses, and reshape narratives around wealth and success, sustainable change becomes possible. Below are key strategies for building economic strength from within, anchored in practical action and community leadership.

Transformational change requires action across multiple sectors. A strong foundation in financial literacy is critical for economic empowerment. With that said, school curricula must be reformed to prioritize essential knowledge about saving and investing, emphasize entrepreneurship, and stress the importance of circulating money within the local economy. Faith-based institutions and community leaders must model transparency and become champions for economic initiatives that are community-centered. These early interventions will help young people see economic participation as both accessible and achievable.

In the realm of culture and entertainment, artists and musicians hold significant influence and must use their platforms to promote self-reliance, investment, and empowerment. Food and business cooperatives, such as community gardens and local markets, can offer models of self-sufficiency and reduce dependence on outside systems. Finally, mentorship is critical! Established business owners

V. Actionable Steps

must take the lead in guiding and supporting emerging entrepreneurs, offering not just advice, but access to networks, opportunities, and confidence.

In addition to education, grants and microloans tailored to local entrepreneurs will diminish barriers to entry for small business creation. Access to capital, especially when combined with training, equips aspiring business owners with the resources they need to start and grow sustainable enterprises. Business training workshops, offered regularly and rooted in the specific needs of the community, will increase long-term capacity and promote self-sufficiency.

Support for local businesses must also extend to visibility and public perception. Organizing "Buy Local" campaigns encourages residents to invest in their own economies, which keeps dollars circulating within the community. Utilizing digital tools, like social media and online marketplaces, allows local entrepreneurs to reach broader audiences and compete in wider markets. Partnering with community leaders, influencers, and trusted voices will further enhance the success of these businesses and build public trust. Rebranding local commerce as high-quality, innovative, and culturally relevant builds pride in local achievement and increases sales.

Physical environments shape economic behavior as well. Investment in infrastructure (street lighting, accessible parking, public spaces that are inviting and aesthetically appealing etc.) will transform how people engage with local businesses. When commercial districts feel safe and welcoming, they attract both customers and investors. In tandem with physical upgrades, strengthening community-based policing and safety initiatives will reduce crime and increase the sense of security necessary for commerce to thrive. Urban development projects that revitalize neglected commercial areas will breathe new life into local economies, particularly when driven by community vision and participation.

Economic empowerment also involves shifting the cultural narratives that define what success looks like. Highlighting the stories of community-based entrepreneurs, particularly those who have succeeded through local collaboration and sustainable practices, helps reshape aspirations. Creating media platforms that celebrate these achievements will inspire the next generation of change makers. Storytelling through film, music, art, and literature is a powerful tool in rewriting the narrative of inner-city and historically marginalized communities. These stories show that wealth isn't only about personal gain but about reinvesting in the community, building legacy, and fostering collective growth.

The reluctance of impoverished communities to invest in themselves and their preference for external spending is deeply rooted in historical trauma, psychological barriers, consumer conditioning, and financial limitations. Therefore, economic empowerment isn't a one-size-fits-all solution, but a multifaceted approach rooted in local wisdom, cultural pride, and practical tools. By weaving together education, investment, infrastructure, storytelling, and leadership, communities can break cycles of economic exclusion and build futures defined by shared success and sustainable prosperity.

<u>Value the Humanity in Each Other</u>

In a world marked by rapid change and persistent injustices, the need for empathy in public life has never been more urgent. Empathy allows individuals to understand and appreciate the experiences of others, leading to policies and behaviors that promote fairness and inclusion. When empathy becomes a core social value, it transforms how communities make decisions, how leaders govern, and how individuals relate to one another. A society rooted in empathy does more than just encourage kindness; it develops more intimate connections, more thoughtful leadership, and creates the conditions in which ecosystems for equity thrive.

V. Actionable Steps

A truly empathetic society begins by valuing diverse perspectives. When people with different backgrounds, experiences, and worldviews are part of influencing the decisions being made, communities become richer and more innovative. Diversity of thought and experience fuels creative problem-solving, ensuring that policies and initiatives reflect the realities of all, not just a privileged few.

In addition to embracing diversity, an empathetic society actively concentrates on institutional injustices. Empathy enables individuals, organizations, and entities to recognize the deep-rooted inequalities that exist due to history, policy, and prejudice. This awareness is not passive! Through empathy, your soul is moved to confront racialized inequality, poverty, and exclusion – not as distant problems, but as urgent, shared responsibilities. Corrective measures, such as policy reform, reparative investments, and inclusive practices, become possible when society sees inequity through a human lens.

Empathy also lays the foundation for compassionate leadership. Leaders, guided by empathy, understand that their decisions affect real people with complex needs and lived experiences. Rather than serving the interests of entities and individuals in positions of power, influence, status, and wealth, empathetic leaders prioritize the well-being of all members of society. They listen, adapt, and act with care to nurture trust and unity, especially in times of crisis.

To cultivate empathy as a cultural norm, communities must adopt intentional strategies. One powerful approach is community dialogue and active listening. Open forums where individuals speak honestly about their concerns, identities, and aspirations create opportunities for mutual respect and inclusive decision-making. These dialogues not only promote empathy but also empower communities to shape their futures collectively.

This strategy also incorporates storytelling and shared narratives. When people share personal experiences, others are given the opportunity to step into someone else's shoes, breaking down stereotypes and replacing judgment with understanding. Stories are powerful mirrors, windows, and sliding glass doors[16] – they humanize issues that statistics alone cannot.

Finally, long-term change requires educational initiatives centered on social and emotional learning. Schools and organizations must integrate lessons on empathy, emotional intelligence, restorative practices, and ethical leadership into their programs. Teaching children and adults how to recognize emotions, resolve conflicts, and care for others lays the groundwork for a more compassionate and resilient society – it's about R.A.C.E. (Reflective Attitudes Cultivating Empathy).

I believe becoming an empathetic society isn't a "pie in the sky" utopian ideal. It's a practical, powerful vision rooted in justice, connection, and care. By valuing diverse voices, confronting institutional harm, and fostering compassionate leadership, communities will build structures that reflect the dignity of all people. And with the help of storytelling, dialogue, and education, empathy can be cultivated not just as a feeling, but as a driving force for societal transformation.

<u>Shift to a Collaborative Mindset</u>

Sustainable ecosystems thrive when knowledge and resources are passed from one generation to the next. Encouraging mentorship, apprenticeships, and cultural preservation ensures that future generations inherit pillars for success. Education in marginalized communities is often shaped by a scarcity mentality, amplified by limited resources, underfunded schools, and the pressure to achieve solely for personal success rather than collective growth. This encourages competition rather than collaboration and discourages stakeholders from seeing learning as a communal effort.

As society becomes increasingly interconnected, the need for a collaborative mindset within educational spaces has never been more vital. Traditional models that emphasize individual achievement and competition often overlook the

V. Actionable Steps

power of collective growth and mutual support. Shifting toward a collaborative approach in education encourages students to see their success as intertwined with the success of their peers and communities. This shift in thinking cultivates empathy and nurtures a sense of shared responsibility, thus preparing students for a more cooperative world.

One of the foundational elements of this shift is promoting collective learning. When students are encouraged to work together, share resources, and approach education as a communal effort, they begin to see learning not just as a personal accomplishment, but as a tool to uplift others. Collaborative learning environments build problem-solving skills, improve communication, and reflect real-world dynamics where cooperation often leads to the best outcomes. This mindset helps students understand that knowledge is most powerful when it is shared and used to strengthen entire communities.

Equally important is the role of teaching empathy through intentional curriculum design. Incorporating social-emotional learning (SEL) into school communities allows stakeholders to explore and understand diverse perspectives, manage emotions, and build meaningful relationships. By learning to listen deeply and consider the experiences of others, students develop the emotional intelligence needed to collaborate effectively and resolve conflict. Empathy is the cornerstone of a collaborative mindset, fostering inclusion and reducing the divisions that hinder collective progress.

To support this transformation, schools must implement mentorship programs that connect students with trusted guides and role models. These mentors provide academic or career advice, in addition to modeling what it means to lead with empathy, share success, and build trust. Mentorship relationships reinforce the idea that achievement is not a solo endeavor, it's the result of support, encouragement, and collaboration across generations and communities.

Shifting to a collaborative mindset in education is about more than group projects or teamwork; it is about reimagining the purpose of learning itself. When education becomes a tool for communal advancement rather than individual escape, it cultivates trust, empathy, and a desire to reinvest knowledge back into the community. For example, music and art are often seen as competitive fields where individual success is prioritized. The entertainment industry thrives on exclusivity, leading many artists to believe that only a few can succeed while others must struggle. By embracing collaboration in the arts, we will transform creative spaces into environments that foster community wealth, trust, and emotional connection.

In our society, shaped by competition and individualism, the arts provide a power model for how we can progress as a human race – a model rooted in collaboration, empathy, and shared purpose. Shifting to a collaborative mindset within creative spaces means moving away from zero-sum thinking and toward collective expression and mutual growth. The fine and performing arts provide opportunities for students to truly be expressive of their cultural beliefs, practices, norms, and traditions. With intentional planning, the fine and performing arts help break down barriers, build trust, and connect people through shared stories and emotional resonance.

I think back to when we were in quarantine, during the height of the COVID-19 pandemic. We were seeking opportunities and ways to reconnect with friends, families, loved ones, and those we viewed as important to our well-being (baristas, clerks, dog walkers etc.). I recall how the television commercials and advertisements focused on ways to stay connected – cooking together (culinary arts), dancing, singing, and making crafts together. The fine and performing arts were amplified as essential for uplifting our souls, boosting our morale, amplifying hope, and improving the human condition.

Community-based art initiatives are a way to foster this shift to a collaborative mindset. They support spaces where artists are encouraged to work together, rather than compete for recognition or resources. By focusing on the collective creation

V. Actionable Steps

of murals, public installations, workshops, or interdisciplinary projects, communities can reclaim public spaces and build solidarity through shared expression. Such initiatives offer more than artistic value; they become hubs for dialogue, healing, and collaboration, making art a tool for both cultural enrichment and social cohesion.

I'm a witness as to the power that music has for shifting mindsets. When used with intention, it serves as a force for connection rather than division. Using music to build trust involves writing and performing songs that uplift shared experiences, reflect community values, and create a sense of belonging. In contrast to music that reinforces harmful stereotypes or glorifies violence and division, trust-building music invites listeners reflect on our shared humanity. Whether performed at community gatherings, protests, or intimate venues, this kind of music fosters deeper relationships and collective understanding.

Beyond performance, music also acts as a tool for empathy. Through storytelling – whether through lyrics, rhythm, or soundscapes – music offers a unique window into the thoughts, beliefs, experiences, and traditions of others. Songs that highlight diverse struggles and triumphs invite listeners to step outside their own experiences and into the shoes of another. In doing so, they expand our capacity for compassion and challenge the cultural narratives that often keep us divided. Music becomes more than entertainment; it becomes an instrument for social connection and emotional transformation.

Shifting to a collaborative mindset through art and music is about reimagining creative expression as a shared journey rather than a solitary pursuit. When artists and musicians work together, reflecting the richness of collective experience, they contribute to stronger and more empathetic communities. In a time that desperately needs unity and healing, collaborative creativity offers a powerful path forward.

C.E.A.S.E. for Equity

In these times of social division and environmental crisis, communities are increasingly seeking ways to reconnect with the earth and with one another. One of the most powerful and grounded expressions of this shift – moving beyond individual gain toward collective well-being – can be found in the practice of gardening. Through careful cultivation, sustainable education, and a shared understanding, gardens offer more than food – they offer a model for how communities can thrive together. Community gardens exemplify this shift in action.

In many impoverished areas, food insecurity leads to a scarcity mentality, causing individuals to prioritize immediate needs over long-term sustainability. Community members may struggle to trust shared land projects, fearing exploitation or lack of access. By establishing shared green spaces where food is grown not for profit but for collective nourishment, neighborhoods create opportunities for cooperation, mutual care, and food sovereignty. These gardens become habitats where people of all ages and backgrounds can gather, work side by side, and share in the rewards of their labor. They help reframe food not as a commodity, but as a communal right, grown and distributed with equity in mind.

Integral to the success of these spaces is the practice of teaching sustainable methods. As community members learn about soil health, composting, native plants, and biodiversity, they come to understand how long-term abundance depends on thoughtful, regenerative choices. Education about sustainable practices empowers people to take ownership of their environment while emphasizing the importance of working together. In these spaces, collaboration is a social value as well as an ecological necessity.

Beyond the physical benefits, gardens also serve as a powerful metaphor for community building. A strong and healthy community requires time, care, and shared responsibility to flourish, just as a garden does. The process of planting, watering, and nurturing teaches patience and resilience. It reminds you that meaningful change often comes

V. Actionable Steps

from sustained, collective effort –healthy growth is never instant. Tending to a garden becomes a way of tending to each other.

In a world that often prizes speed, ownership, and competition, gardens invite us to slow down, share, and collaborate. They provide a practical approach to speaking and behaving, in addition to nourishment. Gardening presents us with opportunities to transform our way of thinking, speaking, and behaving; actions rooted in care, interdependence, and sustainability. When communities embrace gardening as both practice and metaphor, the residents shift toward a mindset that values collective growth and honors the interconnectedness of all life. Shifting from an extractive to a regenerative approach will help communities build trust and self-sufficiency while ensuring long-term food security.

In many societies, strength is often framed as an individual's ability to dominate, win, or survive alone. We simplify it into one word – power. A survival-based approach to martial arts often focuses on dominance and fear, reinforcing the idea that one must always be on guard against others. I experienced this feeling during most of my visit to India – I was always on guard for pickpockets, hustlers, and anyone seeking to take advantage of me. I began to change my perspective, and consequently my behavior, when my close friend explained it to me this way. She said, "In the States, you're taught 'stranger danger,' so you don't trust anyone until they've proven themselves trustworthy. Here, in India, we teach our children to trust everyone, until they show themselves to be untrustworthy."

This survival-based mindset can extend into daily interactions, creating defensive and distrustful communities. However, shifting to a collaborative mindset challenges this notion by redefining strength as the capacity to uplift, protect, and connect with others. The martial arts, though traditionally associated with combat, offers a powerful pathway to cultivating discipline, mutual respect, and community. When practiced intentionally, the martial arts become a tool for personal growth and social cohesion rather than competition or aggression.

One of the foundational values in this shift is mutual respect and trust. In martial arts, practitioners are taught that true strength lies not in overpowering others but in understanding them. Respect for one's training partners, instructors, and even opponents is central to every session. This type of environment teaches that strength is the responsibility to protect others, offer support, and act with integrity. When you internalize this lesson, you begin to see collaboration and care as integral to your personal development.

Another core aspect of the collaborative mindset is conflict resolution. Contrary to popular belief, the martial arts don't promote violence, they teach you how to manage your language and behaviors. Through disciplined practice, you learn patience, self-awareness, and emotional regulation. Techniques are taught not just to win fights, but to avoid them. In this way, the martial arts cultivate understanding and empathy, helping practitioners respond to conflict with thoughtfulness rather than aggression. You begin to understand that peace often requires more strength than combat.

Furthermore, martial arts training often takes place in group environments where community is built through shared discipline. These spaces emphasize mentorship, cooperation, and mutual encouragement. Whether it's a more experienced student helping a beginner or a class working together to reach a common goal, training in the martial arts reinforces the idea that progress is most sustainable when it is supported by others.

By reframing strength as something that serves others rather than just the self, the martial arts offer a powerful model for shifting to a collaborative mindset. Through respect, disciplined conflict resolution, and shared training environments, you learn that community and connection are at the heart of true power. This collective energy fosters belonging and reinforces the collaborative values that extend

V. Actionable Steps

far beyond the dojo or gym – it reveals the path toward deeper empathy, cooperation, and social transformation.

As a church leader, I think of how many faith-based communities have been shaped by histories of persecution and struggle, leading to insular thinking and divisions even within marginalized groups. Fear-based theology reinforces distrust of outsiders or other faith traditions.

These United States of America are divided by cultural, religious, and ideological differences – the call for deeper connection and shared purpose is more urgent than ever! One of the most powerful, yet often overlooked, vehicles for cultivating a collaborative mindset is faith. When practiced with openness and empathy, faith traditions transcend boundaries and serve as bridges between individuals and communities.

Interfaith and community solidarity is a critical starting point. Rather than allowing theological differences to create division, communities must come together through shared values such as compassion, justice, and service. Building bridges between different religious and cultural groups fosters mutual respect and creates opportunities for collaboration on pressing social issues. Interfaith initiatives (e.g. joint service projects, dialogue circles, or shared worship experiences) model the power of unity in diversity and demonstrate that collaboration is possible and deeply enriching.

This makes me think of the many interfaith services that occurred during 2020, following the murder of George Floyd and others by law enforcement officers. I know of Catholic, Jewish, and Protestant faith leaders who came together in solidarity, encouraging listeners to be peaceful, acknowledge and honor our shared humanity, and be loving toward everyone. I'm pleased to mention there are interfaith initiatives that continue to this day, aimed at identifying and eradicating racialized social issues.

At the heart of this shift to a collaborative mindset is the understanding of faith as a source of empathy. Many spiritual teachings emphasize the presence of the divine in every person. To truly recognize God (i.e. the sacredness) in others requires more than tolerance; it demands love, trust, and a commitment to understanding perspectives that differ from our own. This spiritual empathy breaks down barriers of ignorance, fear, and prejudice, encouraging you to speak and act in ways that affirm the dignity and humanity of all people. Moreover, reimagining the church as a community hub brings this collaborative mindset into tangible, everyday practice.

Making this shifting through faith isn't about abandoning doctrine but about deepening our commitment to unity, justice, empathy, and sustaining ecosystems for equity. Places of worship must serve beyond their traditional roles by becoming spaces for education, economic support, and collective healing. From hosting financial literacy workshops and community organizing meetings, to offering counseling and food distribution, churches and other faith centers have the potential to be engines of local empowerment.

By opening their doors and broadening their missions, these institutions become vital spaces where community resilience and shared progress are nurtured. When spirituality is practiced as a means of collective elevation, rather than separation, faith communities become strongholds of compassion, sanctuaries for the soul, catalysts for social change, and beacons of our shared humanity.

Breaking the cycle of economic hesitation and external spending in impoverished communities requires a multifaceted approach that concentrates on historical ***and*** internalized barriers.

<u>Sustain Ecosystems for Equity</u>

To create a just and inclusive society, communities must move beyond temporary fixes and develop sustainable structures that promote fairness, shared power, financial durability, lasting opportunity, and peace. Ecosystems for equity don't form by chance! Read that part again and let it saturate your soul.... Ecosystems for equity are developed and

V. Actionable Steps

sustained through intentional design, collective ownership, and policy transformation. At the heart of this effort lies a commitment to both justice and institutional accountability.

One of the most impactful ways to sustain ecosystems for equity is through the creation of worker cooperatives. These are businesses owned and operated by employees themselves, ensuring fair wages and shared decision-making. In worker co-ops, power is distributed among those who contribute daily to the business's success, rather than concentrated in the hands of distant owners. This structure helps reduce income inequality, builds a sense of dignity in work, and strengthens local economies.

In addition to worker ownership, communities thrive when they control and benefit from community-owned assets. Housing cooperatives, urban farms, and locally governed public resources provide stability, resilience, and pathways to build generational wealth. These shared assets reduce reliance on outside investors and help insulate neighborhoods from displacement and economic exploitation. They also foster a spirit of mutual care and responsibility that contributes to long-term social cohesion.

Ethical investment strategies are also essential. Redirecting capital toward businesses, initiatives, and infrastructure that prioritize community well-being (rather than short-term profit) ensures that wealth serves people, not the other way around. Investing in 1) renewable energy, 2) affordable and inclusive housing, and 3) appropriate and adequate healthcare services creates cultural and financial returns, while aligning economic growth with community values.

However, truly equitable ecosystems require more than community-based initiatives; they demand institutional changes and policy reforms to eradicate structural inequalities at the root. Governments and institutions must take bold steps to correct historic and ongoing injustices. This includes ensuring equal access to quality, and affordable, education, healthcare, and housing, all of which are foundational to long-term opportunity, stability, and success. Without these rights, individuals and families are unable to participate fully in society or reach their potential.

Moreover, policies must be in place to protect workers and ensure fair wages across industries. This means strengthening labor laws, enforcing workplace protections, and supporting unionization efforts that give voice to marginalized workers. Equitable labor policies create more inclusive and stable economies, and raise living standards.

Finally, it's essential to eradicate discriminatory practices in sectors of housing, employment, healthcare, education, nutrition, and criminal justice. Inequities and disparities in these areas have been reinforced since the inception of these United States of America. Communities will begin to heal and rebuild trust only through deliberate transformative efforts.

Sustaining ecosystems for equity is not a passive endeavor; it requires active participation, structural redesign, and moral clarity. By developing community-driven economic models and implementing policy reforms that challenge inequality, communities will create a future where fairness and opportunity aren't privileges, but shared realities. This work is ongoing, moment by moment. It's rooted in our collective belief that justice becomes possible – it's inevitable – when people have the power to shape their own futures.

By 1) embracing our shared humanity, 2) strengthening social bonds, and 3) nurturing trust, financial literacy, community support and infrastructure development, communities will create self-sustaining social and economic ecosystems that uplift everyone. Through education, mentorship, spirituality, discipline, and the arts, communities will strengthen the social root systems necessary for freedom to saturate every household. Full liberation requires a collective effort. With strategic action and a shift in mindset, sustainable growth and prosperity are within reach.

When we see each other not as competitors but as partners in growth, we cultivate empathy. This reflexive

V. Actionable Steps

attitude will establish communities that thrive not just for today but for generations to come. When individuals see value in investing in their own 'hoods – transforming impoverished communities into thriving hubs of innovation, commerce, and collective prosperity – they empower themselves and future generations to sustain ecosystems for equity. The time to build that future is now.

REFERENCES

1 Collaborative for Academic, Social, and Emotional Learning (CASEL*). Core SEL Competencies.* CASEL, https://casel.org/fundamentals-of-sel/what-is-the-casel-framework/

2 Rizzolatti, G., & Craighero, L. (2004). The mirror-neuron system. *Annual Review of Neuroscience, 27*, 169-192.

3 Singer, T., Seymour, B., O'Doherty, J., Kaube, H., Dolan, R. J., & Frith, C. D. (2004). Empathy for pain involves the affective but not sensory components of pain. *Science, 303*(5661), 1157-1162.

4 Decety, J., & Meyer, M. (2008). From emotion resonance to empathic understanding: A social developmental neuroscience account. *Development and Psychopathology, 20*(4), 1053-1080.

5 Hurlemann, R., Patin, A., Onur, O. A., Cohen, M. X., Baumgartner, T., Metzler, S., ... & Kendrick, K. M. (2010). Oxytocin enhances amygdala-dependent, socially reinforced learning and emotional empathy in humans. *The Journal of Neuroscience, 30*(14), 4999-5007.

6 Barraza, J. A., & Zak, P. J. (2009). Empathy toward strangers triggers oxytocin release and subsequent generosity. *Annals of the New York Academy of Sciences, 1167*(1), 182-189.

7 Figley, C. R. (2002). Compassion fatigue: Psychotherapists' chronic lack of self-care. *Journal of Clinical Psychology, 58*(11), 1433-1441.

8 Dimberg, U., Thunberg, M., & Elmehed, K. (2000). Unconscious facial reactions to emotional facial expressions. *Psychological Science, 11*(1), 86-89.

9 Frith, C. D., & Frith, U. (2003). Development and neurophysiology of mentalizing. *Philosophical Transactions of the Royal Society of London. Series B: Biological Sciences, 358*(1431), 459-473.

10 Premack, D., & Woodruff, G. (1978). Does the chimpanzee have a theory of mind? *Behavioral and Brain Sciences, 1*(4), 515-526.

11 Shamay-Tsoory, S. G., Aharon-Peretz, J., & Perry, D. (2009). Two systems for empathy: A double dissociation between emotional and cognitive empathy in inferior frontal gyrus versus ventromedial prefrontal lesions. *Brain, 132*(3), 617-627.

12 Decety, J., & Lamm, C. (2006). Human empathy through the lens of social neuroscience. *The Scientific World Journal, 6*, 1146-1163.

13 Harbaugh, W. T., Mayr, U., & Burghart, D. R. (2007). Neural responses to taxation and voluntary giving reveal motives for charitable donations. *Science, 316*(5831), 1622-1625.

14 Ice Cube. *"Check Yo Self." The Predator*, Priority Records, 1992.

15 United States Holocaust Memorial Museum. *History of the Swastika*.
https://encyclopedia.ushmm.org/content/en/article/history-of-the-swastika

16 Chappelle, Dave. *Sticks & Stones*. Netflix, 2019

17 Style, Emily. "Curriculum as Window and Mirror." Listening for All Voices, edited by Eleanor L. Lee et al., National SEED Project, 1988.

Bishop, Rudine Sims. "Mirrors, Windows, and Sliding Glass Doors." *Perspectives: Choosing and Using Books for the Classroom*, vol. 6, no. 3, Summer 1990, pp. ix–xi.

18 Connecticut General Assembly. *Public Act No. 17-111: An Act Concerning Hate Crimes*.
https://cga.ct.gov/2017/SUM/2017SUM00111-R02HB-05743-SUM.htm

19 Connecticut General Statutes § 53a-181i. *Intimidation Based on Bigotry or Bias in the First Degree*.
https://www.cga.ct.gov/current/pub/chap_952.htm#sec_53a-181i

20 United States, Congress. *U.S. Code Title 18, § 249 - Hate Crime Acts*.
https://uscode.house.gov/view.xhtml?req=granuleid:USC-2010-title18-section249&num=0&edition=2010

References

21 Angelou, Maya. Collected Poems. Random House, 1994.
22 Scott-Heron, G. *"The Revolution Will Not Be Televised."* On *Pieces of a Man.* Flying Dutchman, 1971.
23 Heinlein, Robert A. Stranger in a Strange Land. Putnam, 1961.
24 Martin, Glenn E. X (formerly known as Twitter) post, 2016.
25 Buscaglia, Leo. Born for Love: Reflections on Loving. Slack, 1992.
26 Franklin, Benjamin. Poor Richard's Almanack, 1748. Various editions.
27 Dawson, Kathryn, and Daniel A. Kelin II. *The Reflexive Teaching Artist: Collective Wisdom from the Drama/Theatre Field.* Intellect Books, 2014.
28 Epler, Melinda Briana. "20 Things You Can Do as an Ally Right Now." *Medium*, 6 June 2020
29 Reed, Louis L. "Get Your Foot Off My Neck: 16 Ways White America Can Revive Opportunities for Blacks." *Medium*, 4 June 2020
30 Collins, Francis S., et al. "Initial Sequencing and Analysis of the Human Genome." *Nature*, vol. 409, 2001, pp. 860–921 https://doi.org/10.1038/35057062
31 Coast Contra. *Legacy*. Field Trip Recordings, 2022.
32 De La Soul. *Potholes in My Lawn*. Tommy Boy Records, 1989.
33 Pathways to Housing. "Housing First Model." Pathways Housing First, https://www.pathwayshousingfirst.org/
34 McIntosh, Peggy. "White Privilege: Unpacking the Invisible Knapsack." *Independent School*, vol. 49, no. 2, Winter 1989, pp. 31–36. Also available via National SEED Project, https://www.nationalseedproject.org/key-seed-texts/white-privilege-unpacking-the-invisible-knapsack.

About The Author

Michael S. Gordon hails from Bridgeport, CT. He is a leader in education, an author, a church leader, a practitioner of the martial arts, and a presenter.

In addition to a passion for immersing himself in other cultures, Michael strives to cultivate empathy and reflective attitudes through practical exercises that focus on confidence, accuracy, self-reflection, and cultural expression.

Michael's life revolves around faith, family, friends, food, and fun. He resides in Connecticut with his family.

Author's Note:
You might be wondering what qualifies me to write on the issues of inequality, injustice, perseverance, and equity?

As the author of this bold and deeply personal narrative, the answer lies in my lived experiences. Raised by a single mother in the heart of Bridgeport's housing projects, my journey is shaped by absence, adversity, and resilience. With rare, complicated connections to a father frequently incarcerated (yet more present in the lives of my siblings than in my own), I forged a different path, one built on a commitment to show up: for my sons, for at-risk youth, and for those often left behind by society. My story isn't told from the sidelines, but from within the trenches of systemic inequality.

www.ingramcontent.com/pod-product-compliance
Lightning Source LLC
Chambersburg PA
CBHW041039050426
42337CB00059B/5056